W9-BSE-594

The

COMPLETE BOOK OF PITCHING

The

COMPLETE BOOK OF PITCHING

Doug Myers
Mark Gola

New York Chicago San Francisco Lisbon London Madrid Mexico City
Milan New Delhi San Juan Seoul Singapore Sydney Toronto

A MOUNTAIN LION BOOK

Library of Congress Cataloging-in-Publication Data

Myers, Doug, 1964–
    The Louisville Slugger complete book of pitching / Doug Myers and Mark Gola.
        p.   cm.
    Includes index.
    ISBN 0-8092-2668-5
    1. Pitching (Baseball).   I. Gola, Mark   II. Title.
GV871.M94   2000
796.357'22—dc21

99-046713

Photos on pages xiv, 3, 6, 8, 12, 53, 92, 104, 112, and 158 copyright © AP/Wide World Photos. All other interior photos courtesy of Mountain Lion, Inc.

10 11 12 13 14 15 16 17 18 19 20 21 22   CUS/CUS   0 9 8

ISBN-13: 978-0-8092-2668-9
ISBN-10:   0-8092-2668-5

Cover design by Nick Panos
Cover photographs (clockwise from top right) copyright © Tom Hauck/Allsport, copyright © Vincent Laforet/Allsport, copyright © Al Bello/Allsport, copyright © Allsport

McGraw-Hill books are available at special quantity discounts to use as premiums and sales promotions, or for use in corporate training programs. For more information, please write to the Director of Special Sales, Professional Publishing, McGraw-Hill, Two Penn Plaza, New York, NY 10121-2298. Or contact your local bookstore.

This book is printed on acid-free paper.

To Ron Guidry for 1978, and to my mom and dad for the red-stitched chromosomes

Doug Myers

To my mom, who may know very little about the art of pitching but will undoubtedly contend that this is the greatest pitching book ever written

Mark Gola

CONTENTS

ACKNOWLEDGMENTS

This book was conceived, developed, and produced by Mountain Lion, Inc., a book producer specializing in instructional and general reference sports books. A book producer relies on the special skills of many people. The following contributed to producing *The Louisville Slugger Complete Book of Pitching*. To all of them we say, "Thanks."

Rob Taylor, editor at Contemporary Books, whose support was instrumental in putting this book on the shelf, and Craig Bolt, senior project editor.

Bill Williams, vice president of advertising and promotion at Hillerich and Bradsby, for his enthusiastic support.

John Monteleone and Randy Voorhees at Mountain Lion, Inc., for their knowledge of the game.

Michael Plunkett, the photographer who took all the high-speed, stop-action, and step-by-step instructional photographs.

Tom Crowley and Matt Golden, Princeton University baseball assistant coaches, for sharing their wealth of pitching knowledge, for modeling during the instructional photo shoot, and for their great friendship.

Larry Shenk, Gene Dias, and Leigh Tobin in the Philadelphia Phillies public relations office for issuing media credentials that allowed us to interview and photograph pitchers and coaches. A special thanks to Leigh Tobin for arranging the interview with Curt Schilling.

To all the major league players, managers, and coaches who gave their time to offer some tips and advice to the many aspiring young pitchers across the country: Curt Schilling, Greg Maddux, Roger Clemens, Tom Glavine, David Wells, Pat Hentgen, Dennis Eckersley, Don Sutton, Billy Wagner, Dan Plesac, Jeff Nelson, Graeme Lloyd, Darren Dreifort, Matt Anderson, Chad Ogea, Sean Bergman, Tom Gordon, Bob Wickman, Bob Tewksbury, Mark Leiter, Dave Steib, Larry Andersen, Jim Kaat, Leo Mazzone, Bob Apodaca, Galen Cisco, Jim Kerrigan, Mel Queen, Charlie Hough, Terry Francona, Jim Fregosi, Johnny Oates, Davey Johnson, Rick Dempsey, Tino Martinez, Tony Clark, Gregg Jefferies, Brian Hunter, and Phil Falco.

A special thanks to "The Professor," The Motel 6 Baseball League, Kerry Wood and Nolan Ryan, Orel Hershiser and Catfish Hunter, and Bill Lee and Satchel Paige.

We'd also like to thank Andy Walker (the weightlifting model); Gerry Green, Fitness Center director at Rider University; Bill Thurston, Amherst College baseball coach, for biomechanical analysis of the pitching motion; Stan Davis; Sonny Pittaro; Edward F. Gola; and "Fast Eddie" Gola.

INTRODUCTION

This book is for anyone who wants to learn about the art and science of pitching. It is divided into nine chapters for ease of use. The first five chapters cover the basic mechanics of the pitching motion, grips for different pitches—fastballs, change-ups, and breaking pitches—and how to detect flaws in your delivery.

The remaining chapters cover more advanced pitching skills, such as pitch sequences, exposing weaknesses in hitters, building arm strength, pitching to game situations, and physical training and conditioning, as well as some of the history of major league pitching.

The cornerstone of our first book, *The Louisville Slugger Ultimate Book of Hitting*, is that—despite the need to conform to a limited group of mechanical absolutes—there is no single correct style of hitting. Pitching is no different. You must find a pitching style that is comfortable and suited to your abilities. Kids often attempt to imitate a big league pitcher they admire, emulate an older brother, or duplicate a teammate's motion. This may be fun during backyard ball games, but most often it's best to do your own thing.

In the classic 1977 baseball film *The Bad News Bears: Breaking Training*, mound ace Carmen Ronzoni is struggling to find the strike zone. Frustrated because he is caught somewhere between his Warren Spahn and Catfish Hunter deliveries, Ronzoni is counseled by his coach. Coach Leak approaches Ronzoni at the mound and says, "Forget Warren Spahn and forget Catfish Hunter. I want to see you throw the ball like Carmen Ronzoni."

The coach's advice may sound ridiculously simplistic. He mentions nothing about balance point over the rubber, hooking during the backswing, overstriding with the lead leg, or throwing from inconsistent arm slots. But Coach Leak's lesson is the first thing every pitcher—regardless of age—must learn: *Don't try to be someone you're not.*

Establish your own pitching style. Not everyone has a 6'4" 220-pound frame like Roger Clemens, and even fewer people have the arm speed of Pedro Martinez or the precision of Greg Maddux. The key to consistent success on the mound, and the focus of this book, is to recognize your strengths and weaknesses as a pitcher, then develop and refine your skills using lessons and techniques in the pages that follow.

Sections of this book dealing with basic pitching mechanics should be read, thought about, tried and practiced, and then reread. By returning to the text and photographs for further study, you will eventually internalize the proper mechanics of the pitching motion and delivery. And when your fastball is sailing high and inside, or your change-up is easily detected by hitters, you'll be able to pinpoint the mechanical breakdown through a process of elimination. This will allow you to become your own pitching coach on the field.

Remember that not every pitcher will have a classic delivery from start to finish. Nearly everyone has some idiosyncratic movements, such as hopping as they stride to the plate or peaking toward the sky at the top of their knee lift (like New York Yankee Orlando Hernandez). As long as these distinct characteristics do not interfere with the basic mechanics of the pitching motion or increase the chances of serious injury, then there's no need to change them.

We cannot stress enough the importance of practicing correctly and often. If you have opened this book, then you must be interested in learning how to pitch. You've taken the first step—learning the basics. But it is only the first step. Aspiring pitchers must practice, experiment, condition their body, and then practice some more. There are no shortcuts to achieving greatness on the mound.

The
Louisville Slugger®
125
Louisville, Kentucky Made In U.S.A.

COMPLETE BOOK OF PITCHING

Greg Maddux

1

PITCHING— OPEN TO ALL

"SIZE, HEIGHT, COLOR . . .
NONE OF THAT MATTERS. IF
YOU BELIEVE YOU CAN PLAY
THIS GAME, AND YOU DEDICATE
YOURSELF AND YOUR TIME TO
GIVING IT ALL YOU'VE GOT,
YOU CAN MAKE IT."

—Tom Gordon, Boston Red Sox pitcher

There is no one way to pitch and the mold for pitchers comes in many sizes and shapes.

When asked to provide a scouting report of the ideal pitcher, most will tell you that someone 6′4″ and 220 pounds with powerful legs, an easy delivery, poise, competitive fire, mental toughness, and a hopping 95-mile-per-hour fastball (and a good idea of where it's going) would be nice. But Roger Clemens only comes along about once every generation. What if that doesn't describe you? You're not alone. Most pitchers don't come close to that description.

That's one of the aspects of pitching that makes it perhaps the most appealing and intriguing position in sports. Short or tall, fat or skinny, gawky or athletic, lefty or righty, hard thrower or spinner, dabbler in multiple pitches and arm angles or master of a precious few, the position is open to anyone who can find a way to get batters out.

"Great pitcher's body—tall with long arms and legs. . . . Very agile and graceful. . . . Fastball tails in on right-handed batters. Curveball thrown hard with bite. . . . Catlike action off mound. . . . Not much effort required on fastball. . . . There is no telling

Dwight "Doctor K" Gooden took the National League by storm in 1984. Armed with a blazing fastball and knee-buckling breaking pitch, Gooden struck out 276 batters in 218 innings pitched during his rookie season.

Randy Johnson is 6′10″, Ron Guidry about a foot shorter—though Guidry could be every bit as dominant with basically the same repertoire as the Big Unit. Harry "the Cat" Brecheen weighed in at 165, while Mickey Lolich was probably carrying 260 on his 6-foot frame toward the end of his career—but both are on the short list of pitchers who've won three games in a World Series.

Brecheen and Lolich have plenty of counterparts today. Compare the success of blade-thin Pedro Martinez and Mariano Rivera to not-quite-svelte David Wells and Rod Beck and you won't find much difference.

Dan Quisenberry saved 244 games pitching underhanded, Dennis Eckersley won 197 and saved 390 throwing sidearm, and 6′8″ J. R. Richard dominated hitters in his all-too-brief career with overhand pitches that left his hand more than eight feet above home plate.

Don Drysdale certainly had the competitive fire scouts look for, taking ownership of the inside half of the plate with an unmatched belligerence. But Tom Glavine has been every bit the competitor and consistent winner that Drysdale was, though it's the outside half of the plate he stubbornly calls his own.

how good this young man could be. . . . In scouting the state of Florida for eight years he is the best-looking pitcher prospect I've seen. . . . A surefire major league draft who should develop into a power pitcher par excellence."

> —Joe McIlvaine's scouting report on 17-year-old Dwight Gooden, who two years later struck out 276 batters in the major leagues

"Tall, rangy, good athletic body. Poised. Polished. Good tight, quick rotation on curve. Straight change major league now. Delivery coordination good. Competitive. Command of pitches very good for 17-year-old. Throws weak slider, which he does not need. Fastball needs another foot on it to be major-league. All he needs is pitching experience in pro ball and [to] get a bit faster. Has good pitching potential."

> —Scouting report on Cal Ripken, who did all right by himself standing alongside home plate with a Louisville Slugger in his hands

"I hate all hitters. I start a game mad and I stay that way until it's over. I guess I'm a perfectionist. When I throw a curve that hangs and it goes for a hit, I want to chew up my glove."

> —Hall of Famer Don Drysdale, who won 208 games in his career and threw 58⅔ consecutive scoreless innings in 1968

Glavine is just one of many pitchers who succeed by "keeping it simple," throwing mostly fastballs and change-ups with a streamlined pitching motion. David Cone, on the other hand, seems to be making up pitches as he goes along—baffling hitters by throwing fastballs and breaking balls from a variety of deliveries and arm angles for strikes.

"I think a lot of pitchers are afraid to be creative on the mound. They're afraid to improvise. They think they have to stay with one certain slot, a certain type of pitch. I'm never afraid to create on the mound or try different angles or different speeds. To me, that's always been the fun part of pitching."

—David Cone, whose 20 wins in 1988 and 1998 gave him the longest stretch between 20-win seasons in baseball history

Greg Maddux and his simple, fluid delivery makes things look easy, but his pitches hit 85 miles per hour rather than 95 on the radar gun—like Whitey Ford before him. Robb Nen brings the heat, but does so with one of the more unorthodox pitching motions you'll ever see—just like Goose Gossage used to do.

Here's the bottom line. *There is no right way to succeed as a pitcher. But regardless of how you choose to pitch, there are certain fundamentals that you will have to master.* In other words, your objective is not to learn how to be Nolan Ryan. You can't be and shouldn't try. But from the pages of this book you will learn why Nolan Ryan succeeded—as well as countless other great pitchers past and present. Doing so will reveal what *all* pitchers—regardless of style or stuff—need to do to get batters out.

Being a successful pitcher means

- developing the proper pitching motion, building arm strength, and establishing command of your pitches
- hitting spots, changing speeds, and knowing how your mechanics can aid or undermine movement, velocity, and location
- understanding the mental demands of the position, so that you can hone your concentration skills, improve your pitch selection, and harness your competitive nature.
- making the commitment to being a well-conditioned and well-prepared athlete

No pitcher in major league history brought the heat like Nolan Ryan did throughout his 27-year Hall of Fame career.

In short, it means recognizing that pitching is not just a sport, but both an art and a science.

"I think the one thing I've always done well is listen. You may think you know yourself best, and a lot of pitchers do, but it never hurts to hear what somebody has to say."

—Curt Schilling, 1999 National League All-Star Game starting pitcher

DOES THIS SOUND LIKE YOU?

There is no rigid formula you need to follow to succeed as a pitcher. There is plenty of room for you to be yourself—provided that "yourself" sounds at least a little bit like this:

STRAIGHT A'S

The scouting report on a 20-year-old pitcher for St. John's University reveals that this left-hander had nearly all of the ingredients to be a successful pitcher very early on.

"He is a very knowledgeable pitcher. Good mound appearance. Moves his ball around with good location. Has a good live fastball with changing speeds. Ball sinks at times. Has good motion on change-up. Good spin on curve. Throws a live hard slider. Has enough equipment to go all the way. Good competitor."—Twins scout Herb Stein

Knowledge. Movement. Control. Ability to change speeds. Excellent repertoire. Competitive nature. That's as close as you're going to see to a perfect report card. Frank Viola went on to win a Cy Young Award in 1988 after pitching his team to a championship in 1987.

- You'll do the repetitive work necessary to make the somewhat unnatural pitching motion and release feel so natural that you no longer have to even think about it.
- You are willing to make the physical commitment to being a well-conditioned pitcher. A tired pitcher isn't of very much use to his team.
- You can harness your concentration skills and can keep your mind from wandering while you're on the mound.
- You're able to outsmart your opponent and not simply "out-athlete" him.
- You don't mind being the center of attention. The idea of the game revolving around you is appealing; you want the responsibility and you like the challenge.
- You can rely on your catcher and teammates to do their job, and you won't try to do everything yourself.
- You're confident.
- You're open to instruction.
- You're aggressive—you *want* to compete.
- You can maintain control of your emotions.

Take another look at the above list. You'll see that having what it takes to be a successful pitcher requires that you become a "master of opposites." You can make the unnatural feel natural. You need to be in excellent physical *and* mental shape. You know when to challenge hitters and when to trick them. You want to be the most important player on the field, but you don't try to do everything yourself. You believe in yourself while still being open to constructive criticism from those you trust. You're aggressive without losing control of your emotions. Your demeanor on the mound is important, but it may be influenced by the type of pitcher you are and your own personality.

Bret Saberhagen won the American League Cy Young Award in 1985 and 1989 while playing for the Kansas City Royals.

By comparing veteran middle reliever Dan Plesac and young gun Matt Anderson (also a middle reliever), it's obvious that there is more than one mind-set that can breed success. Plesac is a cerebral type who relies on quiet confidence and experience to get the best of opposing hitters. "When you're pitching well, it's almost boring. Your concentration is focused on the glove and the pitch you're about to throw. You can't get emotional out on the mound, because it begins to influence your performance in a negative manner. The biggest reason guys go awry during a game is because they allow their emotions to affect their motion and delivery. You have to take whatever emotion you're feeling and calm it down."

Occupying the opposite end of the spectrum, Anderson utilizes his competitive fire to fuel his smoking fastball. "On the mound, your attitude should be that the hitter is your ultimate enemy. You want to bury him. You want to humiliate him. You want him to walk back to the dugout knowing that you just overpowered him. I may tend to get a little crazy on the mound, but that's the state of mind where I feel I compete at my best. Off the field I may be a nice guy, but when I'm on the mound, I can get a little psycho."

Give the benefit of the doubt to Plesac, who has pitched in the major leagues since 1986. But Anderson has turned a lot of heads in his abbreviated major league career. His blazing fastball has been clocked at over 100 miles per hour.

Other aspects of being a successful pitcher will be addressed in the following chapters. Controlled aggressiveness and being open to instruction will be covered now, because these are attitudes that must permeate everything you do as a pitcher.

Curt Schilling has developed into one of the top power pitchers in major league baseball.

On most days, pitching will be the deciding factor in whether your team wins or loses. That's why pitchers get wins and losses and left fielders don't—and it puts pitchers under tremendous pressure.

> "It is made clear to the pitching staff that they are the biggest factor in determining the success of the program. This can be considered pressure, but that's what a pitcher's job is: facing pressure situations and coming out on top."
>
> —Andy Lopez, University of Florida baseball coach

Aggressiveness is the best way to approach pressure situations. Take hold of it rather than let it take hold of you. Keep in mind what former Orioles scouting director Dave Ritterpusch said:

CONTROLLED AGGRESSIVENESS

> "Never let the failure of your last pitch affect the success of your next one."
>
> —Nolan Ryan, Hall of Fame pitcher

"The pitcher determines when the ball is thrown, how fast it moves, where it goes, the sequence of pitches. All the hitter can do is select." In other words, you're in control out there. Realizing that makes it a lot easier to go after hitters aggressively.

Regardless of the sport, the most intimidating defenses are the aggressive ones. Pressing in basketball, forechecking in hockey, and blitzing in football all put offenses back on their heels, and some take them right out of their game. But these are riskier defenses that can allow layups, breakaways, and bombs, and they require brains and conditioning to be implemented effectively. Does it take superior athleticism to make these defenses work? No. In fact, many teams implement aggressive defenses because they don't have the best athletes and can't rely on them to simply make plays. Bobby Knight's Army team that won the NIT basketball tournament in the 1960s comes to mind. Knowing that they weren't as talented as their opponents, they forced the action and capitalized on mistakes.

The same holds true for pitching. The well-conditioned pitcher who challenges hitters without being foolhardy about it will also put batters on their heels and occasionally take them right out of their game. Roger Clemens is a perfect example of a pitcher who goes on the offensive. "All they do is tell pitchers what not to throw at hitters, but it's the defense that's the offense in baseball. The pitcher has the ball, and what the hitter does is predicated on what the pitcher does, not vice versa."

> *"The great thing about pitching is that I'm the one holding the ball. The hitter can only react to what I throw. He has to adjust to what I throw, where I throw it, and how hard I throw the ball."*
>
> —Pat Hentgen, 1996 American League Cy Young Award winner

When Hall of Famer Don Sutton broke in as a rookie in 1966, his teammates were Sandy Koufax, Don Drysdale, and Claude Osteen. When asked what he learned from such successful—and

Hall of Famer Sandy Koufax once said, "Pitching is the art of instilling fear by making a man flinch."

very different—pitchers, Sutton cited the aggressive attitude they all brought to the mound. Their advice: "Pitch to your strength instead of their weakness, stay ahead of the hitters, and back up third if you have to."

You don't even have to be an overpowering fastball pitcher like Roger Clemens or have a knee-buckling curveball like Don Sutton to be aggressive—though it certainly helps! Here's what the legendary Satchel Paige said when making his major league debut at the age of 42, his best fastball and sharpest curve only memories: "I wasn't afraid of anybody I'd seen in that batter's box. I'd been around too long for that. I wasn't as fast as I used to be, but I was a better pitcher."

The attitude that you can't be beat—that you want to be the one that the game revolves around—has been described by many successful pitchers. Though all come at it from a slightly different angle, the common thread—confidence and competitiveness—is very evident.

"You have to be brash and intimidating on the mound. You have to think that you are the best there is for those particular couple of hours. If you expect to lose, you will. The easiest thing in the world to do is to lose. I believed that you had to do whatever is necessary to win, and that started with a good mental outlook. You had to be very positive about what you were doing."

—Denny McLain, baseball's last
30-game winner

Nolan Ryan might have appeared calm and easygoing on the mound, with his relaxed expression and fluid pitching motion, but he was a fierce competitor for all 27 seasons he played. It's well-known to baseball historians that Denny McLain was kind enough to throw "batting practice" fastballs to Mickey Mantle so the aging star could pass Jimmie Foxx with home run number 535, but Ryan offered no such charity. In 1981, on the eve of the players' strike, Pete Rose was two hits away from breaking Stan Musial's National League record of 3,630 hits. He tied it in his first at-bat against Ryan, who then proceeded to bear down and strike him out three times. Rose had to wait nearly two months to break the record, but Ryan kept himself from being the answer to an unfavorable trivia question.

The challenge for many pitchers is how to maintain their aggressiveness without losing

BOB GIBSON: AGGRESSIVENESS

"I guess I was never much in awe of anybody. I think you have to have that attitude if you're going to go far in this game." —Bob Gibson

The consensus of most ballplayers is that no one was more aggressive on the mound than Hall of Famer Bob Gibson. He was 7–2 in World Series play, winning Game 7 in 1964 and 1967 (and losing Game 7 in 1968 when center fielder Curt Flood misplayed a fly ball into a triple). His 251 wins, 56 shutouts, 3,117 strikeouts, five 20-win seasons, and 1.12 ERA in 1968 got him into Cooperstown, but it was his competitive drive that made him a legend. Just listen to what some of his opponents and teammates said about him.

Don Sutton: "I thought Sandy Koufax had more velocity and a better curveball. But Gibson's demeanor on the mound was such that you were fairly certain you were in a fight. You were not in a ball game. You were in a *fight*."

Joe Torre: "Bob wasn't unfriendly when he pitched. I'd say it was more like hateful."

Mike Shannon: "I don't think that Gibson wanted to *win* so much. He despised *losing*. There's a difference. He took winning in stride. It was no big deal to Bob. He expected it. What he despised—I mean *despised*—was losing."

Tim McCarver: "No part of Gibson's drive can be overplayed. You had to experience that to really believe it. He was the fiercest competitor I've ever played with, or against, or seen since. You hated him, playing against him, and loved him, playing with him. He was a teammate that guys *revered*."

Bob Gibson was very difficult to beat, or even to knock out of the box. He went the entire 1968 season without being relieved in the middle of an inning. The Pirates discovered that his desire to stay on the mound and finish the job was almost superhuman: Roberto Clemente hit him with a line drive just below the right knee in a game in the summer of 1967. Gibson then walked Willie Stargell, retired Bill Mazeroski, and walked Donn Clendenon before collapsing.

He'd pitched to three batters with a broken leg.

Bob Gibson pitching at Yankee Stadium during the 1964 World Series. Gibson won two games and was the series MVP as his Cardinals copped the world championship.

control of their emotions. You need to harness it. Part of maintaining your emotional control is being able to handle adversity without melting down, bearing down rather than unraveling when things get tough—and that's all in having the right attitude.

For example, few pitchers have experienced more highs and lows than Kerry Wood. As a rookie, he produced perhaps the most dominating performance in major league history with his 20-strikeout effort against offensive powerhouse Houston, but also got roughed up more than a few times along the way to light-hitting units such as Minnesota. Wood said, "I'm not going to be good every time. I accept that. It's part of baseball. You get knocked around, you lose, and you come back. That's the way it is."

"You throw the ball to the same spot, with the same velocity, and for months the hitters can't smell you. Then you have a stretch when you're throwing the same pitches to the same batters, but now they're kicking the crap out of you. If we could figure out the reason for that, there would be no baseball. Pitchers would throw nothing but shutouts."

—Bill Lee, former Boston Red Sox pitcher

Hall of Famer Jim Palmer took a similar view: "You must accept that you'll give up runs. The pitcher who gives up runs one at a time wins, while the pitcher who gives them up two, three, and four at a time loses. I've given up long home runs that I turned around and admired like a fan. But the ones I admired were all solos."

Palmer wasn't kidding; he pitched 4,000 innings without yielding a grand slam. But even an eight-time 20-game-winner like Jim Palmer couldn't always keep his cool. He was known to commit the cardinal sin of getting on his fielders for defensive lapses behind him.

Blowing up on the mound has happened to some of the best of them. Roger Clemens got himself tossed in the second inning of Game 4 of the 1990 ALCS when he unleashed a stream of profanity at the home plate umpire. The A's ended up completing their sweep of the Red Sox that day. Dwight Gooden got himself ejected in the first inning of Game 2 of the 1998 divisional series against the Boston Red Sox arguing a play at home plate. Perhaps the most famous pitching ejection in history took place in 1917, when a hotheaded young lefty named Babe Ruth got himself run after walking the first batter he faced. In the melee that followed, Ruth took a swing at the umpire and got himself a 10-day suspension on top of the ejection. Ernie Shore came in to relieve Ruth, his manager telling him, "Go in there, will you Ernie, and try to hold them while I get somebody ready." Shore threw five warm-up tosses, the base runner was thrown out stealing, and Shore set down the next 26 men he faced for one of the strangest perfect games in history.

Controlled aggressiveness is a delicate balancing act. Former Orioles scouting director Dave Ritterpusch sums it up well. "[A starting pitcher needs] a tough attitude, the belief that he *owns* home plate. The starting pitcher's problem is to sustain that aggressive role, and that's where emotional control comes in. It may not be so crucial for relief pitchers . . . but the starter needs *low* emotionality, because his job is more mechanistic. Guys like Carlton, Seaver, Palmer, Valenzuela—when they're on the mound, they're inside their own bub-

Kevin Brown combined an explosive arm with competitive fire to become one of the best pitchers in the major leagues.

PITCHING CONTRADICTIONS

The need to be aggressive without being emotional is just one of many apparent contradictions that good pitching requires. Here are some others to keep in mind as you read further:

- You add power to your pitching motion by slowing down rather than speeding up.
- You pitch with your lower body as much as, if not more than, your upper body.
- Throwing hard requires a firm grip and a relaxed wrist.
- Velocity is the least important element of a good fastball and the most important element of a change-up.
- Perhaps the game's most effective pitch is a slow fastball thrown over the plate (a.k.a. a change-up).
- The less you throw a breaking ball, the more effective it can be.
- The less you try to make a breaking ball move, the more it *will* move.
- One of the best ways to take care of your arm is to throw.

ble. If you could ever program a robot to play baseball, the position you'd pick for it is starting pitcher . . . a machine that throws strike after strike to the corners of the plate, with an occasional brushback to keep those human hitters honest."

ACCEPTING INSTRUCTION AND CRITICISM

"Every time you learn something, it help—

anyone else does, so that they can make adjustments in the middle of a game if necessary. But they also need to be willing to accept instruction and criticism from their managers, coaches, and teammates—at all levels, no matter how talented or successful they might be. No one, no matter how talented, is born with perfect form and mechanics. And no one, no matter how successful, ever perfects the craft of pitching.

Consider what was said in the high school college scouting reports of some of the e's best pitchers, including more than a few nt or future Hall of Famers:

Overstrides in delivering ball. Real long e. Lands on left heel. Curve flat. Needs help st phases of pitching starting with delivery (Vida Blue, winner of the AL MVP and Cy g Awards as a 21-year-old.)

Slider is not consistent. Slows arm and on on change." (Kevin Brown, owner of perthe most unhittable stuff in his prime years.)

Improving your craft on the mound requires open ears and an open mind.

READER'S NOTE

Throughout this book, features titled "Throw It Again" appear. They summarize valuable information from the most recent text. Please take note of each box to remind yourself of the most important information.

Listed below are brief summaries of each upcoming chapter.

Chapter 2: Proper Mechanics Equals Consistency and Success. Without the proper pitching motion—"mechanics"—nothing much else matters. If you aren't delivering the ball properly, you won't get as much on your fastball, you'll tip off your change-up, and you'll hang your breaking balls. You won't be able to hit your target consistently with any of these pitches. And you'll probably injure yourself. That's why the discussion of pitching will begin here.

Chapter 3: Challenging the Hitter: The Fastball. The fastball is your most important pitch, regardless of how hard or soft you throw. If you can throw strikes with it, you can get batters out—while also setting up your change-up and breaking ball. Location, movement, and velocity—in order of importance—come from the right grip, a relaxed arm, and proper mechanics. Velocity, in particular, also comes from arm strength, which comes from throwing.

"Control was only fair. Didn't see a straight change. Fastball doesn't have much movement when in strike zone." (Roger Clemens, winner of five Cy Young Awards.)

"Throws across body. Curveball needs more consistency." (Dwight Gooden, who was dominating the National League less than two years later.)

"Fastball straight and hittable. Needs movement. Slider—no drive to it. Curve not good. Split-finger might help, but not very soon. Delivery easy to follow. Breaking ball needs help, as does fastball for movement." (Pete Harnisch, a successful big leaguer who has bounced back from arm injuries and clinical depression.)

"Drops arm at times. Fastball is straight at times. Should use change more." (Greg Maddux, winner of four consecutive Cy Young Awards.)

"From his performance in this game, I could not consider him a prospect." (Tom Seaver, Hall of Famer and member of the 300-win club.)

In most cases, these excerpts came from very favorable reports. The success that all of these pitchers experienced is due in large part to being coachable.

Tom Seaver won 311 games and three National League Cy Young Awards during his 20-year Hall of Fame career.

arm as you throw it—with the proper grip, a simple turn of the wrist before release is all you'll need.

Chapter 6: Fielding Your Position. You're not just a pitcher, but one of nine defensive players who must know what to do when a ball is hit: making the play, covering first, backing up third, or directing traffic. Critical to these and other defensive responsibilities is anticipation. To anticipate, you will need to understand some of the inner workings of baseball strategy—so you can think along with the opposing manager and base runners while still being able to concentrate on retiring the batter.

Chapter 7: Preparation and Conditioning. Without the proper conditioning, you'll find it hard to develop proper mechanics and nearly impossible to maintain them. That means no control, no endurance, a lot of walks, a lot of fat pitches, and most likely some arm injuries down the road. To be successful as a pitcher at any level, you will need strength, flexibility, and stamina—not just in your throwing arm, but the rest of your upper body as well as your legs, hips, and lower back. Pitching is a full-body workout.

Chapter 8: Game Day. Since pitching is both a physical and a mental task, you will need to develop a fairly comprehensive between-starts and game-day routine to get yourself prepared. On game day, you will need to find an appropriate way to get mentally prepared for the intense concentration to follow—without getting so pumped up before the game starts that you're drained by the time you take the mound.

Chapter 9: Advanced Pitching: Mastering the Mental Game. No pitcher reaches his potential without learning how to get a batter out with his head and not just his arm. That means learning how to "work" a hitter; how to adjust to a ballpark, an umpire, or even to yourself, depending on your stuff on any given day; how to approach pitching in long, middle, or short relief differently than starting; and how to recognize—and get—the most important outs in a game.

Chapter 4: Pulling the String: The Change-up. After the fastball, the change-up is the next pitch for you to master. It doesn't take as much out of your arm as other pitches, and for most pitchers it is easier to throw for strikes than a breaking ball. Even if you're a very hard thrower, you need to learn how to use a change-up grip to take something off of your fastball (without tipping the batter that a change-up is coming). "Pulling the string" will become more and more important as you move to higher levels of competition, where hitters can handle your fastball and breaking ball.

Chapter 5: Making It Break: The Curve and Slider. Early in your pitching career, you should have good mechanics and two pitches (a fastball and change-up) in which you have great confidence. Then it's time to learn a breaking ball—a curveball or slider—though you shouldn't try to master both at the same time. Proper mechanics are critical to throwing a good breaking ball without injuring yourself. Do not try to do too much to the ball by bending your wrist or twisting your

Roger Clemens

Proper Mechanics Equals Consistency and Success

Mechanics is a one-word description of the correct sequencing of the pitching motion—that is, the knee lift, arm swing and cock, leg stride, foot plant, hip turn, torso flex, and arm arc that are integral parts of a pitcher's motion. It is critical to master the mechanics of a proper pitching motion. Sound mechanics are the foundation of pitching. They will help you develop control of your pitches, allow you to throw with maximum velocity and movement with optimum effort, and give you your best chance for playing injury-free.

Great athletes with powerful arms have failed miserably as pitchers because of improper throwing mechanics, which hampered their ability to consistently hit spots and gain command of their pitches. Others, such as Nolan Ryan, have enjoyed successful careers and pitched nearly injury-free due in large part to efficient mechanics. Establishing good throwing mechanics at an early age is important, because poor techniques often cause unnecessary stress on the shoulder and arm. Also, bad habits, that is, poor pitching mechanics, become much harder to change as you get older.

"Without proper mechanics, it would be impossible for Nolan [Ryan] to generate enough force to accelerate a baseball to 90 miles per hour. Likewise, without good

mechanics, he'd be unable to repeat these forces thousands of times without serious trauma to the arm and shoulder."

—Dr. Eugene Coleman, Houston Astros conditioning coach

The key to good mechanics is "informed repetition," that is, understanding what proper mechanics are and throwing this way so often that it becomes second nature. Another absolute of good pitching is concentration, the ability to focus on the task at hand, which is virtually impossible to maintain in a game situation if you have to *think* about your mechanics.

Pitchers experience slumps just like hitters. Any number of factors can bring on a slump. Pitchers can lose rhythm. They can fail to bring their throwing arm into the correct delivery position (or slot) where they release their pitches. They can fail to keep the proper pressure on the ball. With a complete understanding of proper mechanics to enable you to identify and correct the flaw that has brought on the slump, you will work free of it more quickly.

FOUR PHASES OF THE PITCHING DELIVERY

To understand mechanics, you need to break the pitching delivery into four integrated phases:

1. Windup
2. Stride/Arm Swing and Cocking
3. Front Leg Bracing/Arm Acceleration
4. Deceleration/Follow-Through

In each of these phases the legs and torso play major roles in enabling you to throw properly. The legs form a firm base or platform for the torso to twist and flex. The strong back, chest, and abdominal muscles of the torso must efficiently transfer the power of the leg muscles to the shoulders and pitching arm. To get the lower body coordinated with the arm motion, you must use the torso, that is, you must rotate at the hips to create a whiplike action of the shoulders, pitching arm, and hand.

"Coaches have always told me to keep things as simple as possible. Keep it simple with my mechanics and just think about throwing one pitch at a time. My pitching coach at Wichita State used to always say, 'Work fast, throw strikes, and change speeds,' and that's about as simple as you can get."

—Darren Dreifort, Los Angeles Dodgers starting pitcher

GRIP THE BALL COMFORTABLY

The hitter has to hit it, all you have to do is throw the ball. Even if he does make contact with it, the odds are about two in three that your fielders will catch it. He doesn't know what pitch is coming, where it's going, and how fast it will be moving—and even on off-speed stuff he doesn't have much more than a half second to decide whether to swing. Make the hitter feel the tension of trying to accomplish this extraordinary feat of timing. All you're doing is playing what Tim McCarver calls an "elevated form of catch."

You hear about hitters who grind their bat into sawdust as they try to send one 500 feet. Don't be the pitcher who tries to crush a ball with his fingers. Treat it like an egg—securely in the hand with a firm, stable grip but with a loose wrist.

While taking the sign from the catcher, some pitchers hold the ball with their throwing hand in their glove, others hold the ball outside of the glove, and some keep the ball in their glove and let their arm hang loose. The first option is best for most pitchers. Hand-in-glove allows you to establish your grip and pressure points on the ball *before* beginning the delivery, while shielding it from the view of enemy base runners and coaches. You may find that you're more relaxed with the ball in the glove and your arm hanging free, but very young pitchers may have a hard time establishing the proper grip on the ball during their delivery this way. Keeping the ball outside of the glove presents the same problem; Goose Gossage used to hold the ball behind him, spinning it in his fingers as he took the sign (not

Maintain a firm grip and loose wrist on the baseball when pitching. Hold the ball out in your fingers, not in the palm of your hand.

David Wells holds his pitching hand in his glove while taking the sign from his catcher.

a good idea when runners are on base, as a ball dropped from this position is a balk) so no one could tell if this was the one time in ten when a hitter would be getting something other than a fastball.

You don't want to prepare differently for different pitches. Rather, keep your preparations the same, every time, or else you'll start to tip your pitches. Develop a brief ritual if you need to, if that's what's necessary to make sure that you take the sign from the catcher and begin your delivery in the same way every time. That will not only help you to keep from slipping into telltale patterns, but will help your rhythm and concentration. Think of it like the routine every basketball player goes through before shooting a foul shot. Take a second to visualize your pitch hitting the target, just as basketball players see the ball dropping through the rim.

An example:

1. Take your stance on the rubber.
2. Pick up the catcher's sign and pitch location.
3. Nod agreement.
4. Visualize the location and the pitch traveling from your hand to the target.
5. Begin your motion.

Just don't do anything too elaborate. Coaches and fielders like fast workers.

TIPPING YOUR PITCHES

Sometimes the simplest, unconscious mannerisms can let the batter know what pitch is coming. It is critical to stay out of patterns, but it's easier said than done. Here are some common ways that pitches are tipped. Are you doing any of them?

1. Holding your pitching hand inside the glove differently when gripping one pitch than another.
2. Holding your glove differently when gripping one pitch than another.
3. Moving your glove differently when throwing one pitch than another.
4. Lifting your arms to different heights.
5. Lifting your knee to different heights.
6. Shortening or lengthening the backswing of your throwing arm.
7. Throwing from different arm angles.
8. Striding toward the plate with more or less force.
9. Accelerating or decelerating your motion.

PITCHING MECHANICS FROM THE WINDUP POSITION

PHASE 1: THE WINDUP

Take a position on the rubber that is comfortable. A right-handed pitcher usually pitches from the right half of the rubber, a left-hander from the left half. These positions aren't mandatory, but they can improve the angle of the breaking pitch when facing same-handed batters.

Take a balanced and relaxed stance, square to the plate. Place your throwing foot (right foot for a right-handed pitcher) on the top and forward edge of the rubber with the toe facing toward home plate; position the ball of your foot slightly in front of the rubber so that the spikes touch the ground. This is your pivot foot and posting leg. Keep your other foot slightly behind the pivot foot, the feet about shoulder-width apart. This is your stride foot and leg. Place your pitching hand and wrist deep inside the glove, thus hiding the grip and ball from the batter and opposing coaches.

The first movement is a rocker step, a soft and short step backward at a 45-degree angle taken with your stride or rear foot (the foot not touching the rubber). Keep your head over the pivot foot and centered over the body. This will shift your weight onto the back foot so that you can pivot your front foot and drop it in front and parallel to the rubber. When you do this, your weight will now be on the front foot and leg, that is, your posting leg.

Keep your weight over the posting leg and lift the knee of your lead or striding leg. Let the free foot hang straight down from the knee; do not swing it to the side, which may cause you to lose balance. As you lift the knee, rotate the front hip closed to at least a 90-degree angle so that your front knee is pointing toward third base. Maintain balance until the stride leg starts to lower. Do not drift forward early or tilt back toward first base. Some pitchers—such as Nolan Ryan or Orlando Hernandez, a.k.a. El Duque—can lift the lead knee up to the chest area and still maintain good balance in this posting position.

PHASE 2: STRIDE/ARM SWING AND COCKING

The stride begins with two simultaneous actions: (1) the downward and drifting forward movement of the lead leg and stride foot, (2) the breaking apart of the glove hand and throwing hand. The throwing hand goes down, back, and up toward the cocked position in a continuous motion. During the cocking phase, the wrist is loose and relaxed and the fingers, on top of the ball, are firmly gripping the ball with the appropriate pressure. At all times, the arm swing and cocking should be fluid and continuous.

When done properly, the lead arm action can be deceptive to the hitter. Extend the lead elbow toward the plate. Following the planting of the stride foot, pull the lead elbow down and alongside the lead hip, which is opened—that is, facing home plate—upon planting of the stride foot. These actions make it possible to generate arm speed and velocity. The trunk or torso, including the chest, arches, then rotates swiftly to square with the hips.

The stride itself is a controlled and aligned sliding of the front foot just above the ground directly toward home plate. Land flat-footed or on the ball of the stride foot with the ball of the stride foot slightly closed, one to two inches across the midline. This will keep the front side—most importantly the shoulders—closed, yet not enough to prevent good hip and trunk rotation. The length of the stride is roughly 85 to 90 percent of the height of the pitcher, but a longer stride is acceptable if the pitcher can get his head and shoulder over the lead leg at the time of ball release. The hips open slightly upon planting of the stride foot, but the shoulders stay closed. Just milliseconds later, they whip open as the hips, trunk, and shoulders rotate and the torso moves forward and down, flexing from the waist over a braced stride leg.

Do not land on the heel first. This can cause the foot to fly open, put the hips in a position that is open too early (for a right-handed pitcher, facing too far toward the first base side of home plate), and initiate a premature trunk rotation (flying open).

As the lead foot plants, the upper body and head remain at the top center of a widening triangle of the body. The body does not sit down, it does not leap or jump itself forward. Rather, it moves forward without hesitation and stabilizes over the lead or front foot, which has formed a flexed position at approximately a 135-degree angle. It is now ready to turn on the power.

But the body cannot execute proper pitching mechanics if the arm is not properly cocked at this moment. So where are the arm and hand when the body is at its maximum torque? Earlier in this chapter, we said the path of the throwing hand is down, back, and up. This "down, back, and up" arm swing should be aligned with the body and shoulders, in a line between home plate and second base.

Upon stride foot contact, the pitching hand should be approximately cap high, and the hand should be slightly closer to the throwing-hand-side baseline than the elbow. The hand and forearm are nearly perpendicular to the ground, with the palm of the hand facing second base during the early phase of cocking the arm; upon planting of the stride foot the palm of the throwing hand faces the shortstop (right-handed pitcher) or second baseman (left-handed pitcher). The wrist is in a loaded position, extended slightly back toward the pitcher's head.

PHASE 3: FRONT LEG BRACING/ ARM ACCELERATION

The body stops moving forward when the front leg braces— the hips open slightly but the shoulders stay aligned slightly longer (for only a millisecond) toward home plate. This bracing action of the front leg provides a firm base against which the upper body can rotate. The rapid-fire sequence of opening the hips, then squaring the torso and shoulders with the hips, creates tremendous torque (rotational force), much as the energy stored in a twisted rubber band. As the trunk or torso then unwinds, springing from extension to flexion, and the shoulders square up with the hips, the head and shoulders move over the braced front leg. The body unleashes rotational (shoulders squaring with the hips) and vertical or downward (a flexing of the upper body over the front leg) forces. The result: tremendous arm and hand speed, thus pitch velocity.

As the trunk and shoulder rotate and square off to the plate, the shoulder rotates externally with the elbow leading. The forearm and hand then fire forward, coming outside the elbow. As the trunk goes from extension (an arched back) to flexion (bending over the front leg), the arm and hand accelerate to the release point.

The release point, that is, when the ball leaves the hand, occurs as the hand passes by the stride foot. The fingers are behind and on top of the ball, angled outward close to 45 degrees. Upon release, the hand and arm naturally pronate (turns outward from the body so that the palm is facing foul territory or the baseline).

PHASE 4: DECELERATION/ FOLLOW-THROUGH

Deceleration—the slowing down and stopping of the arm and hand—begins as soon as the ball is released. Here is the correct way to slow the arm and bring it to a safe stop: Bring your throwing arm, hand, and shoulder down, over and outside the lead leg. Complete the motion with your hand and arm down and outside the lower leg. Bring your glove hand up and in front of your body—for protection and to be ready to field a ball batted directly at you. Square off, that is, get both feet on the ground facing the hitter. If your momentum has pulled you off balance, take a short jump forward and get squared. In squaring off, you not only move from pitcher to potential fielder but you also get your body's biggest muscles—those in the legs and back—to help brake the whipping action of the arm, thus taking a strain off the muscles, ligaments, and tendons of the throwing shoulder, elbow, and arm.

Notice the pitching arm is relaxed and at the pitcher's side when throwing a fastball, but the elbow is held up when throwing a breaking pitch. An observant hitter will notice this discrepancy and know what pitch is coming. Always hold your pitching arm and glove the same way when gripping different pitches.

"I wiggle my glove all the time. This leaves the hitter with no idea of what I'm throwing. In the major leagues players on the opposing benches are looking for clues such as holding the fastball higher in the glove or digging (deeper into the glove pocket) for a forkball, so I always wiggle my glove to disguise my pitches."

—Jeff Nelson, New York Yankees
relief pitcher

Though most pitches are tipped through mechanics, others are given away with mannerisms: nodding your head differently, sticking out your tongue, closing your eyes, or looking down, up, or at the batter. You'll need to know your pitching motion well enough that you can see it as if you were watching on television, then ask yourself if you're doing anything differently on a change-up than a fastball or a breaking ball. Better still, have someone film you and study it for telltale patterns.

Holding your glove open to the third base side may give the third base coach a peek at your grip. He may then send a signal to the hitter. Keep your glove closed to hide your grip.

TAKE A RELAXED POSITION ON THE RUBBER

Strive to maintain balance and relaxation. Being off balance robs you of control, while being tense robs you of velocity. Balance and relaxation begin with how you stand on the rubber. Some young pitchers stand with both feet on the rubber, but it may be hard to relax while standing at attention with your feet close together on a 24-by-6-inch slab. Spread your feet shoulder-width apart. Keep your legs slightly flexed; standing ramrod straight with your knees locked will create tension and stiffness. Put your pivot foot on the rubber—right foot for a right-hander—the toes and ball over the front edge. You should be feeling the rubber with your arch. When you begin your delivery, you will be pivoting off the rubber and placing this foot in front of it and parallel to it. The only way to easily do this is with the toes and ball of your foot already in front of the rubber.

Your stride foot—left foot for a right-hander—should be a few inches behind the rubber with your weight forward, on the ball of your foot, and your heel slightly off the ground. As you begin your delivery, this will allow you to bring your weight back in a short "rocker step" before you bring it forward. This is a simple rocking motion similar to what many hitters do. (Hitting requires balance and relaxation, too, so you will find some surprising similarities between striding to throw a baseball and striding to hit one.)

Some pitchers set up in different spots on the rubber for righties or lefties, while others sometimes move around on the rubber to overcome wildness. High school pitchers will occasionally tip their pitches by standing at different places on the rubber for fastballs and breaking balls. Any advantage you might gain from this will be negated tenfold as soon as it's detected. Dennis Eckersley is one of many who cautions against too much movement. "It's not too easy to bounce around on the rubber. Pick a spot and stick with it."

Most left-handers throw from the first base side of the rubber, while most right-handers throw from the third base side. You will need to experiment with different spots in practice, then

Curt Schilling takes a relaxed position on the rubber before making his delivery.

settle on the one that you feel gives your pitches the best path to the strike zone. Since where you stand affects how you approach the plate, it can even have an effect on your movement and velocity.

Left-hander Tom Glavine feels that standing to the extreme first base side works best for him. He throws change-ups and sinkers away to right-handers, and feels he would be getting too much of the plate with his pitches if he pitched from another spot. If Glavine had a screwball or a lot of tail on his fastball, he might not be getting *enough* of the plate, so he might find that setting up on the third base side worked better for him. Keep that in mind as you decide what works best for you.

SHIFT YOUR WEIGHT BACK FOR RHYTHM

The traditional method of initiating the delivery is the windup—bringing the hands together and over the head—though this has changed through the years. Hall of Famer Warren Spahn used a classic windup. He would bend forward at the waist while bringing both arms behind and up. As he stood straight up again, he brought his arms forward and then up over his head, and his hand would enter the glove out in front of him. Many of today's pitchers have dispensed with the elaborate backswing, while more than ever have eliminated bringing their hands over the head at all.

Some believe that a long windup (pumping the hands down at least once and then overhead) helps create power, but pitchers such as Kevin Brown have shown how hard you can throw without it. The no-windup was believed to help a pitcher's control—in part because Don Larsen went to it and threw a perfect game. *The real benefit of the windup is timing and rhythm.* Inspired by Bill Gullickson (an excellent control pitcher with 162 career victories), Mark Leiter went from the windup to the no-windup early in his career to help his control. He's now gone back to a windup to "get a little momentum going, a little rhythm." If you can get that rhythm without bringing your hands over your head, great. Remember Johnny Sain's advice about simplicity. The simpler your mechanics, the fewer things there are that can go wrong.

> *"All the time I was using the windup I was tipping off my pitches. No matter what I threw, [Red Sox coach Del] Baker knew in advance what was coming. So I went to [Yankees pitching coach] Jim Turner and asked his permission to drop the windup. He gave me the* OK, *and I've pitched without a windup ever since. It gives me better control. It takes noth-*
>
> *ing off my fastball, and it keeps the batters tense. They have to be ready every second."*
>
> —Don Larsen, former New York Yankees pitcher

Bring your hands together and lift them over your head, to your chest, or leave them at your belt—whatever helps you to develop rhythm and timing. In general, the younger the pitcher, the lower he should lift his hands. Bringing your hands over your head can make it harder for you to maintain good balance.

Hold your glove so that the back of your wrist is pointed at the batter—this will help you hide the ball in your glove. If you haven't already gotten your grip on the ball, now is the time. If you start your motion with the ball in your glove and your throwing arm free, be certain that you go into your glove for the ball at the same time and in the same way for a fastball, breaking ball, or change-up.

Most pitchers take a step back with their stride foot to shift their weight, what is termed a rocker step. Others simply keep their stride foot in place and shift their weight back onto the stride foot without moving it. When you step back, make it a short step and *keep your head over your pivot foot or posting leg.* Too long a rocker step will bring too much of your weight back, causing you to lose balance and rush your motion. When you step back, move back toward second base and not off to either side, again for reasons of balance. With a short, soft rocker step, you won't need to worry about striding too far back or leaning to either side; it's simpler. Remember: whether you step or just rock, keep your head over your pivot foot to stay in balance.

> *"A pitcher's head should never come off the imaginary vertical line from his pivot foot. In fact, the only time the head should ever be behind the rubber is when the pitcher is picking up the resin."*
>
> —Tom House, former major league pitcher and pitching coach

John Burkett holds the ball outside of his glove as he takes his sign. He takes a lengthy step straight back, but

as you can see, Burkett keeps his head and the weight of his body over the rubber.

LIFT THE FRONT KNEE

Pitching motions have varied dramatically through the years, from the windmilling arms, high leg kick, and catapulting deliveries of Bob Feller and Juan Marichal to the streamlined, no-windup of Roger Clemens and Kevin Brown. Tom Seaver and Don Sutton each won 300 games with dissimilar motions—the squatting power delivery of Seaver and the taller, over-a-stiff-front-leg, curveball delivery of Sutton. Nolan Ryan split the difference between Seaver and Sutton with a tall-and-fall motion over a flexed front leg that suited both his 100-mile-per-hour fastball and his outstanding curveball. He lasted 27 seasons and 5,387 innings before his arm finally gave out at age 46, a week before he planned to retire.

Since the days of Feller and Marichal, the leg kick has become a knee lift. By giving up his very distinctive kick later in his career, Feller was years ahead of his time. Feller said, "In the early stages of my career, I used an extraordinarily high left leg kick, but I gave it up. It tended to destroy balance and it added little speed, if any."

Balance in the delivery must be maintained both side to side and front to back. The more compact the delivery, the easier it is to maintain balance. Kick your left leg straight out in front of you, then compare how that feels to simply lifting your left knee. It is much harder to keep your balance kicking your leg out, and this can force you to move your upper body toward third base or first base to compensate. You want your upper body to remain in line with second base and home plate, head over pivot foot. Dennis Eckersley was one of the greatest control pitchers who ever lived despite a very unorthodox motion and a big leg kick, but he's the exception. The compact delivery of Greg Maddux is much more conducive to throwing strikes. You want to be directing most of your energy into moving from the mound toward home. Think about moving toward home plate while disturbing as little of the air toward third and first as possible. Or imagine you are pitching in a narrow hallway. Stay compact.

Begin lifting your knee after you have shifted your weight back through either a short step or a rocker step. Shift your weight forward onto your pivot foot as you place that foot directly in front of and parallel to the rubber. Keep your back leg flexed very slightly, but not bent beyond 10 to 15 degrees.

> *"When I was in Double-A ball, Larry Harding was my pitching coach. He would use video-tape to show the pitchers on the staff what minor quirks we might have in our motion. Larry would emphasize to me that I get my balance point over the rubber. Once I got there, then I was able to go forward with my legs."*
>
> —David Wells, Toronto Blue Jays starting pitcher

Do not keep your pivot foot on top of the rubber. Drop it in front, keeping the side of your foot in contact with the rubber. A caution: Pushing off the rubber with your pivot foot is erroneously believed to be critical for throwing hard. This is actually a bad habit that can mess up your mechanics. The power in pitching comes from rotating your hips and flexing your torso, thus creating a whipping action of the throwing arm and hand, after setting up a firm base with your foot plant. Once you have rotated and flexed over the front leg, you simply pull the pivot foot away from the rubber toward home plate. You do not push or thrust your body forward. You plant the stride foot, rotate and flex, then pull your back leg forward. Keeping your pivot foot on the rubber after you have released the pitch will simply make it harder for you to stay balanced.

Lift your stride leg and bring it forward in front of the rubber, turning on your pivot foot so that your knees are facing third base (for a right-hander). Your back leg should be flexed slightly at the knee for balance. As you bring your arms down to the belt, lift your front knee up at least

Darren Dreifort employs an extremely high knee lift in his motion. His back leg is slightly flexed, which allows him to store power and energy on his back side. Note that Dreifort's left foot is "toes up," which makes it harder for him to maintain balance throughout his rotation.

that high. Your thigh should be at least in line with your belt, your calf perpendicular to the ground. Your upper body should be straight—don't crouch as you lift, stay tall. Don't kick your leg, lift your knee.

During your knee lift, your toes should be lower than your heel and pointing toward the ground. Raising your knee feels much more natural and relaxed with your toes pointed downward. Conversely, pointing your toes to the sky may cause you to land on your heel, which will adversely affect rhythm and control.

Lift your stride leg straight up until your thigh is at least in line with your belt. Point your toes down (to the ground) and "stay tall" with your upper body.

ROTATE YOUR HIPS AND SHOULDERS

There is some variation in how much a pitcher can rotate his hips (and shoulders) during his knee lift. A right-handed power pitcher may rotate his hips a bit farther, pointing his knee toward the shortstop side of third base and showing his back to the batter. Some, such as Orel Hershiser, do this while pointing the sole of their stride foot back toward second base. You may need to make subtle adjustments such as this to make sure you maintain good balance, but try it first without them. Keep it simple.

Uncoiling or rotating your torso back toward home plate—that is, squaring it with your hips, which are already opened upon the planting of your stride foot—is where the power in your delivery will be generated, not in your arm. Just as the most powerful hitters generate bat speed with the rotation of their hips, torso, and shoulders, the same holds true for pitchers. You will *not* generate this power by *swinging* your stride leg behind you, and an exaggerated leg swing may even cause you to rush your delivery. The power will come with the rotation and flexing of the torso. Lift and rotate, don't kick and swing.

Rotating your hips too much in your knee lift—so that a right-hander is facing more toward shortstop than third base—may also make it more difficult to maintain a direct line from the mound to home plate. In turn, it may also make it difficult to achieve a proper landing of the stride foot. Many pitchers with extreme hip rotation end up in poor fielding position at the end of their delivery, as their horizontal momentum carries them too far off to their glove side. Luis Tiant—who accumulated 229 wins in his 19-year career—turned his back completely toward home plate and looked up at the sky before wheeling and firing. He somehow managed to still find his target, throw strikes without throwing across his body, and be in position to field. However, Luis Tiant was one of a kind—don't copy his style.

> *"He had 60 different pitches that he threw from 90 different angles. . . . Watching him pitch was the most fun I could have in baseball without being on the mound myself. He turned the pitching rubber into a stage, pirouetting and twisting into the most bizarre gyrations, so that the batters had no idea where the ball was coming from."*
>
> —Bill Lee on Luis Tiant

If you don't rotate enough, you may have a hard time generating sufficient velocity. Pedro Martinez rotates his hips a great deal farther and faster than the consummate control artist, Greg Maddux, whose delivery stays more in line with

As Bret Saberhagen executes his knee lift, he turns his hips back to store power. Coaches often tell pitchers to "show the hitter your numbers," or "show them your back pocket," to remind pitchers to rotate their hips.

As he strides forward, his shoulder remains closed until the stride foot is planted.

home plate and second base as he flexes his upper body downward or vertically over his stride leg. Note that a sidearm pitcher gets most of his power through horizontal rotation, or what is termed angular velocity, rather than vertical momentum (downward motion and flexing of the upper body over the front leg), so he needs more extreme hip rotation. He also will get more downward movement because his fingers will come over the ball (as he pronates, that is, turns outward, his arm), thus rotating the ball sideward and downward.

> *"Hip rotation is very important to maximizing your velocity. If you look at most of your hard throwers in the game, they have very well-developed thigh muscles and buttocks. You've got to have a strong lower half to throw hard. They go hand in hand."*
>
> —Mel Queen, Toronto Blue Jays pitching coach

Once the stride foot plants and the lead arm begins to pull in toward his body, the hips forcefully rotate, generating power from his lower half and increasing his arm speed.

Like the hip rotation, the purpose of the knee lift is to build energy that will eventually be transferred through your body, into your arm, and to the ball. You get other benefits with the knee lift and hip rotation. You make it harder for the batter to pick up the ball coming out of your hand. This is called hiding your pitches. In addition to being fast, Nolan Ryan's pitches were difficult to pick up because they were shielded by his front leg and torso. The incredibly flexible Orlando "El Duque" Hernandez lifts his knee just as high as Ryan did, so hitters don't pick up the ball until very late in his delivery either.

DON'T LIFT TOO HIGH

A high knee lift has some disadvantages, however. For one thing, it's tiring. You need to be very flexible and in very good condition to be able to maintain this fairly extreme type of delivery. As the game progresses, you may find it harder to keep bringing your knee to your chin, and this can throw off the mechanics of your entire motion. It doesn't follow Sain's principle of simplicity.

For another thing, it may make it more difficult for you to get comfortable pitching from the stretch (see "Pitching Mechanics from the Set Position" later in this chapter). A high knee lift can't be used with runners on base, but most pitchers who do this in their windup end up having a very hard time using a quicker slide step from the stretch. Dwight Gooden used a very high knee lift as a young major league pitcher, and it basically allowed runners to steal at will. Fortunately for him, when he first arrived in the major leagues very few runners got on base against him.

A high knee lift will make it more difficult for you to stay balanced. Some pitchers try to lift their knee too high and end up tilting their shoulders; the shoulders need to remain level through the first two phases of the delivery. One of the most important tests of your mechanics is to halt your motion at the peak of your knee lift. If you're truly in balance, you should be able to hold that position—knee up and hands together in the glove next to your torso, between your belt and chest—for several seconds. If not, you have to fix it. Being unable to hold your lift is a sign of a very serious mechanical flaw that could undermine all aspects of your pitching.

"My pitching coaches have told me to simplify everything, and I think that has helped me the most. I try not to allow too many things to go on in my windup and stretch—like raising my hands or kicking my leg. I pretty much try to keep things north and south and don't move around side to side. The simpler you make your windup, the easier it will be to maintain sound mechanics, which leads to throwing consistent strikes."

—Billy Wagner, Houston Astros closer

If you have good balance and well-conditioned legs, you might experiment with a high knee lift. If you can throw hard strikes with this delivery—both early in the game and when you're fatigued—keep it. If not, simplify by bringing your knee as high as your belt and take it from there. It's a good idea to pause for a split second at your balance point—this will ensure that you're in balance (if not, you can just stop your delivery provided no one is on base). This very brief pause will also serve as a reminder to keep yourself from rushing (see "Rushing," later in this chapter).

Finally, it's important that you keep your eyes on the target throughout the most critical phases of your delivery, when you are moving from lift to cocking of the arm and hand. Some pitchers, such as Nolan Ryan and Fernando Valenzuela, do not pick up the target until the peak of their knee lift. Here is what to do: As you lift your leg, lift your eyes to locate the target. Move from soft focus—seeing the larger scene of batter, catcher, umpire—to hard focus—seeing only the target. For optimum results, do not zoom in on the glove any later than the end of the lift phase.

Tom Seaver peers down during his knee lift and then picks up his target as he begins his stride toward home plate.

STRIDE TOWARD HOME PLATE

Keep your eyes on the catcher's glove. Lift your knee and point it toward your third baseman (for right-handers). Keep your calf perpendicular to the ground, and your toes lower than your heel. Grip the ball properly in the glove, your hands together inside of your lift leg. Keep your arms relaxed, hanging down, and elbows bent at right angles, which puts your glove somewhere between your belt and chest, in line with your navel. Keep your head over your pivot foot, the back knee flexed very slightly. Pause for a split second (if you can maintain this position, you are in balance).

Do not begin your movement toward home plate until your knee lift has reached its highest point. Moving toward home plate before your leg lift is complete and your arm and hand are fully cocked leads to what is called "rushing." This is when you are moving forward with the throwing hand too low, which causes you to throw upward, rather than downward. This can lead to control problems, lost velocity, and hanging curveballs.

David Wells owns a 90-mile-per-hour-plus fastball, a devastating breaking ball, and an effective change-up. When you couple his menu of pitches with the fact that he maintains excellent command of the strike zone, it's easy to understand why he's one of the most dominant left-handed pitchers in the game today. But even Wells experiences mechanical flaws from time to time. When his fastball is up in the strike zone and the break on his curveball isn't so sharp, he knows he needs to slow things down. Wells says, "My most common mechanical problem is rushing my delivery and lunging forward. When I don't stay back, my arm doesn't catch up and I end up throwing the ball all over the place, especially up

When a pitcher overstrides or "rushes out to the plate," his pitching arm trails behind his body. The result will be pitches that are wild high both in and out of the strike

zone. A controlled fall allows you to maintain balance and stay on top of your pitches. Keep the length of your stride at 85% to 90% of your body weight (from heel to heel).

in the strike zone. So I basically have to slow down my body. When you're in the game, there's no time to consult with your pitching coach and work things out on the side. You've got to realize the mistake you're making, make the adjustment, and go get the hitter."

Achieve balance at the peak of your lift, *then* begin a "controlled fall" toward home plate. Don't jump toward the plate. Some pitchers get into this habit, which can cause mechanical problems. Inexperienced pitchers may also find that they are jumping more for their fastball, less for their slider, and even less for their curveball. Good hitters will pick this up and punish them for it.

TOM SEAVER: DROP AND DRIVE

Hall of Famer Tom Seaver achieved great success with what was termed a "drop and drive" motion. He would deliver his pitch over a bent front leg, but he also dropped his upper body and pivot leg closer to the ground during his stride. This brought him very low at the very end of his deliv-

ery—so low that he would scrape his back knee on the pitching mound. However, in looking at stop-action images of Seaver's motion, it appears that the description "drop and drive" may, in fact, be inaccurate. Stop-action analysis shows that he actually maintained a graduated lowering of his arm and body, similar to the "stand tall and fall" method that is more common among pitchers. Like all power pitchers, Seaver had an unusually long stride. This long stride, along with his superior leg strength, helped him drop lower than most pitchers. Seaver piled up 311 major league victories and pitched relatively free from arm miseries, a tribute not only to his unique ability and exceptional body strength but also to his strict adherence to what worked for him.

There are many reasons why this type of delivery is a difficult model for most pitchers. For one thing, it is more difficult to throw a sharply breaking curveball with it. For another, the bent back leg during delivery can make it more difficult to maintain balance. It also promotes a long push off the rubber to get the body so low at conclusion. A longer stride often leads to rushing. Finally,

Philadelphia Phillies all-star pitcher Paul Byrd has a stride similar to Seaver's famed "drop and drive."

Sutton describes his motion this way: "My delivery gave me more leverage, stressed all of the muscles up and down my body. With the drop and drive you have to have very strong legs, and if you're going to throw that way you're going to have to have your mind made up that you're not going to have a curveball. You're going to pitch down in the strike zone and you're going to be a power pitcher, fastball/slider. My motion seemed to automatically make it easy for me to throw a curveball. I never felt like anything but the big muscles were stressed. It's what came naturally for me. I never had to tinker with it, and I never had an arm problem."

TO PUSH OFF OR NOT TO PUSH OFF?

Pushing off has become a controversial aspect of pitching mechanics. It used to be considered an absolute, with Tom Seaver echoing the sentiments of most students of pitching when he said, "If you want to throw hard and effectively, you must push hard off the rubber." But pushing off led many pitchers at all levels, including the major leagues, to hurl themselves toward the plate in an effort to increase their velocity. For most, this just led to rushing and the inevitable slinging, or to over-striding and a recoiling follow-through. Those who succeeded while pushing off were able to do so while maintaining balance and the other elements of outstanding mechanics. They gained the benefits of increased arm speed without suffering the mechanical consequences. It's not easy to do, and most shouldn't even try. You can get good velocity with control through the much simpler tall and fall delivery. Dwight Gooden in his younger days and Kerry Wood now are both prime examples of that.

"Slowing down your body and thinking 'quick arm' will improve your control and velocity immediately."

—Dave Smith, former Houston Astros closer

dropping down this low to deliver a pitch—so low that your back leg is actually scraping on the mound—is like throwing from a lower mound. Why not force the hitter to contend with a pitch coming to him on more of a downward plane. Why rob yourself of the advantage of height?

DON SUTTON: STIFF FRONT LEG

Don Sutton raised some eyebrows by pitching 23 seasons and winning 324 games without any arm miseries. He pitched with a very tall delivery, unlike the "drop and drive" of Tom Seaver. A key to his success with this type of motion was that he "got over" his front leg, that is, flexed his upper body forward and downward, thus giving him good vertical momentum, extension, and follow-through.

ROBB NEN: STAYING BACK

Robb Nen, the hard-throwing closer of the San Francisco Giants, reaches 100 miles per hour with one of the strangest pitching motions you'll ever see. Despite a great arm, he struggled mightily in the Texas Rangers' minor league system. The Rangers finally promoted him to their major league team on the strength of his potential alone. He walked 26 and struck out only 12 in 23 innings, so they gave up and dealt him to the Marlins for a journeyman reliever. In Florida, pitching coach Larry Rothschild diagnosed him as a classic "rusher" and completely reworked his delivery.

As a result, Nen now succeeds by defying nearly all of the old-school wisdom. He does not use a windup, pitching from the stretch at all times. He does not push off the rubber, going with a tall and fall approach. Tap and fall might be more accurate, considering that he uses a stutter step with his stride foot to keep from rushing his delivery. Immediately after beginning his movement toward the plate, he taps the mound with his left foot to remind himself to stay back and not try to do too much before planting his stride foot. Nen began to throw strikes, gained velocity, and became a dominant reliever almost overnight.

In the controlled fall—or tall and fall—delivery, *you are not pushing off the rubber.* You are striding a distance that is roughly equal to your height. Your leg should be flexed as you land—not too bent and not stiff. Landing on a front leg that is bent at any less than a right angle will not allow you to transfer the energy from your legs up to your arm. Instead, your front leg won't be able to absorb the energy and will collapse. Landing on a leg that is stiff won't allow for a proper follow-through and will damage your arm.

Most of the power that you get on your pitches will not come from your arm but from your hip turn—just as batters, golfers, quarterbacks, tennis players, and boxers do. It's fundamental to many athletic activities, and pitching is no exception. So as you stride, your toes are *not* pointed at the target—this will open up your hips too soon. To use your hips, you need to point your

John Smoltz set in the power position.

toes slightly to the throwing arm side of the plate. This way you land with a slightly closed front foot—for a right-hander, your foot should be at "1:00"—which will allow you to rotate against and over a firm but slightly flexed (at 135 degrees) lead leg, and thus generate more rotational and downward force. By planting too far to the side of the throwing arm, you throw too much against your body; by planting too far to the glove side, you open the hips too far to the glove side, causing a loss of rotational torso speed and ultimately arm speed.

"We want our pitchers to step directly toward the target, to step in a direct line to where we intend the ball to go (but keep the toe slightly closed). If you move off line by planting the lead foot too far to the right, you're throwing against your body, if you move off line by planting the lead foot too far to the left, you're losing power and arm speed."

—Bob Apodaca, former New York Mets pitching coach

Kevin Brown lands with his stride foot slightly closed to home plate. His front toe points to the one o'clock position.

Your stride affects where you land, and where you land affects your release point. If you overstride, your throwing arm will come through lower than it usually does and your pitches will usually be wild high. Think of it as throwing uphill. If you finish with your head behind your landing foot, you are overstriding.

Another source of trouble in striding is landing on the heel of your stride foot rather than the ball of the foot. This can cause a host of problems, including causing you to open your hips too soon and lose power. You want to land flat, not heel first, with the weight on the inside ball of your foot—landing on the outside of your stride foot will throw your balance off to your glove side. If you find yourself rolling over on the outside of your front foot, bend your front knee in slightly and try to land initially more toward the ball of your foot.

Landing with the weight on the ball of your foot or flat-footed rather than on the heel of your foot is critical. Before the conclusion of your delivery, your stride foot will actually be "digging in" with your toes. You can see pitchers who appear to land with their heel first and experience no problems with their delivery. But what they're doing is softly "touching" the ground with their heel, and then "landing" with their weight on the ball of their foot. This is not recommended, but some pitchers are able to do this without affecting their delivery.

Remember: Pitching is just as much a lower body as upper body exercise. If you don't have this deceptively simple lower body exercise down, even the most powerful arm in the world won't be able to bail you out. A beginning pitcher should put in a lot of work getting the stride down before even throwing a ball.

"A simple solution to overstriding is to tell the pitcher to concentrate on sticking his nose out in front of his toes upon release. When the pitcher gets his nose out front, the stride takes care of itself. So when a pitcher gets tired and starts to throw the ball high, have him try to put his nose in the catcher's mitt."

—Spanky McFarland, James Madison head baseball coach

"Efficient athletic movement is not generated from the heels; the human body is not designed to work that way."

—Tom House

If you understride, your pitches will be wild low (you have moved your release point forward of your stride foot, and thus lowered the downward trajectory of the pitch). Where your stride foot lands left or right of the line between the rubber and home plate is also very important. Many pitchers think that they should be pointing their foot directly toward the catcher. This is ok as long as the toe is pointed slightly toward the throwing hand

Landing on your heel is incorrect and produces a stiff, choppy delivery susceptible to loss of balance.

Understriding causes wild pitches in the dirt.

side. For example, a right-hander should be pointing his foot toward the third base corner of home plate in order to give him more leverage in his hip turn. Hitters stride toward the pitcher, but they don't point the toe of their front foot at the pitcher. They keep the foot slightly closed, which keeps the hips from flying open too soon. Try it and see how much less power you get in your swing. You'll feel your arms generating nearly all of the power while your lower body produces very little. This is exactly what you want to avoid on the mound.

When a right-hander lands too far to the right of the midline that leads to the target, the result is that he throws across his body. If your pitches are consistently sailing high and inside to a same-hand batter, check the landing position of your stride foot. If it's several inches to the right of the midline, this could be the problem.

If you find that you can't get your foot to the proper landing position, it may be because you've rotated your hips too much during the knee lift. If you bring your leg too far back behind the pitching rubber, you may not leave enough time to get your stride foot to its correct landing position.

When a pitcher lands too far to the glove side of the target, he is opening up his hips too soon. It's similar to a hitter who "steps in the bucket" and commits his hips too soon. His weight moves outside of his body and his hips have already turned. This diminishes the torque needed to uncoil and flex the upper body and to square the shoulders with the hips. This opening up of the hips too soon and too far toward your glove hand will rob you of your power. It may also force you to slow down your arm to compensate. Your pitches can either go outside to a same-hand batter or hang right over the plate with nothing on them.

When you take the mound, dig a small hole where you want to land your stride foot. If it's your home mound, you should know where this is already. If it's an away or road game, take a few warmup pitches first. If you find that the landscape or condition of the mound is affecting your stride or plant foot, do not adjust your motion. Call time-out and ask the host team to make repairs. It's a simple request that may save you from injury, a horrendous outing, or both. You should not have to adjust where you land or how your foot is pointed on each pitch.

Having a proper stride is critical, but you can't concentrate so hard on it that you aren't focused on the catcher's glove. Throw countless pitches with the proper mechanics until it becomes part of your "muscle memory."

Striding too closed sacrifices power, adversely affects location, and puts strain on the pitching shoulder.

Striding too open sacrifices power, adversely affects location, and puts strain on the pitching elbow.

RUSHING

When a pitcher moves toward the plate too soon, that is, before his throwing hand has moved down, back, and up so that the elbow is at shoulder height, he is said to be rushing. The pitcher fails to get his throwing arm and hand to the release point at the proper time in the sequence of throwing mechanics. The arm arrives late and low, causing the pitcher to throw uphill. This results in erratic control, often high in the strike zone.

"When you're out on the mound, you have to be able to make adjustments on your own so you can focus on pitching. If it's a crucial part of the game, you don't want to walk a hitter or throw a careless pitch because you're worried about your mechanics."

—David Wells, Toronto Blue Jays

GET YOUR ELBOWS UP

As you begin your controlled fall, your stride foot, front hip, lead elbow, front knee, and your glove should all be pointed toward home plate. The shortest—and fastest—distance between two points is a straight line. Keep your body on this line. This is all part of a simple, compact delivery. Doing so will use your body's energy most efficiently, while keeping the hitter from picking up the ball too early in your delivery.

As you begin your stride, separate the ball from the glove. You need to do this at the same place for every pitch, or your timing will be thrown off. Just as you need to get comfortable with a consistent knee lift, you need to get used to holding your hands in the same place. When pitching from the windup, hold them at your center of gravity, which is basically the point where your hands meet when your arms hang down together in front of your body.

Hold your hands against your body during your knee lift. This will help you stay in line with

Joey Hamilton separates the ball from his glove and gets his elbows up in a straight line.

throwing your arms out "off line," you may be compensating for an imbalance in your delivery. If you've achieved balance in your knee lift, you should have no difficulty in taking a long stride toward the plate while holding your elbows straight out from your upper body.

Don't cheat yourself on your backswing. The farther back toward second base that you reach—without shifting your weight backward—the more hand speed you will be able to generate.

Keep your throwing wrist relaxed during your backswing. Avoid "hooking" the ball—bending your wrist down—as you bring your arm back. This is a difficult habit to break and a cause of many injuries. Feel the tension in your upper forearm when you bend your wrist down, then compare that to how your arm feels when you keep your wrist relaxed. This is just the kind of muscular tension that you want to avoid during your delivery. Throwing with a relaxed arm will help you generate more speed and movement with less risk of injury.

second base and home plate. Break your hands as your knee lift starts falling downward. Push your glove hand up and out toward home plate while dropping your pitching hand down, back, and up as you extend both arms during the beginning of your stride. Keep your fingers on top of the ball, your hand pointed at the shortstop if right-handed and at the second baseman if left-handed. Keeping your elbows up—both your lead elbow and your throwing elbow—is part of throwing low strikes.

As you separate your hands and take the ball out of the glove, your backswing should progress in a smooth-flowing counterclockwise motion. Do not take the ball out of the glove and immediately straighten your throwing arm down by your side. Locking the arm stiff with the ball pointed down at the ground and pausing in the backswing is called "sticking." Sticking may not allow your arm to get to your release point in time during the delivery. Some pitchers do stick and get away with it, but remember, the goal is to simplify your mechanics.

Your elbows should remain on the line that extends from second base through the midpoint of the rubber to home plate. If you find yourself

David Wells is an example of a pitcher who "sticks." However, Wells has great balance and is able to get his hand on top of the ball before his arm gets to its release point.

Notice the pitcher is hooking the ball and his shoulders are off line. To correct this problem, take the ball back

toward second base when starting your arm swing. Think about "showing the ball to second base."

"Aim to establish as wide an arc over the top as you can efficiently achieve. The wider the arc, the more velocity and movement you will get on the ball."

—Tom Seaver on bringing the throwing arm back as you begin your stride to the plate

Don't treat your lead arm as an afterthought. It is very important to generating power in your delivery. Your lead arm extends toward home plate, thumbs down, as your throwing arm reaches back toward second base—some pitchers flick their glove in the batter's line of sight as they do this, which can be distracting for a hitter.

When your stride foot lands, it will be your shoulders, pulled around by the hip turn and forward by the flexing of your torso, that help build the power and hand speed that propel your pitches. The momentum built by the big muscles of the legs, abdomen, and back is transferred through the shoulders to your pitching arm and hand, enabling them to sail by your head toward

Get the hand up, fingers on top of the ball, and point the lead elbow toward the target.

home plate. There is no faster human movement than this—like a whip, your hand slings the ball toward the target.

> *"At times my mechanics falter when I don't keep my front shoulder closed through my delivery. You've got to keep your glove-hand shoulder closed. That's your steering wheel, and you point it right at the location of the pitch you're throwing. Your left side is your quiet side if you're a right-handed pitcher and your right side is your power side. Any time that's reversed and the left side becomes my power side I get real jerky and start throwing the ball all over the place."*
>
> —Roger Clemens, five-time Cy Young Award winner

Just prior to release, rotate your throwing forearm outward so that the ball is behind and above your ear, with your index and middle fingers on top of the ball. You have *not* turned your throwing palm up at any point during your backswing. Your throwing elbow is above your shoulder and ahead of your wrist. If your elbow was in line with your wrist, you'd be throwing stiff-armed. If you can watch yourself on a videotape shot from the side, you'll see that leading with your elbow actually creates nearly a 90-degree angle between your forearm and upper arm. This creates a powerful catapulting effect, the culmination of forces built by the rotation of the lower body and flexion of the upper body. Your wrist does not move in front of your elbow until your arm passes your ear.

Deliver the ball the same distance from your ear each time in order to develop control of your pitches. Throwing too close to your ear—a form of "short arming"—hampers velocity and places too much strain on the arm. Letting the ball stray too far from your ear makes it difficult to stay on top, and usually causes you to deliver some very fat pitches.

Elbow over shoulder and fingers on top of the ball are critical checkpoints. Drop either and your pitches will hang. Late in games, you may have to make a conscious effort to keep your elbow up and throw the top half of the ball.

Depending on your arm slot, the arm angle or spot where you bring your hand forward, your upper body will be close to vertical (three-quarter overhand release point), bent toward the pitching hand slightly (slightly below three-quarter overhand release point), or tilted more noticeably toward the throwing arm (sidearm). There should be a slight difference in the mechanics of a sidearm pitcher, since he is relying more on rotational or angular velocity (rather than vertical or downward velocity, generated by flexing down and over the front leg) to generate his arm and hand speed.

David Wells begins his controlled fall to home plate.

"A great many pitchers, and successful ones, too, do not restrict their pitches to one delivery, but often resort to a combination of overhand and sidearm deliveries. Leading pitchers, however, generally use only one style. They develop their assortment of fastballs, curveballs, slow balls . . . from their one delivery to the greatest degree of efficiency in regard to speed, break, and control of the ball. Pitchers who resort to a variety of deliveries do not approximate this perfection with any single delivery principally because there is not enough exercise of one delivery. Walter Johnson, Christy Mathewson, Cy Young, Grover Alexander, and many other immortals were exponents of 'one delivery.'"

—Ethan Allen, former major leaguer and Yale baseball coach

CHOOSING AN ARM SLOT

"I like to have my pitchers use a natural arm action. Whenever I want to see what their natural arm action is, I suggest they they catch a fly ball and then run and throw the ball. Wherever they throw from, right there, I would say that would be the most natural position of their arm."

—Johnny Sain, former pitching coach

Dennis Eckersley threw sidearm because it felt natural to him. Not true of Dan Quisenberry, who closed games for the Royals in the 1980s, baffling hitters with an underhanded delivery he picked up in the minors to compensate for a lack of velocity.

Former scout Al Kubski said, "Quiz was the kind of pitcher you would let play catch in your backyard because if he threw one wild, it wouldn't break any windows. . . . His fastball was nothing. Maybe 80 miles per hour if that. When he was in the minors, a bullpen catcher told Quiz that he would never make it with that kind of speed. He said Quiz should try something different and suggested that he try pitching underneath. Quiz did and he had a great career and became a millionaire by using that confusing delivery. . . . He was still pitching 78 miles per hour as a major leaguer, but they couldn't hit his junk."

Most pitchers are better off finding their natural arm slot and sticking with it. However, it is important to know the advantages and disadvantages of each type of delivery.

Many of the game's most dominant power pitchers pitched closer to overhand (which actually is at one o'clock), such as Sandy Koufax and the 6′8″ J. R. Richard. In general, you will be able

As Wells plants and rotates, his elbow is above his shoulder and ahead of his wrist.

Part of what makes Kevin Brown so effective is that he throws a variety of pitches from several different arm slots. Here he is shown throwing from a three-quarter delivery and then from a sidearm delivery. Notice how his upper body flexes more in the three-quarter delivery and rotates more in the sidearm delivery.

to throw harder from this delivery, though your pitches won't move as much. You also take full advantage of your height and that of the mound, and the vertical momentum you've generated. These factors account for your pitches traveling on a steeper, downward plane. Curveballs thrown from this delivery are called "twelve o'clock, six o'clock" (even though in reality it's a "1:00 to 7:00" arm sweep) because they break down more than sideways. But this sometimes means that a pitcher who throws overhand will need to develop a slider if he wants a pitch that will break away from same-hand hitters. Many overhand pitchers have an easier time making their fastball "hop," but a harder time making it sink or tail away from opposite-hand hitters.

Most pitchers throw some slight variation of three-quarters, which trades off a little power for more lateral movement. Their pitches will tend to have more sinking and tailing action on them—moving down and in on same-hand hitters—than those of "high three-quarters" or overhand pitchers. Their curves will have both a downward and a side-to-side break, ably demonstrated by David Wells in his outstanding 1998 postseason. Steve Carlton threw a devastating slider from a three-quarters motion, as does Randy Johnson, from a low three-quarters delivery position, and many other masters of that pitch. Hall of Famer Walter Johnson didn't fight his natural arm slot—spending most of his career as a pure fastball pitcher with a low, three-quarters delivery.

Most sidearmers trade off speed and power for lateral movement. Even sidearmers with mediocre velocity can get a tailing and sinking action on their pitches, though it is harder for sidearmers to develop a cut fastball with downward break. It will be a rare one who can establish himself as a power pitcher with this delivery. Pitchers who come from the side are usually very tough on same-hand hitters, and often have trouble retiring opposite-hand hitters. Rather than challenge opposite-hand hitters with heat, most have to rely on Dennis Eckersley's recipe for serving lefties: "You have to throw inside to get them off the plate, then get them out with off-speed stuff outside."

"If I have a pitcher who throws from different arm slots and does so with effectiveness, I don't change a thing. But if it starts to affect his control and he becomes wild when changing arm angles, then I would step in and suggest that he throw from a consistent arm slot."

—Mel Queen, Toronto Blue Jays
pitching coach

In choosing your arm slot, the most important thing is to find one that you're comfortable with. It is not true that any one technique puts more or less wear and tear on the arm. If you have sound mechanics in all phases of the delivery, your arm should remain healthy regardless of your release point. A sidearmer without sound mechanics is just as likely as an overhand pitcher to injure his elbow or shoulder.

"I don't throw with my arm or shoulder, but with the base of my spine."

—Hall of Famer Lefty Grove

OPEN YOUR HIPS, ROTATE AROUND A FIRM FRONT LEG

As your stride foot lands, pull your lead elbow down and in to your side—so that your glove is tucked against your ribs, as if you were carrying a football under your arm. Pull firmly and smoothly with your lead elbow, not violently. Any exaggerated movement with your lead elbow may throw you off balance to the glove side.

"Driving your left arm down outside your left hip . . . as though you were trying to knock the wind out of someone behind you, will help establish good off-arm mechanics. Pulling with your hand rather than your elbow will cause you to sling the ball."

—Tom Seaver

This shoulder drive will pull your arm through on that line between home plate and the pitcher's rubber. You have to tuck the glove to your ribs, because as the lead arm goes so goes the lead shoulder. When the glove isn't tucked under and the lead arm flies off toward first base (for right-handers), this is called "flying open." It will make it harder for you to throw strikes, while also putting strain on your throwing shoulder.

Pulling down with your lead elbow while opening your hips drives your throwing arm toward the plate. Here is where timing is perhaps most critical. You need to have the ball ready to deliver just as you turn your hips and drive your shoulder through. If you deliver the ball too early, you are throwing the ball with nothing but arm. If you are late with your arm, you rush to catch up and lose control.

Detroit Tigers reliever Matt Anderson tends to struggle when he exerts too much energy during his motion in an effort to maximize his velocity. "My biggest thing is keeping my body under control throughout my motion. Sometimes I get ahead of myself and think about throwing the ball too hard. When that happens, I have to take a step back, regain my focus, and concentrate on throwing one pitch at a time."

"Dizzy Dean and Lefty Grove . . . were big men; but they did not derive their effectiveness from their bigness, but from their ability to control the muscles used in pitching. . . . Much of it can be credited to their faculty of putting something on the ball without apparently making a maximum effort. They presented perfect pictures of grace on the mound, and delivered the ball to the catcher with such freedom and ease that they expended much less energy than other pitchers of similar proportions who apparently do not know the meaning of the word relax."

—Ethan Allen

Pulling your lead arm away from or across your body opens your front shoulder prematurely. A flying front shoulder adversely affects control and velocity.

Stepping too far to the throwing hand side forces you to throw with a restricted uncoiling and flexing of the torso.

FOLLOW THROUGH

The objective in your follow-through is to land in good fielding position while keeping your throwing arm from absorbing too much of the brunt of decelerating. Fortunately, one leads to the other.

If you've done everything properly to this point, your follow-through should take care of itself. If you throw overhand, your pitching hand should come to rest between your glove-side ankle and knee. Some long-striding, over-the-top pitchers have been known to wear a pad on their knee to cushion the blow of their elbow. If you throw three-quarters, you should come to rest between your glove-side knee and belt. A sidearmer should finish between his waist and chest, since there is almost no vertical momentum in this delivery.

As you deliver the ball, your torso bends and your back leg rises up as a natural response. Do not drag your back foot as you deliver the ball. This will take velocity off of your pitches. Some pitchers do this on their change-ups, but it's a bad habit to get into; instead, pull your foot away from the rubber. Depending on the force of your delivery, letting your back leg rise could bring your back foot above your head. Hard thrower or not, keep your back knee close to your stride leg during the follow-through, rather than letting it fly off toward your throwing-arm side.

Don't try to hit the brakes on your throwing arm—let it follow through naturally. Some pitchers snap their pitching hand back up after releasing the ball, which forces too much of the energy they've generated to be borne by their throwing arm. Just let the follow-through happen—but observe the results. If your throwing hand ends up too high, you may not be keeping your elbow up. Or you may not be getting enough of your back into your release, which could be due to your lead shoulder flying open. If your throwing hand ends up between your legs rather than to the glove side, you may be throwing across your body. You need to know your delivery well enough that you recognize when something's not right—and why. Remember, more arm injuries occur during the follow-through than in any other phase of the pitching motion.

Dan Plesac gets full extension and a strong follow-through.

"You've got to finish your pitches. In order to maximize your velocity and keep your pitches down in the strike zone, you must extend and follow through."

—Mark Leiter, major league reliever

Observe your feet, too. Power pitchers should land one inch to the throwing hand side of a line directly between home plate and the rubber. Finesse pitchers should land straight on the line or one inch to the left of it. Your back leg should come to rest more or less in line with your stride foot, about 24 inches to the throwing-arm side. This is called "landing square," and it puts you in excellent fielding position. Your weight should be a bit more heavy on your stride foot. If you land too heavily on your pivot foot, you may be throwing across your body.

Just as you want to have balance at the beginning of your delivery during the lift phase, you want balance when you finish up. If you find yourself falling off the mound to the glove side, you could be throwing across your body or flying open with your lead arm. Or you could simply be a pitcher like Hall of Famers Jim Bunning or Bob

A poor follow-through: lack of flexing and bending over front leg.

In proper follow-through, bring your throwing arm, hand, and shoulder down over the lead leg. Bring your glove hand up and in front of your body after it passes down and behind your plant leg.

Gibson, whose three-quarters deliveries were so powerful that they were thrown off balance. Not only does this put you into poor fielding position, it is an indicator of significant horizontal momentum—and horizontal momentum doesn't do anything for your velocity. You're launching a ball at your catcher, so you want all of your energy to be concentrated in that direction. Think about how you can make that happen.

"The head may be the most important component of the pitching delivery, for direction. Wherever the head goes, the body follows. . . . When a pitcher falls off toward first base, it is often because his head pulled him in that direction. The head should always go directly at the plate."

—Spanky McFarland

PITCHING MECHANICS FROM THE SET POSITION

Much of the mechanics employed in the windup motion is replicated in pitching from the set position. However, two techniques—lifting of the leg and arm action—are different. Pitchers must master these new techniques if they are to successfully keep runners from stealing bases.

The right-handed pitcher especially needs to adapt. He must reduce the height of the leg lift and speed it up slightly. And he must unload his pitch quicker. He does this by not only speeding up the leg lift but also by breaking his hands apart earlier and quickening his backswing. The important thing is to get the throwing arm into a consistent and proper cocked position.

STANCE AND STRETCH

Stand with the shoulders aligned between home plate and second base, the pivot or back foot in front of and parallel to the rubber. Keep the outside edge of your foot in contact with the rubber. The lead or stride foot is forward toward home plate, about shoulder-width or less (minimum 12 inches) apart.

Stand upright, balanced and relaxed, hands apart with the pitching hand alongside or in back. Hold the ball in your pitching hand. This allows you to adjust the grip for various pitches as you bring the hands together, and it allows for quick pickoff moves.

Rock forward, then backward, returning the feet to about shoulder-width apart. Stop with your hands together, pitching hand inside the glove. The most efficient position is between the letters and chin, because this position enables you to move immediately into the downward and backward arc that is necessary for cocking the arm and hand.

While stopped with your hands together held chest high, or in the set position, keep the front shoulder and front hip aligned toward home plate. Position your head so that you can see the runner on first base and the catcher's target by moving your eyes.

LEG LIFT, HAND BREAK, AND ARM ACTION

Right-handed pitchers must lift the knee quickly, reducing the height to about the thigh level of the pivot leg. Rock back quickly. This shifts your weight over the pivot leg—you go back before moving forward.

As you lift and rock backward, break the hands and move the pitching arm down, back, and up, the same as in the windup. In fact, the rest of the motion is the same as in the windup.

A good pickoff move for a left-handed pitcher depends on deception, not on speed, as is necessary with a right-handed pitcher. Take the sign with the pivot foot in front of and touching the rubber, feet shoulder-width apart and pitching hand alongside or in back. Confirm the sign with the catcher and check the runner. Rock forward and bring your hands together in front of the chest or abdomen. Keep your eyes looking at a point halfway between the runner and home plate. You can see both with your peripheral vision and the runner will not be able to read your eyes.

Lift your lead leg the same as if you were throwing to home plate. Keep your body balanced over the posting leg. Vary your head movements. For example, look at the runner, then to the plate. Then, look at the plate, then to the runner, then to the plate. Change your pattern so the runner cannot learn with any certainty when you're delivering the pitch to home plate. Do not swing the leg behind the rubber; this would be a balk. Instead, as the throwing arm begins its down, back, and upward swing, change your arm direction and throw to first. You may drift slightly, but you must plant your stride foot before it passes beyond a point that is 45 degrees toward home plate.

Aim your throw to arrive at the first baseman's knee closest to the base runner. Finish the throw by moving toward first base. This will help with accuracy and help convince the umpires that you didn't move toward home plate and throw to first base.

WHEN TO PITCH FROM THE STRETCH

Generally speaking, you pitch from the stretch when a runner is on first or second with an open base in front of him. There are other times when you may also want to pitch from the stretch, such as when there is a runner on third with less than two outs and a squeeze play is possible. Anytime your infield is playing up to get the runner at the plate, you need to pitch from the stretch to give them a chance to make the play. You may also want to go from the stretch when you have the bases loaded, a 3-2 count, and two outs. The runners will be moving on the pitch, and going from the stretch will keep them closer—which may mean the difference between an inning-ending force play and a run-scoring infield single.

When pitching from the stretch, just about everything should remain the same except the starting point. Your pivot foot is already in place in front of the rubber, with your stride foot about eight inches ahead. You want to be able to shift your weight back and forth quickly with your stride foot to save time on your delivery to the plate. Being "closed" in this manner will help your balance and will keep your shoulders and hips from opening up too soon. Your knees may be flexed slightly more when pitching from the stretch than the windup, which will allow you to move more quickly to first base.

You have to take the sign from the catcher with your pivot foot along the front of the rubber and your throwing hand at your side or behind your back. You then have to reach a "set" position with your hands together, in front of you, above the waist and below the chin, and come to a complete stop.

When taking your sign, you can bend at the waist or stand relaxed; the latter is less fatiguing as the game goes along. Remember the "keep it simple" principle. It doesn't just have mechanical benefits, it delays the effects of fatigue as well.

Many pitchers hold their hands together at the belt when in the stretch position, but there are advantages to coming set at the letters or even higher. You will break your hands and go directly into the elbows-up, thumbs-down position, rather than having to come up and then back down again. This will accelerate your delivery to the plate. Coming set high will help a right-hander develop a quicker move to first base for the same reason.

Some pitchers choose to pitch from the stretch whether there are runners on base or not. Most of these are relief pitchers who are used to working with men on base. Several have chosen to do it because they find it easier to throw strikes from the stretch. Dispensing with the rocker step and hand lift, they can go right into the knee lift. They find it easier to stay in balance.

Though it's important to deliver the ball quickly, be careful not to rush when delivering the

When taking the sign while in the stretch position, do not bend at the waist and put pressure on your stride leg. The

additional wear and tear on your leg is unnecessary. Stand tall and evenly distribute the weight of your body.

ball. Also, avoid landing with your stride foot open and pointed directly toward the plate rather than landing slightly closed.

Don't try to create two completely different motions for the windup and the stretch. Your command will suffer greatly. Practice the stretch as much, if not more than, your regular windup. After all, your biggest pitches in any given game are likely to come while in the stretch.

DRILLS

There are different drills you can use to help you with all aspects of your delivery. Many don't even involve throwing. Those that do don't require hard throwing.

MIRROR DRILL

Practice your delivery in front of a mirror, stopping it upon completion of each of the three phases.

At the knee lift, check that your head is over your pivot foot, the back leg flexed slightly with your weight on the ball of the foot, shoulders level, front knee lifted at least as high as the belt and pointing somewhere between third base and shortstop (for right-hander), toes lower than the heels, and hand and glove together and next to the body at your center of gravity.

At the end of the fall phase, check that your stride foot has landed flat to the glove side of the target with the toes closed off slightly and the weight on the ball of the foot, the front knee is bent but no more than 90 degrees, lead hip and shoulder are both pointed at the target, glove is over the elbow, the lead elbow is no higher than the shoulder, throwing elbow is ahead of the wrist, fingers are on top of the ball, your head is on line toward the target, and your eyes are on the target.

At the end of the follow-through phase, check that your throwing arm has finished to the glove side of your stride foot and that your pivot foot has come to rest 24 inches to the throwing-arm side of your stride foot. Feel whether your back bent forward and your back foot came up prior to landing.

You should get to know your delivery so well that you can immediately recognize flaws when reviewing video of your pitching—or recognize differences when comparing it to other pitchers you play with, against, or watch on television.

"Seeing myself on video has always helped me correct my mechanics. Advice from a pitching coach can certainly help, but when you can see yourself making a mistake with your own eyes, you get a better perception of what the problem is at hand."

—David Wells, Toronto Blue Jays

BALANCE DRILL

With a coach standing alongside the pitching rubber, begin your delivery without the baseball and pause at the peak of your knee lift. Your coach should then place a baseball in your throwing hand and you should continue your delivery. No matter how long your coach takes to hand you the ball, you should be able to maintain your balance. Without a coach, you can pause and wait for your catcher to yell "Go!" before continuing. Without a coach or a catcher, you can throw against the wall with an exaggerated pause in your delivery. However you do it, your objective is to make certain that you have established balance.

Balance Drill

Swing Drill

SWING DRILL

If you have trouble with leg swinging during the knee-lift phase, use this drill until you've eliminated it. Pitch from the stretch position, with your stride leg crossed in front of your back leg and your stride foot *on* the rubber. Lift your knee and pitch. Pitching from this position eliminates the ability to swing your leg. Do this until lifting feels natural.

LIFT DRILL

If you are having trouble lifting rather than kicking, set up an obstacle on the side of the mound near the rubber, such as a chair or trash can. Place it so that the only way you can pitch without contacting it is by lifting with your stride foot under your knee. Pitch until you've established a proper lift—doing so should lead naturally to lifting with your toes lower than your heels.

Lift Drill

STAY-CLOSED DRILL

When Nolan Ryan first came to the California Angels in 1972, pitching coach Tom Morgan broke him of the habit of flying open by simply standing in his way at the base of the mound. The only way that Ryan could pitch without hitting him was with a proper stride and by keeping his front shoulder closed. If you're having trouble staying closed, you can get the same results by practicing your motion alongside a padded wall in a gym.

STRIDE DRILL

Throughout this chapter there have been references to the line from the pitcher's rubber to home plate. Use lime to actually draw this line down the center of the mound. Mark your desired landing area as well: stride foot on the line (but toe closed, that is, pointed toward throwing-hand side) or slightly to the glove side of the line for finesse pitchers and one inch to the throwing hand side for power pitchers, with the stride length roughly equal to your height. If you have trouble with overstriding, use the Back Foot Drill discussed later in this section.

Hip Drill

HIP DRILL

Pitchers must constantly remind themselves that pitching is a lower-body exercise. This drill eliminates the upper body completely, so that pitchers can focus on their hips. Place a bat behind your back and keep it there with your elbows. Now go through the lift, fall, and pull phases of your delivery, pausing at the end of each. The bat should point toward the plate at the end of both the lift and fall. The hips should not turn the bat (and the upper body) until the pull phase.

FRONT SHOULDER DRILL

This drill will help you to keep your shoulders level until release and to use your front shoulder to drive your throwing arm. Kneel on your back knee. Your front leg should be in front of you, bent at 90

Front Shoulder Drill

degrees, with your stride foot to the glove side of the target and closed off. Your arms should be extended in front and behind, with your elbows up and shoulders level. Your glove should be facing the target and slightly above your elbow, while your fingers should be on top of the ball. Pull your glove down and to the side, driving your arm through. Finish with your chest over your stride knee. You can't get much on your throws from this position without using your lead arm and bending your back. As you get more comfortable with this drill, you can begin it with your upper body at the end of the lift phase—hands together, next to the body, at the center of gravity.

FOLLOW-THROUGH DRILL

This drill will force you to bend your back and roll your pivot foot. Stand about two feet in front of a chair, with your stride foot in proper landing position. Place your pivot foot on the chair, inside down. Come to the set position, with hand and glove together at the center of gravity. Break your hands, elbows up, thumbs down, then throw to the target as if you were delivering a pitch. By removing the back leg from the delivery, this drill will force you to use your back and finish properly—your head ending up ahead of your stride

foot, your throwing arm ending up to the glove side of your stride foot, and your pivot foot rolling over and rising.

BACK FOOT DRILL

If you're dragging your back foot rather than rolling it as you deliver the ball, or if you're over-striding, practice with a brick or small piece of wood a few inches in front of the rubber. The only way you can pitch without hitting the object is if you keep your pivot foot back during your stride and roll it over and up in your follow-through.

CONTROL

"Control comes from concentration and mechanics. You need to know why a pitch ended up where it did. If it's low away, maybe you're flying open. If it's high, maybe your stride is too short. If it's low, your stride might be too long. You need to correct this on your next pitch or it's more balls and you're out of the game."

—Bob Tewksbury, former major
league pitcher

There is no one section in a book on pitching where control should be covered. It belongs in *every* section, because it is the most important aspect of pitching—more than movement, more than velocity. But control is inextricably linked with mechanics. Without proper mechanics, you'll never have consistent control. Without consistent control, you'll never come close to achieving your potential as a pitcher.

Roger Clemens may go down as one of the greatest power pitchers the game has ever seen, but he feels his command of the strike zone is equally attributable to his success. Clemens did not have a "rocket" for an arm in high school. His velocity became a factor later on when he developed a strong lower body and built up his arm strength. He says, "Any kid who believes that throwing hard is all he needs to do to be successful on the mound is mistaken. The reason I performed well in high school was because I threw strikes. I've carried that with me throughout my career. You can turn the lights out in a stadium and I can still throw strikes. But I didn't develop velocity until I matured and understood that the power comes from my lower body."

University of Florida baseball coach Andy Lopez classifies his pitchers by three levels. Level 1 pitchers throw strikes. Level 2 pitchers throw low strikes. And Level 3 pitchers throw low strikes both inside and outside. Nothing about velocity or movement. For him it's about location.

The keys to throwing strikes are:

Good balance. Begin and end your delivery in balance, with your head on the line from the pitcher's mound to home plate.

Easy stride. Do not rush to the plate. As former Los Angeles Dodgers pitching coach Red Adams put it, "Do not run off and leave your arm."

Compact delivery. Eliminate any swaying, that is, side-to-side movement, in your delivery—stay firmly over your posting leg. Lift your knee, don't kick your leg. Bring your arm straight back toward second base. Don't fly open with your lead arm and shoulder.

Consistent release point. Even with great balance, a perfect stride, and a compact delivery, if you can't release the ball at the same distance from your ear time after time it will be very difficult to throw strikes consistently.

Eyes on target. Satchel Paige developed from a wild rookie into a dazzling control pitcher who would literally use a gum wrapper, matchbook, or bottle top for home plate and still throw strikes. The mechanical adjustment he needed early in his career was simply to keep his eyes on the target. Some pitchers have helped their focus in practice by pitching with a patch over their non-dominant eye.

"If I had to give one piece of advice to a young pitcher, it would be to work on the location of your fastball. You need to be able to throw it for strikes when you need a strike. So command—or being able to throw it to specific areas in the strike zone—is the most important thing to learn."

—Chad Ogea, Detroit Tigers pitcher

Most right-handers have a dominant right eye, left-handers a dominant left eye. You can determine this for certain by forming a triangle with the thumbs and index fingers of your hands, and holding that out in front of you at arm's length. Focus on the image inside the triangle, then close one eye and open it, then close the other eye and open it. The image when viewed through your dominant eye will appear nearly identical to the image when viewed through both eyes. The image when viewed through your non-dominant eye will appear to move when viewed with both eyes.

Concentration. Block out your surroundings and focus on the glove, not the plate. Visualize the pitch hitting the target.

No fear. You can't be afraid of getting hit. This will lead you to nibble around the edges of the strike zone and walk too many batters. If you want to be afraid of something, be afraid of bases on balls, deep counts, and fielders back on their heels.

Staying aggressive on the mound even when you're getting hit is a lesson Jim Kaat learned early on in his 25-year major league career. During his first full major league season in 1961, Kaat and the Minnesota Twins held a 6–0 lead over the Kansas City Royals. Kaat surrendered back-to-back homers to Joe Pignatano and Deron Johnson, but induced the following hitter to pop up on a hard fastball down the middle of the plate. Upon returning to the dugout, Kaat was surprised to receive kind words of advice from his pitching coach, Eddie Lopat. Kaat said, "I sat on the bench and Eddie Lopat told me that I had made big strides that inning. I was a little confused by the compliment, but he went on to explain that the tendency with young pitchers in that situation is to get timid. You give up a couple of home runs and all of a sudden you become afraid to throw the ball in the strike zone. Lopat and Johnny Sain were influential in teaching me that even when you start getting hit, you have to get more aggressive instead of becoming more passive."

Reputation. The best way to get close pitches called strikes is to throw strikes. Umpires at all levels will unconsciously expand the strike zone for pitchers who are consistently around the plate.

> *"Once a pitcher has proved to the umpire and the hitter that he can throw strikes, he can start expanding the strike zone a little bit because they're used to seeing strikes."*
>
> —Scott McGregor, former Baltimore Orioles pitcher

Informed repetition. Know what you're doing and why, then do it over and over again. Eventually the plate should become less important and you should be focusing completely on the glove.

Throwing off the mound with a batter in the box is the best way to work on pitch location.

CONTROL DRILL

With each warm-up pitch, have your catcher set up a target on one of the corners: low-away, low-in, up-in, up-away. Have a batter stand in, if necessary. Work on your fastball, concentrating on location first then building velocity. Mix in your change-up and then your curve, aiming for the low corners or down the middle. As your control improves, you can add middle-in and middle-out to the four corners. Your catcher can set up six inches outside or inside to practice fastballs and breaking balls off the plate. Let your head determine location by throwing with your nose to the glove. If you don't have a catcher handy, use a wall and tape.

SURGICAL PRECISION

Through 1998, only 12 men have topped 10 strikeouts per nine innings for an entire season, and they've done it 30 times. Their names are very well known to most baseball fans: Sandy Koufax, "Sudden" Sam McDowell, Nolan Ryan and the "Ryan Express," Mike Scott, Randy "the Big Unit" Johnson, Hideo Nomo, David Cone, Dwight "Doctor K" Gooden, Pedro Martinez, Curt Schilling, Roger "the Rocket" Clemens, and Kerry Wood.

Well, it just so happens that walking fewer than one batter per nine innings for an entire season has been done even fewer times—only 29 times since the mound was moved back to 60 feet, 6 inches in 1893. A few present and future Hall of Fame pitchers have done it (Cy Young, Christy Mathewson,

Grover Alexander, Addie Joss, and Greg Maddux). But the remaining names are a bit less familiar: "Babe" Adams, "Tiny" Bonham, Bill Burns, Lamarr Hoyt, "Red" Lucas, Deacon Phillipe, Bret Saberhagen, "Slim" Salee, Jesse Tannehill, and Bob Tewksbury. It's as difficult a feat as blowing batters away, yet it remains almost entirely uncelebrated.

Now consider this. These control artists actually put up a better winning percentage in *their* extreme seasons than the overpowering strikeout pitchers—.654 to .619, which is enough to coast home with a six-game lead in a 162-game season!

The vast majority of the control artists plied their trade in the deadball era, when the cost of a walk was at its highest point. But there's been a control renaissance in recent years, as Bob Tewksbury showed what could be done when a below-average fastball and a good change-up are put exactly where you want it. Greg Maddux did the same thing with a bit more velocity, a lot more movement, and an even better change-up.

"Because Clemens throws so hard and has three or four nasty pitches makes him a tough pitcher to face. Throw in the fact that he's got pinpoint control and he becomes a hitter's nightmare."

—Seattle Mariner Brian Hunter, talking about the toughest pitchers to face in the major leagues

"Bases on balls is the curse of the nation."

—Satchel Paige, Hall of Fame pitcher

"When he's in the strike zone, he's definitely overpowering at this level. This kid has a lot of God-given talent, that's for sure. When he perfects his pitches and learns how to be in the strike zone all the time that he wants to be, and out of the strike zone when he wants to be, he's going to be dominating."

—Joe Cunningham, Class A manager, on Cardinals prospect Rick Ankiel

THE SECRET TO THEIR SUCCESS

Here are some quotes from pitchers, catchers, and batters involved in perfect games. When they talk about how it happened, they talk about location.

Yogi Berra on Don Larsen: "Don's biggest asset was his control. It was the best control he ever had. Anything I called for, he threw over. Everybody knew he was primarily a fastball pitcher, but on that day his slider was really working for him. Because he was able to get it over, his fastball was all the more tougher for the Dodgers to hit."

Harvey Haddix: "I used two pitches mainly—fastball and slider. I was hardly behind on anybody, and I was only 3–2 on one man."

Buck Martinez on Len Barker: "I've seen him throw a lot harder before, but he never knew where it was going to go."

Ron Hassey on Len Barker: "Lennie had a great curveball, and he always has an excellent fastball. But his control was the big thing. It was amazing. He threw almost every pitch right where I called for it."

Bob Boone on Mike Witt: "Today he just made great pitches. He was throwing everything for strikes. He put it on the corners. I asked him to make some perfect pitches and he did it every time."

Tom Browning: "For once, I had total concentration. It never drifted once. I was consistently on the corners, and they were up there hacking. Every pitch was where I wanted to throw it."

In 1998, David Wells became only the second pitcher in baseball history to toss a perfect game at Yankee Stadium. It was the first thrown by a Yankee during the regular season. (Larsen tossed his in the 1956 World Series and David Cone threw one in the 1999 regular season.) Wells didn't have a good bullpen session that day and actually had thoughts of survival rather than domination as he entered the game. But he tossed a one-two-three inning in the first, and the rest, as they say, is history. Here is what he recalls.

When I was warming up in the bullpen, I was upset. I was really agitated about my stuff, angry to be honest. [Yankees pitching coach] Mel Stottlemyre was watching me and asked me if I was crazy. He usually doesn't say too much when I get angry, because when I'm fighting myself I'm my own worst enemy. But I felt like I had a terrible bullpen. [Manager] Joe Torre usually asks Mel how the pitcher looks before the game, and when he asked, Mel just turned to him and said, "Wow!" I didn't hear him say that, and I probably wouldn't have cared anyway. I just took the mound hoping my stuff would come together when I began facing hitters.

So when I went out, I got in a groove right away. You never expect that groove to last nine innings, but that's exactly what happened. All I was doing was getting strike one, strike two, and getting guys in a jam. When you get ahead in the count and you've got good stuff, you can pretty much throw hitters anything and they'll swing, even at balls in the dirt. When you get in that type of groove, it's almost like you can feel what pitch should be your next.

As difficult as throwing a perfect game sounds, it was a fairly easy day. Only one ball was hit real hard all day, and that was when Ron Coomer lined out to [second baseman] Chuck Knoblauch. Not to knock the Twins—I mean, they had some great hitters in their lineup—but I simply stayed ahead of the hitters and kept them guessing. I had great focus that day and threw pitches in the right spots and let the fielders take care of the rest.

When I reflect on the game, it was an unbelievable experience, but not in the way most people would expect. When you think about no-hitters and perfect games, you think about guys making diving plays and the pitcher having unhittable stuff. But for me, I just got locked in a zone and threw good pitches. It was just doing a good job with the hitters every inning out. It was literally like having a one-two-three inning—nine innings in a row.

In 1968, "The Year of the Pitcher," Bob Gibson threw 13 shutouts and registered a 1.12 ERA while Denny McLain won 31 games. The secret to their success?

Denny McLain: "The bottom line was I never walked a lot of guys. In '68 my control became better. I think with experience you have a tendency to relax more out there."

Bob Gibson: "I'd say control has been a big thing. I haven't walked many. And I haven't been making as many mistakes as I used to."

Tim McCarver elaborated on the success of his batterymate, Bob Gibson. McCarver said, "It seemed like in 1967 and '68 everything came together as far as his control was concerned. His control was almost perfect. He could put the ball in a space of about four inches on the outside part of the plate with his slider or his fastball. Any time you wanted it. Plus, he was so consistent with that pitch the umpires started giving him pitches just off the plate—almost unreachable for right-handed hitters. When a left-hander came up he would raise it about six inches and put it right on the hands. His stuff was already established. Your stuff is more or less God-given. It's corraling it that makes the difference."

THROWERS VS. PITCHERS

Are you a thrower or a pitcher? A thrower throws hard with little idea of where it's going. A pitcher has a plan and takes more pride in hitting his spot than in making the catcher's glove pop. But you can also tell a thrower from a pitcher by looking at their mechanics. A pitcher delivers the ball with little to no wasted effort, the same way every time. A thrower delivers the ball with an inconsistent motion, usually all arm and always inefficient. A thrower can make it all the way to the big leagues, if his arm is good enough, but he can't stay there very long.

"My fastball is my bread and butter pitch because I'm a power pitcher, but understand the second part of that is 'pitcher.' When I'm not overpowering, I can still beat you."

—Roger Clemens, New York Yankees pitcher

David Wells is carried off the field by his teammates after completing the first-ever perfect game thrown during the regular season at Yankee Stadium.

Pitchers who think that the only way they can impress scouts is by throwing hard aren't entirely correct. True, there is a bias toward hard throwers—with Vida Blue just one example of an unpolished high school pitcher with a live arm and poor mechanics who was aggressively pursued anyway. Blue's teammate, Hall of Famer Catfish Hunter, however, attracted scouts with his fluid delivery far more than his fastball. So did Bret Saberhagen. Here's how scout Al Kubski described Saberhagen during high school: "He wasn't fast . . . but he had a good delivery, threw strikes, and didn't walk anybody."

When high school power pitchers draw not just a favorable review but a "can't miss" rave, it will be based almost as much on their delivery as their arm. Pro scouts rate prospects on the chances of faulty mechanics causing injury. If there is too great a risk, they do not pursue the player. It's one thing to put up big numbers on the radar gun, but it's another to see those pitches fired out of an effortless delivery. Consider high schooler Josh Beckett from Texas, who throws 97 miles per hour with a great curve. Mike McGilvray, who coached Kerry Wood in high school and coached against Beckett, says, "Beckett reminds me of Kerry. Similar build, same fluid motion. No wasted energy in his delivery."

No wasted energy in the delivery. If you're pitching with scouts in the stands, messing up your mechanics trying to hump the ball up there is one of the biggest mistakes you could make. Scouts will pass on a pitcher—even a hard thrower—who appears to be working too hard.

"I would say that in my rookie season, I was definitely a thrower and not a pitcher. I would just rear back and try to blow the ball by people. To a certain extent right now, I'm still a thrower. But I'm making a nice progression toward becoming a pitcher. I'm learning where to throw my fastball in certain situations and where not to throw it. I've added a second pitch and I'm working on a third. Becoming a pitcher is not something that happens overnight. It's a learning process that requires experience on the mound."

—Matt Anderson, Detroit Tigers
relief pitcher

SANDY KOUFAX AND NOLAN RYAN: MECHANICS

"[Pitching coach] Joe [Becker] would have Koufax pitching with a windup and without a windup, trying to discover some method that would put rhythm into his delivery. And just like that they found it one day—all at once—just a little rocking motion on the pitching mound. Suddenly he was a pitcher, not a thrower."

—Walter Alston, former Dodgers manager

"It was exhausting work, mechanical work, boring at times, but those days turned around my career. To accomplish anything in life you need faith and you sometimes need help."

—Nolan Ryan on working on his mechanics
in 1972

Sandy Koufax was a thrower who became the greatest pitcher of his generation, stringing together four of the most dominating seasons any pitcher has ever produced before retiring at the age of 31, at the peak of his game, due to an arthritic elbow. When people speak of Sandy Koufax, they talk about his left arm, his fastball, and his curveball. The secret to his success can be found in his mechanics, before his pitch was even thrown.

Koufax always had great stuff, but for the first six years of his career he was a losing pitcher who had a hard time just staying in the Dodgers' rotation. It wasn't until he developed a rhythm to his delivery that he could consistently throw strikes. It wasn't until he could consistently throw strikes that he could win. His fastball actually slowed down a bit and his strikeouts decreased, but he became a living legend and one of the few men to ever make the Hall of Fame on the strength of so few successful seasons.

The key to Koufax's mechanics? The same for most pitchers: the legs. Right from the rocking motion he placed at the start of his windup to give him rhythm and momentum, to the explosive hip turn that gave him the arm speed necessary to throw a baseball in the upper 90s. Pitching is location, movement, and velocity, with location and velocity driven more by the *lower* body than the upper body.

Like Sandy Koufax before him, Nolan Ryan had been a thrower who didn't become a pitcher until he worked out his mechanics. It didn't happen until he was traded to the California Angels in 1972, after he'd been in the majors with the New York Mets for several seasons. Fortunately for Ryan, a brainy catcher named Jeff Torborg (who caught one of Koufax's no-hitters, coincidentally) was with the Angels then. He diagnosed Ryan's difficulties very quickly: overthrowing, rushing, working too hard to deliver the ball. As a result, Ryan was often wild high. Ryan worked hard to simplify, smooth out, and slow down his motion until it became perhaps the *ideal* motion—relaxed, fluid, with a high but controlled knee lift, an explosive hip turn, and a smooth follow-through. It carried him until the age of 46, through more than a few 200-pitch games, a power pitcher until the end, without any serious ailments.

THE COST OF POOR MECHANICS

The flawless delivery is nearly as rare as a 97-mile-per-hour fastball. Don Gullett pitched for division winners, pennant winners, and world champions in seven of his nine seasons in the big leagues. He retired at the age of 27 with 109 wins and a winning percentage of .686, succumbing to arm injuries that had begun very early in his career. He threw across his body, which virtually guarantees an arm injury eventually. It was a problem that dated back to high school, but was never corrected.

Thanks to a very unorthodox pitching motion, Rookie of the Year and Cy Young Award winner Rick Sutcliffe had his career frequently interrupted by arm miseries. He committed two cardinal sins by hooking his wrist as he drew his arm back toward second base, and landing on a stiff front leg. When he was healthy, he could be the best pitcher in baseball. He went 16–1 in little more than a half season for the Cubs in 1984 after coming over from the Indians in a trade, and followed that up with a league-leading 18 wins in 1987. In between he went 8–8 and 5–14 in partial seasons.

Ewell Blackwell won 22 games for the 1947 Reds at the age of 24. He hooked his wrist on his backswing and threw with a sidearm motion that earned him an ominous nickname, "the Whip." He suffered an arm injury in 1948, and arm miseries ailed him throughout his career. After his brilliant 1947 season, he pitched only seven more seasons, going 51–57.

Young, hard-throwing Jaret Wright of the Cleveland Indians was in the high 90s from his first days in the major leagues, but his arm practically snaps like a whip as he delivers the ball. If his mechanics don't improve, those days in the major leagues could be unfortunately short—as they were for another hard-throwing pitcher with a recoiling throwing arm, Rob Dibble.

"Learning simple, solid mechanics was the most important thing I learned growing up as a pitcher. It takes a lot of stress off your arm and allows you to develop consistency and accuracy. If you've got a good coach making adjustments in your delivery, it may feel a little awkward at first and take a while to get used to, but it will be very beneficial to your success in the long run."

—Sean Bergman, Minnesota Twins starting pitcher

SUMMARY

Proper mechanics are critical to getting the most on your pitches while taking the least out of your arm. Improper mechanics have short-circuited countless careers, while other pitchers such as Nolan Ryan, Sandy Koufax, and Robb Nen have found almost overnight success through improvements in how they deliver the ball.

Control is a function not just of concentration but of mechanics. Once you've mastered the ability to consistently hit the target with your pitches, you will be able to get outs even without an overpowering fastball or a knee-buckling curve.

One of the best ways to develop good mechanics is "informed repetition": knowing what works and why, then practicing it over and over again until it becomes second nature.

In describing the delivery of a pitch, you can't help but look at several parts of the body separately. But to execute a perfect delivery requires that you get these body parts all working together. Following is a summary of the major body parts used in pitching a baseball and what their primary responsibilities are.

Starting from a relaxed position on the rubber, Curt Schilling takes a small step back with his left foot to

start his motion. His weight and head stay over the rubber as he brings his

glove and pitching hand back over his head.

His eyes pick up the target.

He continues to stride out toward home plate (a controlled fall).

Schilling keeps his body closed to home plate as he extends his lead arm to the target.

His throwing elbow is above his shoulder as he pulls his lead arm into his body while rotating his hips.

He releases the pitch with his fingers on top of the ball and hand out in front of his body.

His throwing arm continues to extend outward and then down, pronating after release.

Schilling's mind's eye focuses on the target as he pivots his back foot and places it in front of and against the rubber.

As he begins his knee lift, he lowers his hands slowly until the bottom of his glove meets his thigh. He has rotated his hips back slightly and maintains slight flex in his back leg.

As Schilling lowers his stride leg, he separates the ball from the glove. He continues lowering and moving his stride leg forward.

His pitching arm continues to swing upward to the throwing position while his glove hand pulls down, leading the front shoulder toward home. (The

across-the-seams grip means that Schilling is throwing a four-seam fastball.) His shoulder is closed upon planting of stride foot.

Schilling lands with a slightly bent front leg. His foot is slightly closed to the plate as he begins the pull phase of his delivery.

His front leg stiffens after release.

His stiff front leg and upper body are nearly at a 90-degree angle as he follows through.

His back leg swings forward and lands next to his stride leg, putting him into fielding position.

	Role	Checkpoints
Front (Stride) Foot	Initiates delivery with step back.	Initial step is short and toward second base at 45-degree angle.
	Minimizes effort of knee lift.	Toes lower than heels during knee lift.
	Positions body for hip turn just prior to release of ball.	Land flat, weight on ball, foot is in straight line to plate, toes slightly closed.
Back (Pivot) Foot	Helps maintain balance during lift.	Head over pivot foot during step back and lift.
	Helps keep hips closed during fall.	Foot parallel to rubber until throwing arm comes forward.
	Puts pitcher in good fielding position.	Land square, 24 inches to throwing-arm side of stride foot.
Front Leg	Generates power through knee lift and hip turn.	Knee at least as high as belt and pointed toward third base.
	Establishes proper stride.	Fall to same spot on mound, stride roughly equal to height.
	Absorbs momentum of delivery without locking or collapsing.	Land with knee bent, but no more than 90 degrees.
Back Leg	Helps maintain balance during lift.	Flexed slightly—not locked or bent.
	Transfers weight to front leg during fall.	Flexed slightly—not pushing off the rubber.
	Helps maintain balance during pull.	Kicks up as arm follows through—does not stay anchored, drag, or swing off to either side.
Lead Shoulder	Helps maintain balance throughout delivery.	Level with rear shoulder during lift and fall, aligned toward plate.
	Generates power during pull.	Pointed toward plate during fall.
Lead Elbow	Generates power during pull.	Elbow below glove, no higher than shoulder during fall.
Lead Hand	Shields grip from batter and helps maintain balance during lift.	Glove moves in falling arc toward batter.
	Keeps front shoulder from flying open during pull.	Glove and ball come together inside front leg, next to body, and at center of gravity during knee lift.
		Glove over elbow during fall, at glove-side ribs during pull.

	Role	Checkpoints
Throwing Shoulder	Helps maintain balance throughout delivery.	Level with rear shoulder during lift and fall, aligned toward plate.
	Transfers power to throwing arm during pull.	Below elbow during fall.
Throwing Elbow	Helps ensure maximum velocity and rotation on pitches.	Elbow over shoulder, in front of wrist during fall.
		Never stiff.
Throwing Hand	Establishes grip.	Grip ball firmly, relaxed wrist.
	Helps ensure maximum velocity and rotation on pitches.	Fingers on top of ball.
	Determines release point.	Consistent distance from ear to hand during pull—not too close, not too far.

THE GOLDEN ERA OF PITCHING I: FROM THE BEGINNING THROUGH THE DEADBALL ERA

Pitching has undergone dramatic changes from the nineteenth century, when a pitcher existed merely to initiate play, to the end of the twentieth century, when the range of his repertoire is matched only by the scale of his challenge. As you trace the evolution of pitching, you realize that baseball has been in a continual state of adaptation—pitchers adjusting to hitters, hitters adjusting to pitchers. Knowing "how we got here" will help you better understand *why* things are done a certain way—or perhaps even inspire a burst of creativity that will trigger the next great pitching innovation.

THE NINETEENTH CENTURY

In the early days of baseball, before the National League existed or the American League was a gleam in Ban Johnson's eye, pitchers were *expected* to be hittable. Their objective was to get the action going by giving the batter something to hit—more like a sparring partner than an opponent. The called strike in organized baseball didn't even exist until 1857. A formal strike zone wasn't in place until 1867, but it came as part of a code that instructed pitchers to "deliver the ball as near as possible over the center" of a plate that was only 12 inches wide.

Pitchers were required to throw underhanded. Some tried to add velocity by throwing from a running start, but they were eventually reined in by restraining lines and later a "box" in the center of the diamond. Their predelivery movements were limited even further when they were required to have both feet on the ground when releasing the ball. To put a stop to the hitter-unfriendly tactic of snapping the wrist in delivering the ball—popularized by Jim Creighton, whose not-quite-legal pitches came from somewhere around his shoe tops—pitchers were required to deliver the ball "with the arm straight and swinging perpendicularly" from the body. Pitchers are resourceful types, however, and some would bend this rule by wearing their belt somewhere just south of their throat.

There were no starting rotations until the 1880s, and relief pitchers did not exist—only "change pitchers," who could only be called upon in case of severe injury. Otherwise, a struggling starter was left out there to die—and expected to start the next game and the game after that and the game after that.

As if all this weren't enough to neutralize the pitcher, a rule was established in 1871 that forced him to throw low or high depending on the wishes of the hitter. It lasted through the 1886 season. The rule prohibiting the overhand delivery lasted until 1884. As for the foul strike, that wasn't even established until 1901 (1903 in the American League).

Changing the rules to constrain pitchers was pretty much an annual event during the 1880s. In 1880, the number of balls to walk a batter was lowered from nine to eight. By 1881—when the distance from home plate to the pitcher's "box" was moved back from 45 feet to 50 feet—it was seven, and by 1884 it was six. It went back up to seven in 1886, but was then brought down all the way to five in 1887—a season in which batters enjoyed the luxury of a fourth strike; hit batsmen were finally allowed to take their base; and a pitcher was required to "hold the ball, before delivery, fairly in front of his body, and in sight of the umpire" and forced to deliver his offerings from the back of his box, 55½ feet from home plate. In 1888 it was back to three strikes for a strikeout, and by 1889 it was four balls for a walk. Flat-sided bats were allowed from 1885 to 1893.

Through it all, some pitchers managed not just to survive but to thrive, as the austere conditions in which pitchers had to ply their trade prompted a number of self-preserving innovations. Depending on who you ask, in 1870 Fred Goldsmith, Deacon White, or Candy Cummings was the first to figure out how to make a ball curve. Albert Goodwill Spalding was a master of control and changing speeds who dominated professional baseball during the 1870s. In 1880, Chicago White Stockings ace Larry Corcoran—a 120-pound power pitcher, believe it or not—developed the first system of signs with his catcher. He was also part of one of the game's first—and best—pitching rotations, combining with Fred Goldsmith to pitch the White Stockings to three consecutive pennants from 1880 to 1882. In 1886, Toad Ramsey invented the knuckleball, winning 38 and fanning 499 in 589 innings! John Montgomery Ward did some rudimentary physics and figured out that he'd be better off if he built himself a mound of dirt in his pitcher's box and threw off that. The practice spread, and mound heights eventually had to be capped at 15 inches in 1903.

But it wasn't until 1890 that the first high-kicking power pitcher appeared in major league baseball. His name was Amos Rusie, and he sired a long line that extended through Lefty Grove, Dizzy Dean, and Bob Feller, then on through Juan Marichal and Sandy Koufax. Rusie, "the Hoosier Thunderbolt," led the National League in strikeouts five times, winning 245 games in nine seasons.

> *"He was to baseball then what Babe Ruth was to baseball later."*
>
> —Clark Griffith, Hall of Fame pitcher, manager, and owner, on Amos Rusie

Perhaps it's no coincidence that the catcher's mitt as we know it made its debut in the same season as Amos Rusie. In 1893 the pitcher's box was moved back to its present distance of 60 feet, 6 inches and marked by a rubber slab. Legend has it the change was made because of Rusie. His strikeouts dropped a bit, as they did throughout the league, but his control actually improved. The biggest casualty of the new pitching distance was Chicago's Wild Bill Hutchison, who dropped from a league-leading 37 wins and 316 strikeouts to a mark of 16–24 with 80 strikeouts.

Despite all the changes made to the rules since 1880, by 1892 the league batting average had dropped back to its 1880 level (.245), while strikeouts had actually increased by 10 percent. But when the pitchers were moved back in 1893, the rulesmakers' objective of unleashed offenses was finally realized. In 1893, at the new distance, strikeouts dropped by 50 percent while the league batting average shot up 35 points to .280. The following year it was up to .309, and it remained at .290 or above for the next three seasons.

One pitcher thrived regardless of rules, distance, or league. He won 30 games at 55 feet as well as 60 feet, 30 games in the National League and 30 games in a new entity, born in 1901, called the American League. In looking for the secret to Cy Young's success and his 511 wins, many have pointed to his speed. Like all great power pitchers, though, he had more than just a fastball: after his playing career was over, Young described a repertoire that included not just a good fastball but a sweeping curve and what sounds like an early slider ("a narrow curve that broke away from the batter and went in just like a fastball"). Yet despite his great stuff, he was not a strikeout pitcher. His strikeouts are only a little better than average relative to his time, while his control stands out: 1.5 walks per nine innings, fourth all-time among 60-foot pitchers. "Control," Young said, "is what kept me in the big leagues for 22 years." As for his longevity—22 seasons and more than 7,000 innings without breaking down—Young, like many durable pitchers who would follow him, chalked it up to legs and efficiency.

> *"You have to have good legs to pitch, and I always took care of them. . . . then I had good control. I aimed to make the batter hit the ball, and I made as few pitches as possible. That's why I was able to work every other day. That and having good legs and keeping them good."*
>
> —Hall of Famer Cy Young, winner of 511 games

THE DEADBALL ERA

With pitchers throwing overhanded from a rubber 60 feet, 6 inches from home plate, pitching as we know it began in 1893. With the foul strike, 15-inch mounds, and the appearance of a 17-inch wide, five-sided home plate in 1901, the transition to the modern era of pitching was complete. By then, pitchers had already adjusted to the longer distance, and the game would quickly become one in which the pitchers dominated. In the so-called "deadball era" of 1901–1919, teams scraped and bunted for runs in 3–2 games.

There weren't that many strikeout pitchers in the early 1900s because hitters concentrated on putting the ball in play, hoping to either reach base on an error or at least move a base runner along. With extra-base hits at a premium, the cost of striking out was simply too high. In this era of swinging bunts and short strokes emerged one of the most overpowering pitchers to ever play—a hard-throwing flake named Rube Waddell. His 349 strikeouts in 1904 remained a major league record until Sandy Koufax struck out 382 in 1965. What Waddell did in 1903 and 1904 relative to the average pitcher of the day would be like a modern flamethrower such as Kerry Wood going out and fanning 14 batters per game and 400 in a season. And then doing it again the next year. Waddell was *that* dominating.

Yet it was Mordecai Brown who was the more prototypical hurler of the day. He's known today more for his colorful nickname (Three-Finger, a tribute to a pitching hand mangled in a childhood farming accident) than his mound exploits. If it's possible for a Hall of Famer to be underrated, Mordecai Brown is. At his best, he was the equal of the great Christy Mathewson—going 127–43 with 38 shutouts in a five-year span from 1906–10 in which his ERA ranged from a high of 1.80 to a low of 1.04. He did it with a nasty curveball—Ty Cobb called it the most difficult pitch he ever faced—excellent control, and faith in the terrific defense that played behind him. Brown was also the game's first "closer," saving 13 games for the 1911 Cubs (while winning 21), a National League record that stood for 20 years—though no one called it a save until the stat was officially established in the 1960s.

Christy Mathewson had his share of dominating seasons, too, winning 20 games for 12 consecutive seasons from 1903 to 1914. Yet Mathewson changed his entire approach to pitching during the course of this awesome stretch. In 1903, he struck out more than six batters per nine innings, but by 1914 he was barely over two. In 1903, he walked 2.5 batters per nine innings, but in 1913 he set a modern major league record at well below one —at one point going 68 consecutive innings without issuing a free pass. After a disappointing—by his standards—1906 season, Matty recast himself as one of the greatest control pitchers in history and became more economical with his pitches. His out pitch—the "fadeaway," an early version of the screwball popularized by Carl Hubbell and Fernando Valenzuela—took a lot out of his arm to throw. As he describes in his classic 1912 book, *Pitching in a Pinch*, he began to pace himself better and only use the fadeaway when he really needed it. Compare Mathewson's difficult 1906 season to what he accomplished in 1913, once he'd perfected the art of throwing strikes rather than striking batters out.

CHRISTY MATHEWSON, 1903–14

	W-L	ERA	K/9	BB/9
1903	30–13	2.26	6.6	2.5
1904	33–12	2.03	5.2	1.9
1905	32–8	1.27	5.5	1.7
1906	**22–12**	**2.97**	**4.3**	**2.6**
1907	24–13	2.00	5.1	1.5
1908	37–11	1.43	6.0	1.0
1909	25–6	1.14	4.9	1.1
1910	27–9	1.90	5.2	1.7
1911	26–13	1.99	4.1	1.1
1912	23–12	2.12	3.9	1.0
1913	**25–11**	**2.06**	**2.7**	**0.6**
1914	24–13	3.00	2.3	0.7

"Many persons have asked me why I do not use my fadeaway oftener when it is so effective, and the only answer is that every time I throw the fadeaway it takes so much out of my arm. It is a very hard ball to deliver. Pitching it 10 or 12 times in a game kills my arm, so I save it for the pinches."

—Hall of Famer Christy Mathewson

The greatest power pitcher of the deadball era was Walter Johnson, who dominated for years with an overpowering fastball that came out of an effortless, low, three-quarter motion. He threw so hard, he never even used a curveball until late in his career. Unlike other strikeout legends like Bob Feller, Sandy Koufax, Nolan Ryan, Randy Johnson, and Kerry Wood, Walter Johnson never struggled with his control. Though he struck out 300 batters in a season in 1910 and 1912, his greatest season came in 1913 when he fanned *only* 243 batters. That year he walked a mere 38 in 346 innings, as he went 36–7 with a 1.14 ERA and 11 shutouts. In 1924, at the age of 37 and coming off four subpar campaigns, Johnson had enough left in the tank to lead the American League in wins, strikeouts, and ERA in the Senators' only championship season.

> *"This boy throws so fast you can't see 'em . . . and he knows where his pitch is going, because if he didn't there would be dead bodies all over Idaho."*
>
> —anonymous telegram to the Washington Senators about a prospect named Walter Johnson

Walter Johnson excelled by throwing hard with control, while Grover Cleveland Alexander put himself in the Hall of Fame by changing speeds and developing exquisite control. He won 28 games as a hard-throwing rookie in 1911 and only got better. By 1920, he was a shell-shocked, epileptic, alcoholic veteran of World War I enjoying his last dominating season. He won 27 games and led the National League in strikeouts. From that point forward, he did it all on guile. Pitching without an overpowering fastball for a series of bad Cubs teams, he still managed to win 80 games over the next five seasons with experience, control, and trust in his defense. At 39, with the St. Louis Cardinals, he won the second and sixth games of the 1926 World Series against the Yankees, then was called on in the seventh inning of Game 7 to protect a 3–2 lead. He struck out Hall of Famer Tony Lazzeri with the bases loaded, wrapping up the series with 2⅓ scoreless, hitless innings.

> *"Alex pitched to Lazzeri's strength, something neither Tony nor the other Yankees expected. Just before the third strike, Lazzeri hit a long ball that was barely foul. But that didn't bother Alex. He threw one down Tony's alley again and surprised him right out of there. He won that one with his head—and that razor-sharp control."*
>
> —Frankie Frisch, Hall of Fame second baseman

SWINGING FOR THE FENCES

By becoming a master of the change-up, Alexander survived as a pitcher into his late 30s despite the offensive explosion that began with Babe Ruth's 54 home runs in 1920. The ball was livelier, and Ruth was showing what could be done by swinging harder and with a decided uppercut—obliterating his own record of 29 home runs set the year before and banishing pitching-dominated baseball for more than 40 years.

Even more significant to pitchers was the fatal beaning of Cleveland Indians' shortstop Ray Chapman, who was killed by a pitched ball thrown by Yankee Carl Mays on August 16, 1920. As a result of this tragedy, the pitcher's most reliable weapon—the unpredictable and ball-defacing spitball—was banned, and darkened baseballs were thrown out of play. The world had changed, and the first golden era of pitching was over.

"The strike zone was wider, fences longer, ball deader, and we always pitched a dark ball. We never threw the ball until we added something to it first, a little tobacco juice and dirt to blacken and liven it up."

—Cy Young on deadball pitching

Kevin Brown

CHALLENGING
THE HITTER:
THE FASTBALL

"ANYONE CAN GET BATTERS OUT
WITH BREAKING STUFF ALL THE
WAY THROUGH HIGH SCHOOL.
WORK ON GETTING THEM OUT
WITH YOUR FASTBALL. IT'S STILL
THE BEST WAY TO DO IT MORE
THAN 100 YEARS AFTER THE
GAME WAS INVENTED."

—Bob Tewksbury

It may seem odd to begin a chapter on the fastball with a quote from one of the softer throwers the major leagues has seen. A control specialist who throws in the low 80s and only half-jokingly states that "If I went to a high school field now, I wouldn't get signed," Tewksbury's career is an inspiration to pitchers at all levels who haven't been blessed with a tremendous arm. With more than 100 major league victories to his credit, Tewksbury has shown how much a pitcher can accomplish with below-average velocity (by major league standards, of course!). Along the way, he's changed a lot of attitudes among talent evaluators throughout professional baseball.

Regardless of how hard you throw, the fastball needs to be your primary pitch. Whether you're Bob Tewksbury or Randy Johnson, everything works off the fastball. It sets up your breaking and off-speed pitches, gets you ahead of hitters, helps you establish your rhythm early in a game, and throwing it properly builds your arm strength. In fact, the only problem with the fastball is its name. You hear "fastball" and you think it means throwing a ball as hard as you can. A more useful name would be "hard strike," and even that fails to take into account the movement of the pitch or the occasional need to throw it off the plate.

"The fastball is the reason for my success—period. But it's not just because I throw hard. A good fastball is a combination of velocity and location. It's never one without the other."

—Curt Schilling, Philadelphia Phillies starting pitcher

When someone says to you that a pitcher has a "good fastball," what do you think that means? That the pitcher throws fast? No. No matter the level at which you pitch, if you throw a fastball with high velocity that is straight down the middle of the plate, hitters will eventually time it and hit it hard. A pitcher has a good fastball when he has "command" so he can control the speed and location of the pitch. It's a good fastball if he can hit his spots with it *and* put some movement on it—sinking it, or tailing it into a hitter, for example. It's a good fastball if he can locate it with movement *and* velocity. No pitcher can be successful for very long with just one pitch, but you can get through a game with just your fastball if it's a good one. That can't be said of any other pitch.

"Every hitter likes the fastball like everybody likes ice cream. But you don't like it when someone's stuffing it into you by the gallon."

—Reggie Jackson, Hall of Fame outfielder

So when you think about the fastball, you need to think about location, movement, and velocity—in that order. Where it goes and how much it moves are more important than how quickly it happens to get there.

Throw It Again

The most important pitch is the fastball. It's the easiest pitch to throw for a strike. It gets you ahead of hitters, helps set up your off-speed and breaking pitches, and throwing it with proper mechanics builds your arm strength.

LOCATION

"The wildest pitch is not necessarily the one that goes back to the screen. It can also be the one that goes right down the middle."

—Hall of Famer Sandy Koufax

Maybe you've gone to one of those booths at a ballpark, had your fastball timed, and been disappointed with the results. Then again, maybe you've always been able to throw harder than anyone else on your team or in your league. Either way, your first order of business with the fastball should be the same: work on location, *not* velocity. That same advice would be given to a little leaguer or a big leaguer, because location is something that is never perfected. You can always improve—and this is why some pitchers get better with age while others flame out as soon as they face hitters with the bat speed to turn around their fastball.

"Good pitching is being aggressive, having total confidence in yourself, hitting your spots, and keeping the ball down."

—Sean Bergman, Minnesota Twins

"I was as raw as anyone who ever came to the big leagues. I didn't have the slightest idea where the ball was going. I was in the big leagues because of my arm, not because I could pitch."

—Nolan Ryan, looking back on the early years of his career

ESTABLISH YOUR FASTBALL

You would think that a pitcher like Bob Tewksbury, who thrived on guile and precision, would have been experimenting with breaking balls very early on. That's not the case. In high school, his coach wouldn't let him throw any breaking balls. It's something he now credits as helping him learn *how* to pitch very early on: learning how to *locate* his fastball to get batters

SPEED ALONE WON'T CUT IT

The fastball doesn't mean a thing if you can't throw it for strikes. Consider the three most consistently overpowering pitchers in baseball history: Sandy Koufax, Nolan Ryan, and Randy Johnson. Look at what they did before they learned how to throw strikes.

Sandy Koufax	W–L	K/9	BB/9	ERA
1956	2–4	4.6	4.4	4.88
1957	5–4	10.6	4.4	3.89
1958	11–11	7.4	5.9	4.47
1959	8–6	10.2	5.4	4.06
1960	8–13	10.1	5.1	3.91
Nolan Ryan	**W–L**	**K/9**	**BB/9**	**ERA**
1968	6–9	8.9	5.2	3.09
1969	6–3	9.3	5.4	3.54
1970	7–11	8.5	6.6	3.41
1971	10–14	8.1	6.9	3.97
Randy Johnson	**W–L**	**K/9**	**BB/9**	**ERA**
1989	0–4	7.8	7.8	6.67
1990	14–11	7.9	4.9	3.65
1991	13–10	10.2	6.8	3.96
1992	12–14	10.3	6.2	3.77

The Dodgers were patient with Koufax, and he eventually turned into the most dominating pitcher in his generation (though those first five years don't look very much like half the career of a Hall of Famer). The Mets ran out of patience with Nolan—who was only getting wilder with each passing year—and dealt him to the Angels for Jim Fregosi in one of the worst deals in major league history. Ryan's stuff was good enough that once he got the walks down below *five* per game, he started to win. Ryan gave some advice to Randy Johnson, and the 6'10" Big Unit finally got his mechanics straightened out and has dominated ever since.

Now here's what each of these pitchers did in their best seasons. Koufax and Ryan (whose finest season came at age 34 in a year unfortunately interrupted by a players' strike) actually saw their strikeout totals drop almost as precipitously as their ERAs. Koufax actually turned into a control artist once he stopped overthrowing and took a little off. Ryan never did—though when he did have Koufax-like command of his stuff, a no-hitter was almost inevitable. At the age of 44, his walk totals dropped below four per game and he recorded his seventh no-hitter, walking none while striking out 16. When Johnson finally got his mechanics worked out, his walks dropped while his strikeouts shot from 10 per nine innings to the previously uncharted territory of 12.

	W–L	K/9	BB/9	ERA
Koufax, 1963	25–5	8.9	1.7	1.88
Ryan, 1981	11–5	8.5	4.1	1.69
Johnson, 1995	18–2	12.4	2.7	2.48

Kerry Wood blew by Johnson to 12.6 strikeouts per nine innings in 1998, though he walked more than 4.5 batters per game. His stuff was so good that when he did have command of it, he turned in the most dominating performance in big league history in only his fifth career start—20 strikeouts, no walks, and one infield hit against the best-hitting team in the league.

The greatest fastball pitcher of them all, Nolan Ryan.

contact with but harder for most to drive for extra bases. If you can keep your fastball down, you will throw fewer pitches—getting fewer strikeouts but more ground balls and more double plays. You may give up a few more singles, but you will give up fewer home runs. And, with most umpires, if you can keep the ball down you should walk fewer batters because you'll get more called strikes. You'll know you've become this type of pitcher when you get a called strike on a ball above the belt and you're not happy about it because you were aiming for the knees.

> *"Keep the ball down and hope they hit it on the ground."*
>
> —Dennis Eckersley, 1992 American League Cy Young and MVP Awards winner, on pitching in a pinch

The key to throwing low fastballs is proper mechanics. (See Chapter 2 for an extensive discussion of the proper pitching delivery. If you have fundamental flaws in your delivery, you won't be able to throw *any* pitch in the strike zone consistently. If you've read Chapter 2, worked hard on your delivery, and aren't rushing your pitches or flying open, you're ready to start refining your pitches. If not, you've got more work to do before you try to learn how to hit spots.)

out. Throwing fastballs helped him develop all of that guile and precision in the first place.

Pat Hentgen, the 1996 American League Cy Young Award winner, traveled a similar route to Tewksbury during his journey to the major leagues. Hentgen didn't throw a breaking ball until he was 18 years old and pitching in the minor leagues. He says, "My advice to a younger pitcher looking to achieve success is to throw a lot of fastballs at a young age to gain command and build up arm strength. You've got to be able to locate your fastball to be effective."

LOW IN THE ZONE

You first begin to make the transition from thrower to pitcher when you start thinking about location in terms other than strikes and balls. This begins when you start to think about *low* strikes— keeping the ball at the batters' knees. Fastballs low in the strike zone are easier for hitters to make

A good fastball located down in the strike zone is a tough pitch for any hitter to handle.

When you perform proper pitching mechanics, you build the momentum that is necessary for transferring the energy of your lower and mid-to-upper body movements to your throwing arm and hand. This momentum is segmented into three distinct sequences of motion.

The first segment is *forward or linear*, that is, you stride forward and transfer your weight onto the stride leg. Then there is a forceful *rotation of the upper torso* as it squares to the plate. Finally, you move forward and downward over a braced front leg with *the trunk flexing at the waist*. Without these segments properly sequenced, you cannot generate sufficient pitch velocity. You must perform this sequence of motions successfully to master the basic fastball.

Here are the things to look for in your delivery:

A long, comfortable stride. Work on getting your stride foot out as far as you can without over-striding or landing on your heel.

Elbow above your shoulder, fingers on top. A failure to keep your throwing elbow up and your fingers on top of the ball is a common explanation for a hanging curveball. It's just as important in throwing a fastball. As pitching coaches are fond of saying, "throw the top half of the ball."

The pitcher in perfect position: shoulders in line, ball facing second base.

Proper release point. Even with a proper stride, elbow above your shoulder, and fingers on top, you could be all over the place with your fastball simply because you're varying your release point. Even if you're consistently throwing the ball on the same path with every pitch, you could still have release point problems if you're releasing the ball too early (high pitches) or holding the ball too long (low pitches).

Finish the pitch. Maybe you're just not getting enough of your upper body, including the head and shoulders, into your pitches. Drive through and down with your lead arm, flex your upper body over your stride leg, and keep your throwing arm moving downward and to the outside of your knee. If you find yourself finishing high, remind yourself to drive down with your lead elbow, pulling it past your hip, and bend at the waist.

Some pitchers approach throwing a fastball as purely a physical exercise, and they find themselves concentrating more when they throw breaking balls and change-ups. It's critical to concentrate on *every* pitch—*especially* with fastballs, since this is the pitch you will be moving around in the strike zone more than any other. Unlike breaking balls and change-ups, you can and will throw fastballs to all parts of the strike zone. The lower half of the zone, which we've just discussed, is the most important. Your next step as a pitcher is to think not just about balls and strikes and low strikes, but to think about what's called the inner, middle, and outer thirds.

THE INNER AND OUTER THIRDS

You will have more success with your fastball if you can avoid throwing it in the "middle third"— over the heart of the plate. Though some pitchers with exceptional movement and velocity make their living by pitching inside (the "inner third"), most get batters out by pitching away (the "outer third"). Neither approach is better. What's right for you depends on your pitching strengths and your personality. When pitching against teams using aluminum bats, you must pitch away more unless

KEVIN BROWN: LOW FASTBALLS

In his prime and on his game, Kevin Brown is the most difficult pitcher to hit in the big leagues. With perhaps the best combination of movement, location, and velocity in recent memory, Brown can be so nasty that he still has hitters messed up three days later. He's a power pitcher with power pitcher's results—including a 16-strikeout performance during the 1998 postseason—but with a *low* hard one rather than the classic high hard one of Sandy Koufax and Bob Gibson or, of more recent vintage, Troy Percival, Ugueth Urbina, and John Wetteland. Though most hitters will tell you that it's a lot easier to make contact with a low fastball than a high one, there remain a lot of advantages to Brown's way of doing business.

By keeping the ball down, when Brown does make a mistake it rarely ends up getting taken out of the park.

If Brown really tried to air it out, his already-impressive strikeout totals might get even gaudier, but he'd sacrifice some ground-ball outs. In 1998, Brown was the most extreme ground-ball pitcher in baseball not named Greg Maddux. On the flipside was the Angels' closer, Troy Percival, consistently one of the most extreme fly-ball pitchers in baseball. In 1998, Percival did not induce a single double-play grounder.

With today's low strike zone, the low hard one can get you a strike both swinging and taking. Many of the high hard ones Koufax and Gibson relied on in the 1960s would be called balls in the 1990s. Troy Percival and Ugueth Urbina walk more than twice as many batters per nine innings as Brown.

Because Brown is more likely to coax a ground ball than blow a batter away, and because he pitches to the umpire's strike zone, he works a lot less hard for his outs. Brown's typical inning will last fewer than 14 pitches, while Percival's are among the longest in baseball at more than 19. These days, pitchers with the high hard one and the deep counts of a Percival or an Urbina can't make it as starters. They'd consistently be reaching the 100-pitch mark by the fifth inning.

A pitcher with Brown's stuff could certainly be a dominating closer, but instead he's one of the most reliable workhorses in any team's starting rotation.

your fastball is high-velocity, that is, 85 miles per hour or more.

The outside fastball is a very difficult pitch for most hitters to handle, because most hitters are comfortable with pitches that are on the inside part of the strike zone. It's possible to pull an outside fastball, but a hitter intent on covering the inside part of the strike zone will either swing through the pitch or hit it off the end of the bat for a lazy fly ball or a soft grounder. Unless a hitter is excellent at going the other way—a right-hander hitting to right field—he will be very vulnerable to the outside fastball. Greg Maddux and the entire Braves pitching staff worked the pull-happy Cleveland Indians away throughout the 1995 World Series, held them to a .179 batting average, and took the series in six games.

Maddux's teammate Tom Glavine is a master at hitting the outside corner. More so than any pitcher in baseball today, hitters know *exactly* how Glavine will work them. Fastballs and change-ups away, away, away. If he hits the catcher's glove consistently, umpires have been known to give

Throw It Again

Location is more important than movement, and movement is more important than velocity. A good fastball does not have to be 95 miles per hour, provided you can hit your spots with it. An essential of good pitching is to develop the ability to throw low strikes and to hit the inner and outer thirds of the strike zone.

him as much as six inches off the outside corner. He was hitting his spots and getting his calls in the final game of the 1995 World Series, throwing eight innings of one-hit ball, closing out Cleveland 1–0.

The key to pitching outside, Glavine will tell you, is being willing and able to pitch in the "inner third." You can throw any number of pitches outside, but when coming inside it's almost exclusively fastballs. (Off-speed and breaking pitches can be effective when thrown inside, as long as they are down in the strike zone. But in most cases, when you talk about pitching inside, you're talking about fastballs.)

> *"I can be successful pitching away because I keep the ball down and keep them honest inside. I'm going to get guys out down and away, they know I'm going to get them out down and away, and if they don't show me they can beat me I'm going to stay down and away. When I see guys who are starting to make adjustments and start beating me at my game, I'll start pitching inside more. Basically, it's a fastball inside once in a while to straighten them up, then it's back outside."*
>
> —Tom Glavine, two-time Cy Young
> Award winner

At the amateur levels, you'll face hitters using aluminum bats, which have "sweet spots" of four

The "Big Hurt," Frank Thomas, swings and misses at a pitch—low and away.

to five inches. It's a lot easier for a hitter to handle an inside pitch with an aluminum bat because he doesn't have to hit the ball within the sweet spot area of the bat to drive it over the infield. With a wooden bat (sweet spot of one inch) he'd be "sawed-off" and retired. Does this mean you shouldn't throw inside? Absolutely not. But make sure you throw inside off the plate or on the black. Throw to an open area in the hitter's stance, such as under the elbows.

> *"You're still better off letting them hit one on the handle than on the sweet spot. So what if you can't break their bats? You can't just stay away, away, away. Don't try to hit them. Aim for a spot between the inside corner and their belt buckle. Get their feet moving."*
>
> —Bob Tewksbury on pitching to
> aluminum bats

KEEPING IT DOWN

In 1998, Minnesota Twins lefty Eric Milton wasn't able to keep the ball down in the strike zone, ending up the season as the most extreme fly-ball starting pitcher in the big leagues. Not a great plan anywhere, but definitely not a good idea when you pitch half of your games in a stadium like the Twins' that turns fly balls into doubles. He ended up getting tagged for 77 extra-base hits. Just for perspective, low-strike specialists Greg Maddux and Kevin Brown yielded 47 and 40 long hits, respectively, while working about 80 more innings. Another rookie who was much better at keeping the ball down—Steve Woodard of the Milwaukee Brewers—threw far more ground-ball outs and yielded 15 percent fewer extra-base hits than Milton in about the same number of innings. Woodard doesn't throw as hard as Milton, but he is able to keep hitters off balance with his change-up.

WORKING INSIDE

When you see a pitcher with a low number of walks and a high number of hit batters, you've

ERIC MILTON: HARD LESSONS

By the time you read this, Eric Milton may have already established himself as a great Minnesota Twins lefty in the tradition of Jim Kaat and Frank Viola. But in 1998, he was a *very* raw rookie. Having been traded in the off-season from the Yankees for Chuck Knoblauch, Milton spent the '98 campaign learning on the job. Despite a 94 MPH fastball, his results could be put next to "rookie pitcher" in the baseball dictionary (though what may bode well for Milton is how similar his results were to a rookie named Greg Maddux!).

Pitcher/Year	Age	W–L	ERA	BA	K/9	BB/9
Milton, 1998	22	8–14	5.64	.282	5.6	3.7
Maddux, 1987	21	6–14	5.61	.294	5.8	4.3

Milton's biggest mistakes in 1998 were not keeping his fastball down and not throwing inside enough.

got someone who isn't afraid of working inside. The average pitcher hits one batter for every ten he walks. Kevin Brown hits batters much more frequently than that, as he runs pitches in on batters' fists. In 1996, Brown walked only 33 batters while hitting 16! (It's no surprise that a scouting report on him while he was still at Georgia Tech said that he has "some meanness in him.") In 1998, rookie Steve Woodard walked 33 and plunked 9. Eric Milton walked 70 while hitting only 2. When a pitcher with below-average control manages to hit only two batters in more than 170 innings, it usually means that he isn't even trying to establish the inner third of the plate—and that hitters are aggressively going after those outside strikes without any fear in their hearts.

> "I pitch inside to throw strikes. Very seldom do I ever get hurt when I put the ball underneath the hitter's hands. Some hitters you have to be a little more careful with than others—guys with quick bats who may pull their hands in on inside strikes. With them, I pitch them in a little tighter."
>
> —David Wells, Toronto Blue Jays

For a right-handed pitcher throwing to a right-handed batter, it is not difficult to throw a fastball inside. That is your natural arm slot (of release). In general, where the head goes, the ball goes. Stay aligned and keep your head and your stride foot on a straight line to your target. Here are some important "don'ts":

Don't move your release point closer to or farther from your ear. It must stay constant. Throwing too close to your ear robs you of velocity. Throwing too far from your ear keeps your fingers from staying on top of and behind the ball.

Even though taken for a ball, this inside fastball adjusts the batter's eyes up and in, making him vulnerable to pitches down and away.

Don't overcompensate with your stride foot.
You need to step toward your target, with your
stride foot slightly closed. As a result, your stride
varies only slightly even when you are moving
from an outside target to an inside target. If you
are overcompensating with your stride foot to
throw inside—stepping well to the left or right of
your regular landing place—this is a sign of trouble. A right-hander who lands with his stride foot
far to the right of his target will be throwing across
his body and adding stress to his shoulder; landing far to the left of his target will rob him of power
because his hips and torso have opened too soon
(like a batter who is fooled on a change-up and
opens his hips too soon).

Don't miss over the middle of the plate. If you
find yourself consistently getting too much of the
plate when throwing inside to a same-side hitter,
you may want to experiment with a sidearm fastball, since this will have a natural tailing action to
it. (If you do decide to "drop down" occasionally
against arm-side hitters, you can't slip into a pattern of throwing exclusively inside with it. You'll
also want to throw it outside, starting it off the
plate so it will tail over. And with arm-side hitters
who flinch, you can get a lot of called strikes on
balls right down the middle.)

It's not just a matter of being physically capa-
ble of hitting the inside corner; you need to
become mentally comfortable about coming
inside. If you're uneasy about it, you won't do it
enough, and chances are you won't maximize
your potential as a pitcher. Sandy Koufax once
said, "Show me someone who can't pitch inside
and I'll show you a loser." Though not all will be
as blunt as Koufax about it, most pitchers will tell
you that pitching inside is vitally important to
succeeding as a pitcher.

*"If you keep throwing away, away, away, hit-
ters will adjust. They'll lean out over the plate
and drive the ball to the opposite field. You
need to avoid patterns, establish both sides of
the plate, and pitch to both sides of the plate."*

—Pat Hentgen, St. Louis Cardinals
starting pitcher

WALTER JOHNSON'S BEST FRIEND

The legendary Walter Johnson—baseball's strikeout king for 60 years before Nolan Ryan—was
one of the rare few who was great enough to
overcome his tentativeness about pitching
inside. He was just about the only fellow player
that Ty Cobb cared for. Cobb liked him because
he knew that Johnson was afraid to pitch inside
for fear of killing someone with his awesome
fastball, so he could crowd the plate against him
and feast on fastballs over the middle. Cobb
really appreciated that.

As any hitter will tell you, it's not easy to cover
a 21½-inch-wide plate (17 inches in white across
the plate, plus a 2¼-inch black border on each
side) with a bat that has a "sweet spot" of 1 inch
with wood, 4 to 5 inches with aluminum. Most hitters will try to cover the outside half of the plate
first, unless a pitcher makes him respect the fastball inside. That's because most hitters will look
fastball and adjust to the breaking ball. It's virtually impossible to do the opposite. Only a fastball
inside will divert a hitter's attention off the outside
corner. At lower levels, it won't just divert their
attention, it will literally back them up. Get him
thinking inside, get him out outside.

*"For me, nobody is tougher to hit than David
Cone and Roger Clemens. They're both guys
who can throw any pitch with any count to
the spot they are trying to hit. They don't give
in. They make few mistakes and they change
speeds well."*

—Tony Clark, Detroit Tigers first baseman

Reliever Larry Andersen made his living on
the outside corner with his outstanding slider.
Unlike Koufax, when Andersen talks about throwing inside he comes at it with the perspective of
someone who didn't possess an eye-popping fastball. He knows what can happen when a pitcher
without thunderbolt speed throws an inside pitch
that catches a bit too much of the plate. Now
watching from the Phillies broadcast booth, he's

also seen what can happen when hard throwers don't come inside often enough.

Andersen says, "Throwing inside doesn't mean it has to be a strike. You pitch inside because you make your living outside. If you try to live away—even at 95–97 miles per hour—they're eventually going to get you. Even if the umpire doesn't give you the strike on a pitch two or three inches inside, it still sets up the hitter. It takes about an eighth of an inch of fear or doubt to keep him from hitting that fastball away. It takes that much doubt that you might come in again."

> *"When you throw inside, all those other hitters sitting on the bench see that. As a pitcher you need any kind of mental edge you can get, any kind of distraction. Hitters won't be looking for a pitch away if they know I'm coming inside."*
>
> —Hall of Famer Nolan Ryan

Nolan Ryan put a lot more than an eighth of an inch of fear into major league hitters. But Ryan didn't just pitch inside to handle the man at the plate. He was doing it for the ones in the dugout, too. Like nearly all pitchers, Ryan didn't believe in throwing inside to hit someone. He once accidentally beaned Red Sox second baseman Doug Griffin, and it put the infielder into the hospital and out of action for 51 games. Griffin's first game back just happened to be against Ryan. Ryan said, "I was a little sensitive about facing him. I pitched him nothing but away his first two times up, and he leaned in and got two ground-ball hits. I realized then that I had to block what had happened from my mind. I had no choice but to block it out or I'd become a defensive pitcher instead of an aggressive one. The next time Griffin came up I pitched him inside, and I got him out. Pitching inside is part of the game."

Los Angeles Dodgers star Don Drysdale—considered one of the meanest pitchers ever to take the mound—certainly did what he felt was necessary. He was big (6′5″) and threw nearly sidearm, with a fastball that tailed into righties. Drysdale threw *inside* because he was fiercely protective of the *outer* third of the plate. He felt it *belonged* to him. Almost 20 years after he retired, he still took offense at the notion that batters would even *think* about trying to take what was his.

Drysdale said, "You have to move a hitter off the plate. The toughest pitch for a hitter to hit is the pitch down and away from him. That down-and-away pitch is your out pitch. If you give that hitter a false sense of security so that he never anticipates being thrown inside, then he'll be diving outside to take away that pitch, which should be an out pitch for you. They'll go out and take away your out pitch! What have you got left? So you have to pitch inside."

Notice that Drysdale wasn't talking about throwing *at* hitters, and certainly not throwing at their heads or trying to injure them. Every bit as fierce a competitor as Drysdale was St. Louis Cardinals ace Bob Gibson, who put up a 1.12 ERA in 1968 with 13 shutouts. Gibson backed up his share of hitters, but he said his objective was to never hit the batter but "to make him think."

Both Drysdale and Gibson were talking about making hitters uncomfortable, and that can be done by simply making them move their feet on a pitch. You can take away the hitter's "sense of security" by aiming for a spot between the inside corner and the belt buckle. It's *your* strike zone. You own it. You live with it for the entire game. The hitter just rents it for three or four at bats. It's true that if you pitch inside, you will hit some batters. You're not trying to do that, but it will happen. But as long as you keep the ball down and aim for the inside corner and not the batter, you won't be seriously injuring anyone.

> *"You can't pitch inside unless you own the down-and-away strike."*
>
> —Leo Mazzone, Braves pitching coach

Atlanta Braves pitching coach Leo Mazzone looks at the inside pitch from a different perspective. He talks about using the *outside* strike to set up the *inside* pitch, not the other way around. Very hard throwers can have a lot of success pour-

This fastball got into the batter's "kitchen," up and in, and the result was a weak swing.

ing fastballs into the inner third of the plate, but even they will get hurt if they get too much of the plate or if they challenge a hitter who can get the bat head out and turn on a pitch. An off-speed pitcher who can consistently get the down-and-away strike will find hitters starting to dive across the plate. Pitching inside *off* the plate will make them think, but pitching inside *on* the plate can do more than that. If a hitter is looking for a pitch away, an inside strike will either freeze him or break his bat—even if it's only a fastball with average velocity.

When asked what pitcher jammed him more than any other in his career, 500-home-run-club member Eddie Murray named Charlie Leibrandt—a crafty lefty with no fastball to speak of who lived on the outside (and who spent a lot of his career with Leo Mazzone in Atlanta, by the way).

> *"There are control pitchers that I've faced that have jammed me with average fastballs. John Tudor, Bryn Smith, and Bob Tewksbury are all examples of that. They had good slow curveballs, and then they'd jam you with an 84 mile per hour fastball. Those guys knew how to pitch."*
>
> —Gregg Jefferies, major league hitter

Throwing inside without fear is part of pitching. But it's not just the fear of hitting a batter that you need to conquer. It's the fear that you might miss over the plate, and that a hitter might take you out of the yard. It happens to every pitcher who comes inside. It's been known to happen to some good pitchers early in games, as dangerous hitters hit 400-foot solo shots—but those pitchers can even use a negative outcome like *that* to set up an out pitch away later in the game, when the slugger's up again with the tying runs on base.

> *"If you make a mistake away, it's a single. If you make a mistake inside, it's a home run."*
>
> —Hall of Famer Bob Gibson

One way of thinking about working inside is that you're trying to take the unease you feel and transfer it to the hitter. Again, Sandy Koufax was very succinct about it: "Pitching is the art of instilling fear." When you can see that fear, you respond accordingly. Even though Greg Maddux has no qualms about coming inside, he advises young pitchers not to force themselves to do it. "You've got to pitch the way you're comfortable. If you're not comfortable pitching inside, don't pitch inside. Would you be a better pitcher if you pitched inside? Probably. But you have to be comfortable."

Are you uncomfortable about it? Work on pitching to the inside corner of a chalk strike zone on the wall until you can "get comfortable" doing it in a game.

MOVEMENT

> *"I was taught that movement is more important than velocity. That advice came from somebody I trusted. I still believe that today."*
>
> —Greg Maddux on some of the best advice he was given as a young pitcher

If you have a fastball with movement but only average velocity, you will be a lot more difficult to hit than if you have a straight fastball with good velocity. Best of all is if you can develop more than one fastball, with different movement and slightly different speeds, so you force the hitter to make more decisions.

There are many different types of fastballs: sinking, running, tailing, and straight. Some of this movement comes naturally, while other times it's a function of different grips. Regardless of the type of fastball grip, the mechanics of delivering the pitch are the same. You take the same stride at the same speed, turn your shoulders and hips at the same time, and release the ball at the same point. Most importantly, you keep your wrist and forearm relaxed, hold the ball with your fingers (not in the palm of your hand), and keep your fingers on top of the ball. As you release the ball, your wrist snaps forward—this helps your velocity, but it also makes certain that the ball leaves your fingers with the maximum spin. The spinning of the seams determines how much action you get on the ball—more rotations means more velocity.

As we go through the different types of fastballs, it will help if you have a baseball in your hand.

STRAIGHT FASTBALL

The straight fastball is the game's most basic pitch and is thrown with the most basic grip—what is called a four-seam grip. Even though a baseball has only one continuous seam, the rotation of a fastball thrown with this grip appears to show four seams to the batter. Another way to think about it is that the pads of your index and middle fingers contact the seams in four different places. Your fingers cut across the middle of the baseball at one of the four spots where the seams are widest apart. As you look at the seams, the "closed" end or horseshoe end should be closer to the middle finger. This allows the shorter index finger to cross the seams where they are closer together.

The pads of your two fingers—not the fingertips, but the fingerprints—rest firmly over the seams, far enough over that you can get some leverage on the pitch by pulling back on the

seams. If your finger pads are just touching the seams and not covering them—or if they are too far over the seams— you won't be able to get as much ball rotation. Rotation helps you to create velocity.

Spread your fingers about an inch apart. Experiment with different widths. If your fingers are too close together, though, you'll have a harder time controlling the fastball. Too far apart and you lose velocity because the wrist and forearm muscles tighten. Whatever the width you select, center your fingers so that an imaginary line through the middle of the baseball would pass exactly between them. If your fingers are too far to either side of the baseball, you won't be able to get pure 1 o'clock to 7 o'clock rotation. You will grip other pitches "off center," but not the high-velocity fastball.

Place your thumb under the other side of the baseball, between your two fingers. The inside of your thumb between the knuckle and the nail rests on the seam. The ball sits firmly but comfortably in this grip, resting against the inside knuckle of your third finger. A very young pitcher with small hands may need to use this third finger on the top of the ball. If so, the three fingers should be placed so that the middle finger is on the imaginary line running through the middle of the ball.

Don't be afraid to make subtle variations with the grip to see what happens. Just remember the key principles to throwing the straight fastball:

1. Center your fingers for imparting spin, between 12 o'clock to 6 o'clock and 1 o'clock to 7 o'clock.
2. Grip the seams with your finger pads so that you can get maximum rotation when you snap down with your wrist at release.
3. Relax your wrist and forearm muscles to get greater wrist pop at release.

The straight fastball is the easiest pitch to throw for strikes because it has the least movement. This is why you should throw four-seam fastballs to your infielders and to your catcher on

Three views of the classic four-seam fastball grip.

pitchouts. As you move up in levels, a straight fastball will become more and more hittable and—unless you throw hard enough to make it move (see the "Rising Fastball" section later in this chapter)—you will need to work on developing movement on a second fastball by using other grips.

Even at the major league level, a straight fastball has its time and place. It remains a very useful pitch to throw inside against opposite-hand hitters. Trying to get inside on an opposite-hand hitter with a tailing fastball can be difficult, since it can easily move back over the middle of the plate. A straight fastball thrown inside will stay inside. It can freeze the batter for a called strike or set him up for a pitch away.

TAILING FASTBALL

When you've established that you can throw strikes with your four-seam straight fastball, you can work in a two-seam fastball, which will give you tailing movement—moving in on a same-hand hitter—and maybe even some sinking action. It's called a two-seam fastball because the grip gives it a spin that appears to show two parallel seams to the batter. You may prefer to think about it as two seams because your index and middle fingers each run along the inside of the seam.

Your finger pads grip the ball where the seams are closest together. The bottom half of the ball rests on the inside of your thumb between the knuckle and the nail, which is directly between and beneath your fingers. Center your grip, grip the seams for stability, and relax your wrist for greater snap at release. Grip the ball a little deeper in the hand and apply more pressure with the index finger. The two-seam fastball rotates slower and builds up more and uneven air resistance, thus causing it to move or tail.

"I think pitchers can run into trouble when they try to make the ball move. Some guys have natural movement because of their delivery, while others don't. You can create or increase movement by sliding your thumb

up and down directly underneath the ball to up onto the side in your grip. All I do is finish the pitch off. As long as I finish the pitch and get good extension out front, my ball is going to tail."

—Graeme Lloyd, Montreal Expos
middle reliever

Against same-hand hitters, you can start this pitch off the plate and bring it in over the outside corner for a called strike—watch Greg Maddux do this time and time again. You can also start it off down the dangerous middle third and have it break in on a batter's fists for a weak ground ball or soft pop. You should not try to move a same-hand batter off the plate with this pitch, because it could tail in and hit him.

Against opposite-hand hitters you should work this pitch away—in the middle third and breaking over the outside corner for an end-of-the-bat fly ball or in the outer third and breaking off the plate for a swinging strike. It may be effective as an inside strike against opposite-hand hitters, provided the umpire will call it. Against Greg Maddux, you will often see left-handed batters lift their hands against this pitch, only to see it tail underneath for a called strike. The danger is in not starting it off inside enough, which causes it to tail out over the middle of the plate.

Concentrate on throwing this pitch for a low strike. You can then make a hitter chase the four-seam fastball up in the strike zone.

Just as you'll get more rise on your fastball with a high three-quarter arm slot, you'll find that you get more tailing action when throwing from a low three-quarters delivery and even more so from a sidearm delivery. Don't be afraid to experiment with different fastballs at different arm angles. Some pitchers can pull this off, while others will sacrifice velocity and command to get movement. If so, that's not a good trade-off and you're better off staying with one arm slot. If not, you've found yourself another weapon.

SINKING FASTBALL

"It's not just the arm that throws the ball. My whole game is really working around my hand, because my arm coming through is the same every time. The positioning of my fingers creates the spin that makes the ball change direction."

—Orel Hershiser, Los Angeles Dodgers
pitcher

Most of the crafty, low-velocity, ground-ball pitchers through the years have made their living with the sinker, a two-seam fastball that breaks down

The two-seam fastball grip.

and in against same-hand hitters. Joe DiMaggio said that the hardest pitch for him to hit was a right-hander's sinker, thrown down and in—hard to lay off, harder still to hit solidly.

If you pitch in front of a solid defensive infield on a nicely manicured field—especially one with a short outfield fence—you should throw this pitch and have great success with it. If the defense behind you is shaky and the field you play on is rock hard or prone to bad hops, you may need to find another out pitch.

The sinker is basically a two-seam fastball that you hold off center and grip tighter and deeper. This creates the side spin you were trying to avoid with your straight fastball. As with nearly all things in pitching, you trade off some velocity for movement. If you're a right-hander, take your two-seam grip and slide it to the right so that your middle finger and index finger are close together, with the middle finger against the seam on the right. Apply more pressure with your index finger than your middle finger.

An alternative way to throw the sinker is to keep your index and middle fingers in the two-seam fastball grip and, upon release, turn the ball in toward your ring finger. Experiment with different thumb placements. You will find that as the thumb goes higher, velocity decreases.

It's not unheard of to have more than one sinker—a harder one and a slower, bigger-breaking one that can even serve as a change-up. Experiment with different grips and go with the one that is easiest for you to locate. Just remember that the basic principle is to throw the two-seam fastball off center, creating some side spin and movement.

"I guess you could say I have two fastballs. I have a four-seam fastball and a two-seam fastball, which sinks. Then I take my four-seam fastball grip, add the other two fingers, and put the ball back in my palm to throw a change-up. So I have three different pitches I throw from a fastball delivery."

—Chad Ogea, Detroit Tigers

The sinker does not require good velocity to be a great pitch. Kevin Brown's power sinker, which he can throw in the low-to-mid-90s, is an aberration. Most pitchers who try to throw a sinker that hard either lose movement on it or have difficulty keeping it in the strike zone. You don't have to throw it hard to get outs with it. Many sinker-ball pitchers actually get better movement on it with a tired arm—when they're fully rested or overly pumped up, the ball stays up. A sinker thrown with limited velocity can be just as effective, if not more so, than one thrown much harder, because it looks so much more appetizing to hitters. They swing at it and either tap a grounder or miss on a pitch that's out of the strike zone. The same pitch thrown much harder is less likely to be put in play for an out and more likely to be taken for a ball. And sinker ballers care about groundouts, not strikeouts.

"While the rising fastball always has great velocity, the sinking fastball has the least velocity of any fastball. Usually. Kevin Brown throws his sinker ball very hard, and he's therefore about as tough to hit as anyone when he has control of the pitch. That's the catch. The ball's explosive movement downward can take it out of the strike zone."

—Keith Hernandez, former MVP and all-star first baseman

You may hear pitchers talk about "turning over" their fastball to make it sink. This requires that you change the rotation of the ball. It can be done by bringing the index finger down earlier inside the ball, much the way the arm and hand naturally turn so that the palm faces the sideline. Next time they show a shot of the pitcher from behind home plate in super-slow motion on television, watch his hand and not the ball. You will see that his wrist naturally turns in (pronates) as he throws any pitch, turning his thumb toward the ground.

When asked to describe Kevin Brown's stuff, opposing hitters simply call him "nasty." Brown's bread-

and-butter pitch is a two-seam, sinking fastball that moves down and in toward a right-hand batter. The pitch

moves so much and has such late action that it's not uncommon for Brown to break three or four bats per

game. Brown also throws a four-seam fastball (seen here) in the mid-90s when he's looking for a strikeout.

Note how early in his delivery he shows the hitter the number on the back of his uniform, storing power in

his torso. This is the classic position for power pitchers at the top of their knee lift.

It should come naturally. However, if you *try* to pronate your hand and arm too early, you're going to lose velocity and control and possibly hurt your elbow. This is how a screwball is thrown, a pitch that is *very* difficult on the arm. A young pitcher simply does not need to put that much strain and stress into a pitch.

CUT FASTBALL OR CUTTER

There is only one way left we haven't discussed to make a fastball move, and that's running away from same-hand hitters. This is called a "cut" fastball or "cutter," and it breaks in the same direction as traditional breaking balls—though less than a slider, which breaks even less than a curveball. It has less downward movement.

The cutter can be thrown with either a four-seam or a two-seam grip. Take the four-seam grip and slide your fingers and thumb to the right (for a right-hander), and bring your index and middle fingers together. You can also try it from the traditional two-seam grip, where you slide your thumb off center to the middle-finger side of the ball. Experiment with these grips until you find one that gives you the best combination of location, movement, and velocity. Also notice how the ball may break more or less for you when it's thrown up or down in the strike zone.

TOMMY JOHN: THE SINKER

In 1980, Tommy John was a 37-year-old left-hander pitching with the first surgically repaired elbow, having undergone what is now known as "Tommy John surgery," in which a piece of ligament from his right wrist was transferred to his left. Though never an overpowering pitcher, even before his injury, he had to learn how to get by with even less on his fastball than before. (An interesting footnote: John injured his arm in a game just before the 1974 All-Star Game. Though he was 13–3 with a low ERA, he'd been left off the all-star team, perhaps because he wasn't piling up enough strikeouts. In trying to prove that he belonged, he admittedly overthrew in his next start and felt something pop in his elbow.)

Not only did he return to pitch again, he was better than he'd ever been. Forced to rely on his craftiness more than ever, he responded with 20-win seasons in 1977, 1979, and 1980—the first of his career. His performance in 1980 was truly remarkable, as he won 22 games while striking out only 78 batters—2.6 per nine innings. Seventy-eight was the lowest number of strikeouts for a 20-game winner in 27 years and hasn't been repeated since.

Before you write off John's accomplishment to the run support of the division-winning Yankees, bear in mind that John led the league with eight shutouts. He averaged 7⅓ innings of seven-hit ball every time out, and he recorded 16 complete games along the way. How did he do it?

His "money" pitch was a sinker. It looked like a fat, juicy fastball to hitters, who tried to jerk it out of the park but whose timing was messed up by its movement and its slightly slower speed than his already-slow two-seam fastball. It wasn't uncommon for John to record 20 groundouts in a game, as hitters continually tried to pull his appetizing-looking offerings and ended up hitting weak ground balls to Bucky Dent at shortstop.

Like all pitchers who thrive without strikeouts, John's control was impeccable. He walked only 56 batters in 36 games, fewer than two per nine innings. With a fastball that couldn't break glass, he allowed fewer runners to reach base per game that season than Nolan Ryan.

The cutter is a great pitch to use to jam opposite-hand hitters and to get same-hand hitters to chase balls away. You can also start it off the plate against opposite-hand hitters and catch the corner. A right-handed pitcher facing a left-handed hitter should bring it in on the hands or knee. A right-handed pitcher facing a right-handed batter should always throw it low and away, sometimes just off the plate.

Most pitchers use the cutter against opposite-hand hitters who might otherwise be diving out across the plate for a tailing fastball. They also try to throw this pitch to the corners of the plate exclusively, because when it's not thrown properly it's a slow, flat fastball—not as fat as the dreaded hanging slider, but close.

"I always turned the ball over, sunk the ball a little bit. I worked on a cutter to get it to move the other way, but that's tough with my arm slot."

—Future Hall of Famer Dennis Eckersley on getting movement on a fastball with a sidearm delivery

Roger Clemens preparing to throw one of his devastating split-finger fastballs. Notice how he keeps the ball—and his grip—concealed from the hitter.

THE SPLITTER

Unless you're one pitch away from getting to the major leagues, or just trying to hang on in the majors, there is no reason to throw a split-fingered fastball. When it's not thrown properly it can either break in the dirt for a ball or a wild pitch, or it can hang up in the zone. Though it can have devastating downward movement—it's been called a "dry spitter"—the anecdotal evidence suggests that it may be harder on your arm than any other pitch you can throw. The good news for most young pitchers is that their hands aren't large enough to have success with this pitch even if they wanted to.

While strongly advising you not to throw it, in the interest of completeness, we will describe its grip, release, and use.

Take a two-seam fastball grip and spread your fingers so that they are on the outside of the seams. Don't spread your fingers too far or you risk hurting your arm. In gripping it, the ball should be deep between these two fingers. Throw it just like a fastball. It will take awhile to master, and it should be used almost exclusively as a two-strike strikeout pitch.

The splitter rotates slowly—it comes in looking just like a regular fastball, then dives under a hitter's bat. Many hitters are so far out in front of it that the downward movement isn't even necessary. This will be the case at most levels below the major leagues, so you're better off throwing a change-up, which is just as effective and much less stressful on the arm.

RISING FASTBALL

As already indicated, it's difficult to get movement with a four-seam fastball unless you throw very hard—in the 90s, at least. At that speed, it appears to rise. In reality, however, all fastballs are dropping as they travel toward the plate—faster pitches resist gravity more, thus creating the illusion of a "rising" fastball. Hitters expect the ball to be lower than it really is.

Most pitchers with four-seam fastballs throw from a high three-quarter delivery and throw with great velocity. It's a pitch with which they challenge hitters up in the strike zone, where most hitters have a hard time connecting—yet can't resist swinging. However, the danger of the four-seam fastball comes when the pitcher starts to tire and it becomes a high fastball that loses velocity. This is why fastball specialist John Wetteland struggled as a starting pitcher before blossoming into a dominating closer who doesn't have to pace himself.

VELOCITY

"I didn't always have good velocity on my fastball. In high school I threw 78 miles per hour. But in college, I really blossomed and was throwing up and around 98 miles per hour. The thing that helped me the most, quite honestly, was simply throwing. I played a lot of long catch and threw more frequently, which really built up my arm strength."

—Billy Wagner, Houston Astros

Getting the maximum velocity on your fastball does *not* necessarily mean throwing the ball as

hard as you can. There are ways to build your velocity, but you will find that you are faced with complicated trade-offs: What is the maximum velocity at which I can throw strikes? What is the velocity at which I get the most movement on my pitches? Do I get different actions on my fastballs at different speeds? *Never sacrifice location or movement for speed.* Learn to "stay within yourself," that is, perform at your body's capabilities. High-velocity pitchers usually throw at 90 to 95 percent effort, not 100 percent effort, a level at which their body movements would not remain in complete control.

"One thing I've learned is that just throwing hard doesn't get the job done. Hitters will eventually catch up to you. Velocity helps, don't get me wrong. It helps complement other pitches and can get you out of some jams. But you have to be able to spot the pitch or create some movement. If you just rear back and throw a straight fastball down the middle, sooner or later, the hitter will crush you."

—Matt Anderson, Detroit Tigers

The young Dwight Gooden shown here could simply blow hitters away with his fastball. Now, minus the great velocity of his youth, he gets by with better location and a better understanding of changing speeds.

ARMANDO BENITEZ: VELOCITY

Speed is, for lack of a better word, overrated.

Flash back to the 1996 division series between the Baltimore Orioles and the Cleveland Indians. With Baltimore up two games to none in the best-of-five series and the score tied at 4–4 in the bottom of the seventh inning of Game 5, the Orioles' hard-throwing Armando Benitez was facing an extraordinary fastball hitter in Albert Belle with the bases loaded. Getting out of this inning would pretty much put a stake through the hearts of the Indians.

Benitez poured belt-high 98-mile-per-hour fastballs up and out over the middle of the plate, and Belle kept fouling them straight back. Foul balls reveal a lot, and this should have warned Benitez that Belle had him timed and was just below his pitches. Something off-speed and on the plate would have had Belle way out in front or frozen stiff. Benitez reared back, hit 99 miles per hour on the gun, and Belle put the ball in the bleachers in left center.

One of the biggest raps on Armando Benitez has been his obsession with speed—to the point of checking the velocity of his fastballs on the stadium scoreboard during games and pumping his fist when he hits 100 miles per hour. Any pitcher who judges his success by the radar-gun numbers may find himself with plenty of time to watch the scoreboard, from a vantage point other than the pitcher's mound.

Velocity is a function of torso rotational forces, arm speed, and arm looseness. If your goal is to increase the velocity of your four-seam fastball, take the following approach and in the order it's given.

Grip. Are you holding the ball firmly, but with a loose, relaxed wrist and forearm? Are you holding the ball with your finger pads and not choking it in the palm of your hand? Are your finger pads getting good pressure on the seams?

Release. Is your wrist relaxed? Are you snapping your wrist forward naturally as you release? Is the ball far enough away from your head during acceleration that you're getting good arm and trunk extension? Is your elbow higher than your shoulder and your fingers behind the ball?

Backswing. Are you creating a short, controlled circle with your throwing arm? Are you flexing your elbow in your backswing? Are you bringing your hand directly back toward second base, with your fingers on top of the ball?

Posting and Stride. Are you staying balanced in your knee lift and not drifting forward until the stride leg starts to lower? Are you landing flat-footed on your stride foot without under- or over-striding? Are you landing with your toes and shoulders closed?

Pull. Are you turning your hips, transferring the energy from your legs to your torso to your arm? Are you staying aligned with your lead elbow and not flying open? Do you release the ball alongside your stride foot? Are you getting your head and shoulders into your follow-through? Does your back knee pull forward and inward, accelerating the lower body into the pitch?

"If I tried to throw harder than I could, the ball went slower than it normally would."

—Hall of Famer Tom Seaver

In other words, velocity is a function of mechanics. Keep your arm, wrist, and fingers relaxed and loose, then let your lower body create momentum and rotational velocity of the torso, and that will generate arm speed. Some coaches may tell you to push off with your back leg, but this will just cause you to rush, which will actually put you out of sequence and rob you of some velocity. If you have sound mechanics already, the best thing you can do for velocity is to (1) throw a baseball, and throw it mechanically correct (babying your arm will actually hurt you in the long run—you don't build strength in a muscle by resting it); and (2) build lower-body strength with running and weights, upper-body strength and flexibility with light weights and stretching (see Chapter 7).

"Pitchers should use their arms every day. They've got to get the blood flowing through there to help with the healing process. It also helps to keep strengthening those muscles and keeps them stretched out. If you don't throw between starts, those muscles will shrink up and it will be tough to get them stretched out before your next start. If you don't throw, you won't build arm strength."

—Mel Queen, Toronto Blue Jays pitching coach, on starting pitchers

John Smoltz possesses the best fastball on the Atlanta Braves pitching staff, a group known for throwing nearly every day to build and maintain arm strength. Braves pitchers believe that throwing more rather then less has helped them to remain relatively injury free.

If you're looking for reasons why Nolan Ryan was able to play the game longer than any other player, piling up games, innings, and pitches, here are three reasons:

- He threw a lot as a kid, but only fastballs. He didn't have a breaking ball until he was playing professionally.
- Sound mechanics. By 1972, he had developed an outstanding delivery, which allowed his legs to generate and control the bulk of his force.
- Conditioning. Ryan took to rigorous conditioning early in his career and stuck to it. Even at age 44 after his seventh no-hitter, you could still find him riding the stationary bike after the game.

"You don't find too many pitchers grunting the way Nolan does when he throws the ball. Youngsters today say, 'I have only so many pitches left in my arm and I have to save them.' Then you look at Nolan Ryan pitching into his 40s and still blazing the ball after all the pitches he's thrown."

—Herb Score, Indians broadcaster and former overpowering pitcher

Don't fall into the trap of trying to trick batters too early. If you have good velocity on your fastball in high school, why speed up the hitter's bat by throwing him breaking balls? Make him prove he can catch up to your fastball. Even if you don't have good velocity, challenging hitters with well-located fastballs will still take you a very long way.

At the high school level, there is no need to depend on your breaking pitches to get your outs for you. Sure, it's fun to make the ball move and watch a hopelessly overmatched hitter swing and miss, but you'll pay for it later. Here's how:

1. Pitching breaking balls with improper mechanics is easy to do at a young age. The slider especially can be very hard on your arm if thrown improperly.

2. Breaking balls do not help you build arm strength. Your fastball will develop only as your arm strength and arm speed develop. Established pitchers must use it or lose it. Young pitchers must throw it or never develop it. The growth plates and bones of young pitchers are not always fully developed. The ligaments are not firmly attached to the bones, which are softer in young than in mature pitchers. Thus, there is a greater chance for injury, so concentrate on throwing the fastball. It creates less strain on the arm.

3. For the most part, throwing breaking balls at too young an age does not help you learn how to pitch. Remember the Bob Tewksbury quote that started this chapter: anyone can get batters out with breaking balls in high school. At a higher level, those pitches aren't going to fool the hitters, and you haven't developed the ability to locate your fastball. It may be harder to get batters out that way— especially when facing aluminum bats— but it's a skill that *must* be developed if you have any interest in pitching in college or beyond.

"Practice throwing the ball with a four-seam rotation like an infielder and work on getting the ball to carry. When you're young, your muscles are growing and your bones are still growing. Establish proper mechanics early and build your arm strength with fastballs. It's not pivotal to your success to throw breaking balls at a young age."

—Pat Hentgen

More than simply building velocity, you should be thinking about *varying* velocity. The change-up will be covered at great length in the next chapter, but most pitchers take their first steps toward mastering this pitch by throwing the same fastball at different speeds. Rick Reuschel had a long career *after* arm surgery robbed him of his velocity by becoming a master of the multi-speed fastball. None of his fastballs ever seemed to be the same speed. They wouldn't vary by the 10 miles per hour of a traditional change-up, but 3 miles per hour even when you're only throwing 85 can still mess up a hitter's timing. Reuschel is just one of many hard throwers who proved there was life after velocity.

"In high school, college, you're just reaching back and blowing guys away. All of a sudden you get to A ball, and the hitters are a lot better. They're patient. I was falling behind guys. I was overthrowing and guys weren't swinging at it. Then I learned, after having my injuries, how to get ahead of hitters and throw strikes."

—Mark Leiter on being a very hard-throwing young pitcher until arm injuries while still in the minor leagues forced him to change his pitching style

The key is to find a way to change speeds off your fastball without affecting your arm speed or stride or in any other way tipping it off to the batter. The only change you should make is in your grip. Experiment with subtle differences in grips on your two-seam and four-seam fastballs, throwing a few with the ball farther back toward the palm and then a few farther forward, toward the fingertips. Try something with three fingers on top of the ball rather than just two. This may help you to "take a little off" while still being able to locate the ball.

Throw It Again

The best way to build velocity is through proper mechanics, conditioning of your legs, and throwing fastballs. Rather than merely attempting to maximize how hard you throw, you should be thinking about how to vary the velocity on your fastball, and you should be noticing whether less velocity actually gets you more movement.

Experiment. Some of the best pitchers the game has produced stumbled onto their out pitches while trying out different things in practice. That's experimenting, not just messing around. When you try something different with your grip, you need to be aware of what you're doing to the ball and throw the same pitch at least three times. This way, not only will you able to see for certain what effect you're having, you'll remember what you did! See what happens when you grip the ball across the seams diagonally. Remember: it's the grip you're varying, not your arm speed, not your release, and definitely not your delivery. You can experiment with different pressure points—holding the ball the same way, but more firmly with one finger than the other—though you'll probably find that you get different results with different grips.

"Let the grip do the work."

—Bob Tewksbury on varying velocity and getting movement on your fastball

As you experiment with different grips, notice also what happens to the ball when you try to throw it as hard as you can as opposed to simply throwing it less hard. You may find that you actually get more movement on your fastball when you don't try to throw it through the backstop. You're often better off just throwing it with authority and under control.

When you think you've come up with some grips that give you different speeds on your fastball—or when you've come up with a speed that gives you greater movement—try it out when pitching to some friends. You'll be surprised at how bad a few miles per hour or a few inches can make hitters look.

BE AGGRESSIVE

"It's all heart. He's got the biggest heart of any pitcher I've ever caught. It doesn't matter how good his stuff is, he's going to get you out because he's got heart and he's not afraid to come after you."

—Eric Munson, USC catcher, on NCAA record-setting closer Jack Krawczyk

Eric Munson had this to say about his teammate after Jack Krawczyk saved the final game of the 1998 college world series, giving USC the national championship. Krawczyk—who holds two NCAA records for relievers, with 23 saves during the 1998 season and 49 in his career—had come into a 16–14 slugfest in the eighth inning with the tying run at the plate and retired all five batters he faced to preserve the lead for USC. It was no minor feat, considering that the Arizona State lineup he faced had been 16-for-38 in the game prior to Krawczyk's arrival.

Did Krawczyk do this by going after hitters with a 95 MPH fastball? Hardly. He throws about 75 miles per hour, a fastball so slow that opposing hitters call it a change-up. One LSU player described Krawczyk's fastball as a "knuckleball, only it doesn't knuckle," and suspected that "it's almost like he wants to see how slow he can throw it." Krawczyk's coach, Mike Gillespie, continued to

Dodgers right-hander Darren Dreifort doesn't believe in nibbling—he goes right after the hitter. The best fastball is one thrown with an aggressive mind-set.

call on him, underwhelming velocity and all, because "he continues to get outs."

Challenging the hitter with your fastball—however fast it may or may not be—is part of being an aggressive pitcher. And being aggressive is part of being successful. If you're a very competitive person, this just comes naturally. If anything, you may need to resist the urge to challenge the hitter *every* time, even when the situation calls for a breaking ball or change-up. If you're a more laid-back type or you aren't all that confident in your fastball, you will need to undergo a personality transformation when you take the mound.

> *"If I'm facing a fastball hitter, I'm certainly not going to back down from throwing my best pitch. I mean, I have two different fastballs [a four-seam and two-seam] that I can throw to seven different locations. So you can say it's power against power, but I still feel like I own an advantage over the hitter because I can throw the ball where I want. And that's my approach."*
>
> —Roger Clemens

Maybe you can be agressive in a very personal way. View base hits as personal affronts that motivate you to go right after the next hitter. Or maybe you can stoke your competitive fires in a very team-oriented way, taking the responsibility of being aggressive very seriously because your team's chances of winning or losing depend most heavily on you. You can make it a point to exude a relaxed confidence and controlled aggressiveness—even if you have some butterflies—because you know your team will feed off your attitude.

When a pitcher lacks confidence in his stuff, he ends up giving the hitters too much credit. He thinks they will crush just about any pitch he throws over the plate. He "nibbles," which causes him to fall behind in the count and either forces him to come in with a pitch that a hitter is sitting on, or forces him to walk the hitter. When a pitcher nibbles rather than challenges, the tentativeness rubs off on his teammates. Nibbling affects the most important pitching statistic—wins—not just in the additional walks given up, but in all the extra time standing around in the field that you're making your defense do. Over time, it will have a negative effect on defensive play and eventually offensive production. When you see a nibbler losing a lot of close games, that's not a coincidence.

Not all pitchers who work deep counts by staying out of the strike zone are soft throwers who need to be cute to survive. Many nibblers actually have good stuff, but they just don't trust it enough or haven't worked hard enough at developing the ability to "paint the black."

If nothing else, pitching requires having a positive outlook—something that can trouble pitchers at even the highest levels. In 1987, two years after winning 20 games as a rookie, Tom Browning found himself back in the minors. He describes how the pitching coach of the Nashville Sounds, former 20-game winner Wayne Garland, helped him: "He didn't talk mechanics at all. It was all mental stuff. I had no confidence. I was negative. I just knew every time I went out there something bad would happen."

A year later, Browning was back in the majors and throwing a perfect game. Two years after that, he was winning a World Series game that put the Reds up three games to none on a heavily favored Oakland team.

The best way to develop a positive outlook is to work hard at your craft—being able to locate your fastball, being able to make it move, and being able to throw it for strikes at various speeds. If you can do this in practice—regardless of your size, athletic ability, or radar-gun readings—you can get batters out. If you can locate your fastball, be aggressive with it. Good things will happen.

> ········ **Throw It Again**
> You need to be aggressive to succeed as a pitcher, and that means challenging hitters with your fastball. Regardless of how fast you throw, once you've established the ability to locate your fastball—you will be able to get outs.

Pedro Martinez

Pulling the String:
The Change-Up

The change-up is nothing more than a pitch that looks like a fastball but travels at a reduced speed. The hitter thinks he's got your fastball timed and he's going after it aggressively— only to find himself with his weight on his front foot, trying to hold up his swing as your change-up floats over the plate for a strike. That's really all there is to it. Some change-ups have a sinking movement or tailing action, but even a straight change is very effective.

> "You don't just want the hitters to be moving in and out, but forward and back. That's what Greg Maddux does so well."
>
> —Larry Andersen, former relief pitcher

Throw off a batter's timing and you take away his power. As former all-star first baseman Bob Watson said of a particularly vexing change-up artist, "(Scott) McGregor doesn't get you out, he lets you get yourself out." That's why they called McGregor's change-up a "dead fish"—when properly thrown, the batter seemed to be trying to hit one of those rather than a tightly wound baseball.

When Pedro Martinez won the Cy Young Award in 1997—breaking a six-year run by members of the Atlanta Braves staff—his jump from very good to outstanding was due to the addition of

Atlanta's primary weapon: a change-up. There is no better second pitch for you to learn. It will generate a lot of weak grounders or swinging strikes without taking much out of you. It does not strain your arm, it should be easier to throw for strikes than a breaking ball, and the stiffer your competition, the more important it is to have in your reper-toire. It will make your fastball look faster, and it can be psychologically devastating to hitters.

Upon being traded to the Boston Red Sox in 1998, Martinez found himself back under the tute-lage of former Expos pitching coach Joe Kerrigan. Kerrigan preaches that every pitcher will benefit from throwing a change-up, and supports his phi-losophy in a simple, yet convincing manner.

Kerrigan says, "After you learn a fastball, you should learn how to throw a change-up. The rea-son a change-up is so effective is as simple as this: Hitters will recognize the fastball spin on a change-up, but they don't recognize the change in speed. This upsets their timing, and this is the essence of pitching. In addition, the change-up can be thrown more consistently for a strike than any other non-fastball pitch. Without question, the change-up is a powerful weapon in a pitcher's arsenal."

It's no secret that the success of the Atlanta Braves is directly linked to its pitching staff and coach Leo Mazzone. Mazzone is a strong proponent of the change-up.

LEARNING TO THROW THE CHANGE-UP

Many pitchers need time to get comfortable throwing a change-up. It's not an easy pitch to master, but here's the good news: the delivery is exactly the same as your fastball delivery. In fact it has to be. No new mechanics to learn. Lifting your leg lower, shortening your stride, or slowing down your arm would all help you to take speed off your fastball—but they will also let the batter know that a change-up is on the way. So much for upsetting his timing.

It used to be that young pitchers were taught to change speeds by throwing a fastball without pushing off with their back leg. But if you've taken the chapter on mechanics to heart (Chapter 2), you aren't pushing off. You're pulling your arm through with your lead elbow, front shoulder, hips, and lead leg. Some pitchers were even taught to throw a change-up by pushing the ball elbow-first. Absolutely not! You'll tip off the hitter, mess up your mechanics, lack command of the pitch, and possibly injure yourself.

Early on, you can experiment with changing speeds off your fastball by not driving your lead elbow down as powerfully or landing with your stride foot pointed directly at home plate. These slight adjustments will reduce the velocity of your fastball. As for how much you're taking off your fastball, Braves pitching coach Leo Mazzone suggests "the most you can take off without losing arm speed. Arm speed promotes deception; deception gets batters out."

> *"Throw a fastball with something extra on it, then throw a fastball without putting anything on it. Then go from there."*
>
> —Leo Mazzone, Atlanta Braves pitching coach, on the first step for a young pitcher who wants to learn a change-up

Taking something off your fastball is a good way to learn how changing speeds can help you, but eventually you will need to develop a true change-up. That means learning a grip that will enable you to throw a ball over the plate about 10 miles per hour slower than your fastball with the same arm speed. Throw it too fast and you won't put a hitter off balance. Throw it too slow and a hitter might be able to adjust in time to drive the ball.

THE GRIP

To get it right, you need to let the grip do all of the work for you. The grip for the four-seam fastball called for you to put the pads of your index and middle fingers on the seams for leverage. With a change-up, you don't want leverage. You actually want just the opposite.

> *"A pitcher should take speed off the ball by changing his grip, but maintain the same arm speed. Find a comfortable grip that slows down the speed of the ball and throw it like a fastball."*
>
> —Galen Cisco, Philadelphia Phillies pitching coach

One change-up is called the three-finger change-up and is thrown with your thumb and pinkie finger to each side, and your middle three fingers on top of the ball across the wide seams. The ball is held in the palm of your hand rather than with the ends of your fingers. It's also called a palm ball. It will feel awkward at first, but you'll find that it's a very simple way to take something off your fastball.

A more popular change-up is called a circle change. You form a circle with your bent index finger and thumb, then grip the ball with your middle and third finger along the narrow seams with your fingertips inside the seams. Because your thumb is off to one side rather than directly under your middle two fingers, you will naturally end up delivering this ball with your palm out. This will provide a tailing or fading action to the pitch, breaking away from opposite-hand hitters.

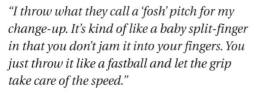

Three views of the three-finger change-up

"I throw what they call a 'fosh' pitch for my change-up. It's kind of like a baby split-finger in that you don't jam it into your fingers. You just throw it like a fastball and let the grip take care of the speed."

—Darren Dreifort, Los Angeles Dodgers

Whatever change-up you use, remember that it's the grip that takes the speed off the pitch. Throw it with the same arm speed as your regular fastball. *Don't try to take anything off this pitch with anything other than the new grip.* If it feels like you're throwing it too hard, most likely you've got it just right.

There are about as many ways to throw the change-up as there are pitchers throwing it. Experiment with different grips when throwing on the side, noticing which ones allow you to throw strikes at a deceptive velocity. You'll need to rely on your catcher or the hitters on your team to help.

"You have to experiment. Don't be afraid to use different grips. We've got four guys here [Maddux, Tom Glavine, John Smoltz, and Denny Neagle in 1998] and four different change-ups. But they're all effective. There's no one set way to throw it. If you need an opinion on whether the pitch is effective or not, the hitters will let you know."

—Greg Maddux on the change-up

Once you have your grip, the next step is practice. Work on it just as much as you work on your breaking ball. Throw it when you're shagging fly balls in the outfield. Throw it when you're having a catch with your teammate. More importantly, throw it in the game. Remember, it's the same mechanics as when you throw your fastball, so there's no risk in hurting your arm.

Three views of the circle change-up

"Our idea is simple: command the fastball and change speeds. The best way to do that is with repetition and feel."

—Leo Mazzone

LOCATING THE CHANGE-UP

The many types of change-ups you can throw offer a variety of movement, but this is the least important aspect of the pitch. Once you have established a good velocity for the pitch—about 10 miles per hour slower than your fastball—you need to focus on location.

The first step is to practice throwing the change-up down in the strike zone. Do not worry about throwing it to either side of the plate until you've established throwing it low. A high change-up, whether it be inside or outside, is a fat pitch. If you miss your spot, miss low.

Once you've established throwing your change-up down, then focus on throwing it "over the plate" for strikes. Keep in mind your intent is to throw low strikes. More often than not, hitters will swing through the pitch, take it for a strike, or hit it weakly on the ground. Anytime your change-up rides high in the strike zone, you're playing with fire.

Do your best to throw your change-up on the outer half of the plate. A hitter can do damage to a change-up on the inside corner even if he's swinging out on his front foot. Despite the fact that the lower half of his body (legs and hips) becomes a nonfactor, he will still be able to generate some power swinging at a ball that is in close to his body.

American League all-star Mike Mussina has a live fastball, a wicked breaking ball, and an outstanding change-
up. The latter makes his first two pitches even tougher.

As you move to higher levels of competition,
you'll need to refine your location of this pitch.
The location keys for the fastball discussed in
Chapter 3 will be just as effective with a change-
up. It comes down to mechanics and concentration. Concentrate on putting the pitch in the
lower half and on the outer half of the strike zone.
If you can add movement, so much the better, but
just velocity and location will take you very far.

*"You've got to keep the change-up down. Aim
to start it out at the hitter's knees. It's going to
look like a fastball to the hitter, which will get
his hands committed to swing the bat. Once
his hands are committed, the best he'll be
able to do is hit a weak ground ball."*

—Sean Bergman, Minnesota Twins

It may be difficult to believe that the best
pitch you can throw is a slow fastball in the strike
zone that doesn't move very much. If you're still
skeptical, try to hit one when you're geared up
for something harder. It's like hitting off a pitching machine. After timing pitch after pitch,
someone turns down the speed without telling
you. With the next pitch, you're coming out of
your shoes. Hitting your spots with your change-
up is the closest any pitcher will come to the
"unhittable strike."

Twenty-one years before Greg Maddux won a
Cy Young Award pitching in Wrigley Field, Hall of
Famer Ferguson Jenkins did the same for the
Cubs. In 1971, he quietly had one of the most

remarkable seasons any pitcher has ever had.
While most successful pitchers end up striking
out two to three batters for every one they walk,
Jenkins was averaging seven strikeouts with only
one walk every time he took the mound. This kind
of command of one's stuff was unparalleled to
that point, and has been exceeded since by only
Greg Maddux. Both pitchers achieved this degree
of dominance through pinpoint control of their
change-ups—their unhittable strikes.

BE AGGRESSIVE WITH IT

Once you've established control of your change-
up, your next step is simply to throw it. Every
pitcher with a good change-up will tell you that
this was a critical step in their development. Don't

> ······· **Throw It Again**
>
> You do not change your delivery in any way when throwing your change-up. Throw it just as you would a fastball—same leg lift, same stride, same arm speed. Changing any of these will tip off the batter, eliminate the element of surprise, and find you backing up third base after throwing it.

throw it because someone else is telling you to do it, throw it because you've worked hard on the sidelines to refine it and you know it's a good pitch. Throw it because it will make your fastball look even faster. Throw it in many different situations, so you don't fall into a pattern with it. In short, be aggressive with it.

Former New York Mets pitching coach Bob Apodaca had a couple of starting pitchers in Rick Reed and Bobby Jones who used their change-up to foil hitters. He wouldn't have minded having a few more pitchers who followed that recipe. Apodaca has to look no further than the Atlanta Braves to witness the positive impact a change-up can have on a pitching staff: "The Atlanta Braves pitchers are all confident in throwing change-ups and off-speed pitches regardless of the count on the batter. That's what makes the Braves pitchers so successful. Human nature seems to be to throw harder when in trouble, but that's not the way to be a successful pitcher."

Throwing a change-up does not make you a passive pitcher. Being aggressive as a pitcher does not mean throwing the ball as hard as you can. It does not mean overpowering your opposition. It means throwing pitches in the strike zone and challenging the hitter to do something with them. Listen to what Seattle Mariners lefty Jamie Moyer has to say about being aggressive. He has a change-up in the low-70s, a below-average fastball, and a record of 45–17 from 1996 to 1998.

Moyer says, "I don't feel like I've ever gone out and dominated a league or a hitter. And I don't want to ever to feel that way. Maybe if I threw 95 miles per hour I'd look at it differently. . . . If I have to go after hitters, I challenge them, but I chal-

lenge them by using different sides of the plate, different speeds, different looks."

It would be hard to find a much more aggressive pitch than the 3–2 change-up Catfish Hunter threw to Hall of Famer Harmon Killebrew in the seventh inning of his perfect game in 1968. Killebrew was so far out in front of the pitch that his bat flew all the way to second base. Hunter's manager, Bob Kennedy, called it "the greatest and guttiest pitch of the game." Not bad for a guy who'd just turned 22.

Nolan Ryan showed that even a pitcher with a 100 MPH fastball can be aggressive with a change-up. In 1975, Ryan was still pretty much a two-pitch pitcher: fastball and curveball. In a game against the Orioles, he found himself without his best stuff but still one out away from his fourth no-hitter. He also had only a 1–0 lead. The dangerous Bobby Grich was up, and he fouled two of Ryan's fastballs straight back, which told Ryan that he was right on the pitch. Ryan didn't *throw* this no-hitter, he *pitched* it—going after Grich

Power pitcher Tom Seaver prepares to "pull the string" with a circle change-up.

with a change-up down the middle, freezing him for strike three.

Next time you're watching Greg Maddux, Tom Glavine, Pedro Martinez, Trevor Hoffman, or any other pitcher with an outstanding change-up, notice how many times they go to their change-up to get a crucial out. And how many times they get it.

WHEN TO USE THE CHANGE-UP— AND WHEN NOT TO

The change-up is a very versatile pitch. You will find that you can use it against just about every type of hitter you will face, with the exception of the batter who simply can't catch up to your fastball. Never throw a change-up to a hitter who is late on your fastball. It simply speeds up his bat. If a right-hander is fouling your fastballs down the first base line or just barely getting a piece of them, he may be able to pull your change-up with authority. Throw this hitter a change-up and he could hit a home run literally by accident.

Here are some other things to look for:

During his practice swings or in the first at bat, notice whether the hitter takes a very long stride and has a hard time keeping his weight back. These are typically very aggressive fastball hitters, and if they connect the ball can go a long way. But it is hard for these types of hitters to keep their weight back (and more importantly their hands back), so you can throw off their timing with a change-up. They will be way out in front of the pitch, swinging and missing, trying to hold up, or connecting weakly because all of their weight is on their front foot.

Most long-striding hitters try to make contact with pitches out in front of the plate to pull the ball, but there are some short striders who try to pull everything as well. If you notice that a right-handed hitter won't try to take your outside pitches up the middle or to the right side, you've got an excellent candidate for a change-up over the outer half of the plate. The path of a pull-hitter's swing through the hitting zone leaves him

B. J. Surhoff is badly fooled on a change-up. His weight has already shifted forward onto his front foot, and he's reduced to swinging with just his arms.

only the end of the bat with which to hit the ball. If he's a pull hitter who "steps in the bucket"—steps away from the plate as he swings—he will be even more vulnerable to a change-up away.

"Developing a change-up has been the biggest adjustment for me. It's a pitch that I have to throw if I'm going to be successful. You've got to change speeds more in the starting role because you're facing hitters three and sometimes four times throughout a game instead of seeing them once out of the bullpen."

—Darren Dreifort on becoming a starter in 1999 after being a relief specialist

More than simply how a hitter strides or what he tries to do with the pitch will tell you whether or not to throw him a change-up. Once you've faced a hitter a few times—or watched other members of your staff pitch to him—you might notice that he is a first-pitch fastball hitter. Once he's gotten a chance to time your fastball, he's a perfect candidate for a first-pitch change-up. But you don't want to throw him a change-up until he's seen your fastball. And you definitely don't want to throw him a first-pitch change-up all the time.

Other hitters may be more patient. They may not go after the first pitch as aggressively, but they still like to work the count, hoping you get behind and have to throw them a fastball. These hitters love to sit on 2–0 and 3–1 counts, look for a fastball in a particular spot, and drive it. Throw them a change-up and you've got a swinging strike or a weak ground ball. Of course, the key to being able to throw change-ups when you're behind in the count is being able to throw your change-up for a strike down in the zone.

SITUATIONAL CHANGE-UPS

The game situation can also determine whether or not to throw a change-up. If a hitter does not want to pull the ball, you may want to throw him a change-up. Say there is a man on second, no one out, and a right-handed hitter at the plate. Chances are, he's going to try to hit the ball to the right side to move the runner along. A change-up down the middle may be very hard for him to hit to the right side. You could end up with a hard grounder to short that forces the runner to remain at second. It's usually a mistake to throw the change-up to a left-hander who is trying to advance the runner, unless you think you can strike him out with it.

Some pitchers use their change-up sparingly. Rather than throw the change-up to just about every hitter, as Glavine and Maddux do, they save it for when they really need to get a tough out late in the game—when the hitter thinks he's seen all of his pitches.

An integral factor in making the transition from relief pitcher to starting pitcher for Darren Dreifort was learning to throw an effective change-up.

"I went from experimenting with it to being confident enough to throw it with the bases loaded and a full count in the World Series."

—Tom Glavine on his change-up

Though some pitchers use it to get strikeouts, the change-up can be a dangerous pitch to throw with two strikes against a contact hitter. This type of hitter will shorten up his stroke and wait longer, so he will have a much easier time hitting your two-strike change-up than a free-swinger will.

Even if the change-up is a pitch that you throw only a few times throughout your outing, it's still effective just to show it to hitters early on in the game. This will plant a seed in their head, which can benefit you regardless of whether you throw the change-up again. Showing the change-up cooks up another side dish for the hitter's brain to digest.

CHANGE-UP MISTAKES

Change-up mistakes boil down to where, when, how, and who. You've already seen some of the "who" mistakes—throwing a change-up to a hitter who is late on your fastball, or throwing a change-up to a left-hander who is trying to advance a runner. Here are the where, when, and how of change-up mistakes.

Where. It is almost always a mistake to throw a change-up inside. A fooled hitter might still be able to get "good wood" on the ball. A change-up away almost always leaves the hitter with nothing but the end of the bat to use. A change-up high in the strike zone is also a dangerous pitch to throw. It's easier for a hitter to detect, and he can generate more power with his arms swinging at a pitch that's waist-high rather than one down by his knees. Change-ups will also move more when thrown down in the strike zone. Finally, a change-up out of the strike zone serves no purpose. Sometimes you may want to throw a change-up off the plate, but most of the time you want the hitter to swing. Miss with a change-up and, though you've fooled the hitter into thinking it's a fastball, he lays off because it's out of the strike zone. Don't waste a good change-up by missing the target with it.

> *"The change-up is never purposefully thrown inside. Never. The reason is simple: If the change-up does what it's designed to do and gets the hitter off stride, about all he can do with the pitch over the outside part of the plate is to hit it weakly toward the end of the bat."*
>
> —Keith Hernandez, all-star first baseman

When. Because the change-up is designed to fool hitters who are looking for your fastball, it is a big mistake to throw this pitch to a batter until he has seen your fastball. You need him to be "replaying" one of your fastballs in his head when you "pull the string" on him. Once a hitter has seen your change-up, there are plenty of times to use it. The key—as with all pitches—is to not get into any predictable patterns. If a hitter is confident that you will throw the change-up in a given situation, he can take the high-risk, high-reward approach of sitting on your change-up. Then it becomes a batting-practice fastball.

How. The biggest mistake most pitchers make with their change-up is not who they throw it to, where they put it, or when they use it—it's *how* they throw it. Throwing it improperly will either hurt your ability to control it or will let the batter know that it's coming. Both of these can lead to big innings. The biggest delivery mistakes that most pitchers make are slowing down their arm, shortening their stride, or changing their delivery in some other way (how they lift their hands, how high they lift their leg, etc.). The best way to keep this from happening is to get comfortable with a change-up grip, and then go into your delivery

A change-up thrown above the knees on the inside part of the plate is enough to make a hitter salivate.

telling yourself that you're throwing a fastball. This will keep your mechanics consistent and let "the grip do the work."

Some coaches tell young pitchers to actually speed up their motion when throwing a change-up, in order to deceive the hitter. No, no, a thousand times no! This may work for Bugs Bunny, but not when facing astute hitters. A smart hitter will pick up any change in the pitcher's motion, then sit on a change-up as if the catcher told him it was coming.

THE BENEFITS OF CHANGING SPEEDS

"I don't put any strain on my arm because I don't have to throw the ball harder to change speeds."

—Doug Jones, who pitched into his 40s without being sidelined with a sore arm

So how come everyone doesn't throw a change-up?

Many pitchers just don't feel comfortable "taking a little off their fastball" and putting it over the plate. It scares them. They prefer to try to throw the ball by the batter or get him to chase something off the plate. Others get more enjoyment out of making a ball move, relying on a curveball or slider instead. Some want to learn it, but find themselves having to do so at a high level because they never felt they needed it in high school. In college, the minors, or even the majors, learning on the job can be a very scary proposition. If you tip your change-up, it's batting practice.

Ask any veteran major league pitcher what advice he'd give himself if he were pitching in high school again, and most will tell you, "Learn a change-up." That's what Dennis Eckersley said when asked this question in the middle of his last season: "I didn't start changing speeds until I got to the big leagues. That's a little late." As for when he got comfortable throwing the change-up, the 43-year-old pitcher laughed and said, "I'm still not comfortable with it." Dave Steib, who returned to the big leagues in 1998 after a four-year absence,

echoed Eckersley's thoughts on wishing he'd learned how to change speeds as a young pitcher. Take it from them.

Many pitchers have such good fastballs and sliders in high school, they don't think they need an off-speed pitch. If the batter can't catch up to the heat or handle the breaking stuff, why throw them something slow? That's true, but only in the short run. A short-term advantage is almost always a long-term disadvantage. Perhaps the game's greatest change-up pitcher, Greg Maddux, recognizes the problem that the change-up poses to pitchers in high school: "A lot of kids that age have success throwing breaking pitches. And these guys probably throw really hard, so they've got guys late anyway. The change-up won't really help you until you face older, better hitters. I threw my change-up in high school, gave up a home run on it, and got second-guessed. My coach told me, 'You've got a good fastball and a good curveball, so why are you letting the hitter off the hook by messing around with a change-up?' So I stopped throwing it in high school."

Home run and all, do you think Greg Maddux's decision to throw change-ups in high school was such a bad idea? After going 6–14 in 1987 in his first full season in the majors, with an ERA well over five runs per game, Maddux went 18–8 in 1988. What happened? He started dusting off his change-up and using it more often.

SEEING THE FUTURE

"Doubt if he'll be the overpowering type, but should throw a lot of ground balls."

"Change shows promise."

"Good control for a high school pitcher."

"Potential to be a front-line pitcher."

—comments from two scouting reports on Greg Maddux in 1984

Maddux says, "I started throwing my change-up more after my rookie season when I started facing guys who could hit the fastball and recognize the curveball. As hitters get older, they learn how to hit the curveball better and the slider better, and that's where the change-up comes in. Often, the better the hitter, the more effective the change-up."

Maddux's teammate and fellow Cy Young Award winner Tom Glavine had to learn his change-up at the big league level. It took him a year, and he didn't begin to feel comfortable with it until the end of 1990 and the beginning of 1991. His fortunes mirrored those of his team. The Braves went from last place to the World Series. Glavine went from 10–12 to 20–11 and a Cy Young Award.

Unlike Maddux and Glavine, many pitchers reach the upper levels of the minors or the majors, realize that they need a change-up, but can't learn it quickly enough. So if you have any desire to compete at the college or professional level, learn a change-up now. Down the road, the best hitters you face will have the hardest time with a good change-up on the outer half of the plate. Especially the dead-pull power hitters; Tom Glavine says he prefers to face hitters who are trying to take him deep rather go the other way. Unless you face a very disciplined lineup full of hitters that are willing to go with a pitch, the change-up on the outer half will get you plenty of end-of-the-bat grounders and fly balls.

Without his change-up, Tom Glavine would be just another pitcher. With it, he's won two Cy Youngs and the 1995 World Series MVP award.

> *"I learned I had to give in, to go to the opposite field against him, to wait on the ball a split second longer, or I wouldn't have had a chance."*
>
> —Hall of Famer Stan Musial on facing Hall of Famer Warren Spahn and his outstanding change-up

Even the hardest throwers against the most overmatched competition will find some use for a change-up at least a few times per game. As good as your fastball may be, there should be at least one hitter in the opposing lineup who can catch up to it. If you can locate a change-up on the outer half of the plate, there's not much he'll be able to do with it. And if for some reason you think that throwing a change-up to a hitter is "giving in," remember that the game's greatest fastball pitcher—Nolan Ryan—threw one. Ryan threw two no-hitters in the 1990s after he turned 40, in part because of the change-up he first began to feature more prominently in Houston in the 1980s. When some National League hitters saw it for the first time, they looked out to the mound as if in protest. Trying to catch up to a Ryan fastball only to find themselves lunging at a high-80s change-up? This isn't fair! In short, if Nolan Ryan had use for a change-up, so do you.

"Pitching is just an illusion. You're dealing with a man's eyes. Make him think he's getting one thing and give him another and you've got him."

—Alvin Jackson, former Red Sox
pitching coach

The change-up is also a great weapon even if you don't have the size or velocity that scouts drool over. Greg Maddux and Tom Glavine were outstanding athletes in high school, but they're not very big and their velocity has never been great by major league standards. This hasn't kept them from winning six Cy Young Awards between them. And it didn't keep Glavine from pitching arguably the greatest championship-clinching game in history, a 1–0 one-hitter in 1995 to close out the Indians in the World Series.

"I'm average at best when it comes to velocity, but my ability to throw the ball where I wanted to and my ability to change speeds were what enabled me to throw that kind of ball game."

—Tom Glavine on his one-hitter in Game 6
of the 1995 World Series

Maybe you're more like these two star pitchers than you realize. You have enough on your fastball to overmatch some of your high school competition, but not enough to take you as far as you could go. If you fail to learn how to change speeds, here's a glimpse into your not-so-distant future at the next level of competition:

The leadoff hitter has a quick enough bat to foul off your fastballs and a good enough eye to lay off your breaking pitches, eventually working out a 10-pitch walk. With the runner moving on the pitch, you throw a hard fastball away and the hitter drives it through the hole vacated by your second baseman to put runners on the corners. When you were in these spots in high school, all you needed to do was throw your fastball on the inner half or your curveball over the plate to get out of it. So you jam the number-three hitter with your fastball, but he's quick enough to get the bat head

out and line a run-scoring single over the shortstop's head. You get two strikes on the cleanup hitter, then throw a curveball over the plate that always got you the called third strikes. He stays back on it and drives it into the gap to clear the bases.

Kind of unsettling, isn't it? You've got your velocity, your curveball is breaking, and you're throwing strikes—but you're still getting rocked. When you had this kind of stuff before, you knew you were on your way to a four-hitter. Now the batters are strong enough that they can hit inside fastballs off the fists with their aluminum bats and send flares over your shortstop's head. You need another pitch, and you need it quickly. Something that will take the quickness of a hitter with an aluminum bat and use it against him, while being just as effective against wooden bats. Maddux and Glavine are living proof that good control and learning how to change speeds will make you a more devastating pitcher than any straight fastball, no matter how fast it's thrown.

"They can just work the outside half of the plate, and (batters) who try to pull them hit ground balls . . . or fly balls instead of going up the middle. That kind of pitcher doesn't really need speed, and size isn't even an issue."

—Pat Gillick, then Toronto Blue Jays
general manager, on pitchers with good
change-ups

Tom Glavine's change-up and control are so good that he can get by on basically two pitches and one location. He works the low-and-outside

> **Throw It Again**
> Location is critical to a change-up. Ultimately, you want to command the pitch so well that you can place it on the outer half of the plate and in the lower half of the strike zone. You want the pitch over the plate, so that a fooled hitter won't be able to lay off and take it for a ball.

SUTTON ON GLAVINE

Hall of Famer Don Sutton has had the opportunity to watch future Hall of Famer Tom Glavine for several years from the broadcast booth in Atlanta. Sutton began his pitching career in the 1960s, when pitching inside early and often was considered to be essential to success. Sutton has observed Glavine defy this cardinal rule of pitching, living on the outside corner and thriving.

When asked how Glavine can do it, Sutton says that the key for any pitcher to succeed by pitching almost exclusively on the outside corner is the change-up. "You need to be able to put two pitches with different speeds and different movement in the same spot. They both look the same coming out of his hand. Most hitters don't adjust. The hitter can never sit there knowing that he's going to get two or three pitches in a row in the same spot at the same speed. It's never going to happen."

Getting outs all comes down to what Sutton's former teammate, Hall of Famer Don Drysdale, said: "What you're trying to do as a pitcher is keep the hitter off balance. Don't let him keep that same stride, that same motion, that same grooved swing all the time, as a golfer would."

Drysdale was a power pitcher and master of the inside pitch, but his formula works just as well for a crafty outsider like Glavine.

corner with a high-80s fastball and a high-70s to low-80s change-up, and hitters simply can't pick up the difference in velocity quickly enough to do anything with it. If you're skeptical, try this formula yourself when pitching to friends. Executed properly, it can make you a very frustrating pitcher to face. Master it and you can be unhittable.

THE ALL-SOFT TEAM

"Scouts, on both the pro and the college level, just love to see those big studs who can throw the ball through the wall. This often causes them to overlook the finesse player who really knows how to pitch."

—Bill Lee, former Boston Red Sox pitcher

Here are some words of wisdom from change-up artists through the years.

"I've got three pitches: my change, my change off my change, and my change off my change off my change."

—Preacher Roe, former Brooklyn Dodgers pitcher who won 127 games in his 12-year career. He went 22–3 in 1951 at the age of 36.

"Teams can't prepare for me in batting practice. They can't find anyone who throws as slow as I do."

—Dave LaPoint, who won 80 games in his 12-year career and went 9–3 as a swingman for the 1982 world champion St. Louis Cardinals.

"The harder you throw, the less time you have to duck."

—Doug Jones, who has recorded over 250 saves in a career that began in 1982.

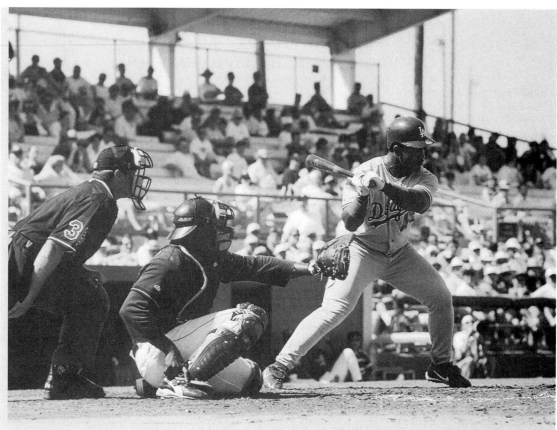

Aggressive fastball hitters, like Raul Mondesi, have trouble keeping their weight back on change-ups. The reduced velocity will often "freeze" hitters, and earn you an easy called strike.

"I'm getting by on three pitches now—a curve, a change-up, and whatever you want to call that thing that used to be my fastball."

> —Frank Tanana, 1978. He won 240 games in his 21-year career—176 of them after an injury forced him to change from a flamethrower who struck out more than a batter per inning as a 21-year-old to a crafty junkballer who pitched until he was 40.

"Frank Tanana had a 78 MPH fastball for the last four years he was in the majors, but he knew how to pitch. Guys like Stu Miller and Eddie Lopat were famous for having nothing. Yet they won."

> —Al Kubski, former scout. Nothing but a great change-up, that is. Stu Miller pitched for 15 seasons, winning 105 and saving 154. Lopat won 166 games in 12 seasons, leading the American league in ERA in 1953 at the age of 35.

······· Throw It Again

A change-up is an excellent pitch to use against aggressive, pull hitters and hitters who are expecting a fastball. You should never throw it to a hitter who can't catch up to your fastball.

HOME RUNS AND STRIKEOUTS: FROM THE BABE TO RAPID ROBERT

Babe Ruth outhomered every team in the American League in 1920, but he also struck out 80 times—a very high number back then. His larger-than-life exploits and his team's success were eroding the stigma of going down on strikes, and slowly this new style of swinging for the fences caught on around the league. The following year, Ruth's teammate Bob Meusel hit 24 home runs while leading the league in strikeouts with 88. In 1926, a young first baseman on the Yankees named Lou Gehrig got 83 extra-base hits at the cost of 73 strikeouts while the team's second baseman, Tony Lazzeri, led the league in strikeouts with 96. The Yankees team fanned 25 percent more times than any team in the league, yet led the league in scoring and won the pennant. They duplicated the feat in 1927 while going 110–44 with the league's top three home run hitters. In this new era of big innings and extra-base hits, the cost of striking out wasn't as high as it used to be.

With the success of Ruth and the Yankees came imitation. Hack Wilson of the Cubs—who'd been farmed out by the Giants in 1925 for striking out too much—led the NL in both home runs and strikeouts every season from 1927 to 1930, fanning even more times than Ruth the final three years of the stretch. In 1929, Jimmie Foxx brought power and strikeouts to an Athletics club that ended the Yankees' three-year run at the top of the league. Even line-drive-hitting Rogers Hornsby, who hit .424 with only 32 strikeouts in 1924, got into the act, hitting 39 home runs for the pennant-winning Cubs with a career-high of 65 strikeouts.

Overall, however, strikeout totals were nearly flat, though the number of home runs went through the roof, and wouldn't return to deadball levels until the 1950s. Pitchers were throwing a livelier, easier-to-see baseball, and were struggling in all facets of the game.

TIMES CHANGE

American League	Runs	Home Runs	Walks	Strikeouts	Batting Average	Slugging Average
1908	530	14	347	610	.239	.304
1919	631	33	463	483	.268	.359
1930	834	84	497	511	.288	.421

National League	Runs	Home Runs	Walks	Strikeouts	Batting Average	Slugging Average
1908	512	19	378	517	.239	.306
1919	562	28	361	452	.258	.337
1930	875	111	460	479	.303	.448

Average team, 154-game season.

Before the 1920s ended, Walter Johnson and Grover Alexander rode off into the sunset—and there weren't many pitchers able to follow in their fairly large footsteps. Only two hard throwers—hard-and-straight Lefty Grove in the AL and the late-blooming Dazzy Vance in the

NL—were able to consistently dominate hitters in this pitcher-unfriendly era. On the short list of consistently effective pitchers in the NL during the roaring 1920s was Burleigh Grimes, one of a handful of spitballers who'd been given special dispensation to continue practicing his craft after the pitch was outlawed in 1920.

The most significant pitching innovation of the 1920s wasn't made on the mound but in the dugout, as Washington Senators manager Bucky Harris established the first relief special-ist. Firpo Marberry led the league in saves five times, including 22 in 1926, a mark that wouldn't be topped for 23 years. He helped pitch the Senators to their only world championship in 1924, as the bullpen was transformed from a home for failed starters to a valuable resource. The innovation wouldn't catch on throughout the big leagues, however, for another 30 years.

Hitting peaked in 1930, when the entire National League batted .300 and only Vance in the NL and Grove in the AL were able to manage ERAs below 3.00. Pitchers were chucking and ducking, and disgusted Giants manager John McGraw, a veteran of the deadball era, was call-ing for the mound to be moved in two feet.

"It's not the pitching. It's that new jackrabbit ball. The pitchers have had their stuff. But with that jackrabbit ball, they haven't a chance. All a batter has to do is meet it, and if the ball is not hit right at somebody, it's a base hit. That ball travels like a bullet, and unless you are in front of it, you haven't a chance to stop it. Just tap it and it lands in the stands. It's making a joke of the game."

—John McGraw, New York Giants manager, 1930

In 1933, a 30-year-old screwball artist named Carl Hubbell burst into superstardom in the NL with a 1.66 ERA, 10 shutouts (one an 18-inning affair), and 46 consecutive scoreless innings. The following year he would cement his reputation by striking out five future Hall of Famers in succession at the All-Star Game. That same year, Dizzy Dean became the last National League pitcher to win 30 games. Their years as dominant pitchers were brief, however. Dean went 28–12 in 1935 and 24–13 in 1936, but a line drive off of his toe in the 1937 All-Star Game caused him to change his pitching mechanics, and he blew out his arm as a result. Hubbell's pitching arm was so twisted out of shape by the screwball that his palm faced permanently out; he won 20 games five years in a row, then faded quickly.

"We gotta look at that all season."

—NL catcher Gabby Hartnett to the AL bench during Carl Hubbell's legendary 1934 All-Star Game performance, referring to "the Meal Ticket's" unhittable screwball

Meanwhile, outstanding black pitchers such as Satchel Paige, Bullet Joe Rogan, and Smokey Joe Williams (who was 23–7–1 in games against big leaguers, beating both Walter Johnson and Grover Alexander and no-hitting the 1917 world champion New York Giants with 20 strikeouts in 10 innings) were forced to conduct business outside of the major leagues. Paige fanned 13 in six no-hit innings against the world champion St. Louis Cardinals in 1934, beating Dizzy Dean 4–1. Dean's comment: "Satch, if you and Josh [Gibson, the "black Babe Ruth"] played with me 'n [Dean's brother] Paul on the Cards, we'd win the pennant by July 4 and go fishin' the rest of the year."

In the AL, the 1930s saw the emergence of another free-swinging slugger in the Jimmie Foxx mold—Hank Greenberg of the Tigers, who hit 58 home runs in 1938 while striking out 92 times. With Greenberg, Foxx, and Gehrig to contend with—and Joe DiMaggio and Ted Williams on the horizon—the AL remained a hitting league for the rest of the decade. When Lefty Grove blew out his arm in 1934, there was no one with his kind of stuff until a 17-year-old named Bob Feller arrived in 1936.

"Rapid Robert" fanned 15 in his first major league game against the St. Louis Browns, then followed that up with 17 strikeouts against the Philadelphia Athletics three weeks later. But Feller walked more than six batters per nine innings during his first three seasons—leading the league in strikeouts *and* walks in 1938. He threw in the high 90s and was the first pitcher to be timed with a radar gun, clocking in at 98.6 miles per hour. His fastball once beat a motorcycle in a bizarre speed contest.

"Go on up there and hit what you see. If you can't see it, come on back."

—Bucky Harris, Washington Senators manager, offering advice to his hitters on facing Bob Feller

In looking at Bob Feller's career, five years stand out. In 1939, he finally started winning consistently as he got his walks below five per nine innings, going 24–9. By 1940, he had his walks down below 3.5 and he won 27 games. His wins had steadily climbed just as his strikeouts per nine innings steadily dropped. He missed 3½ seasons during the prime of his career due to military service, but returned in 1946 without missing a beat—winning 26 games for a bad team, with an ERA of 2.18, 10 shutouts, and excellent command of his devastating fastball and curve. After that season, he began to lose the hop on his fastball and the snap on his curve. But 1951 showed that the prodigy of 1936 had made the transition from thrower to pitcher; he won 22 games while striking out only four men per nine innings. As impressive as that performance was in the twilight of his career, three years later in 1954 he went 13–3 with better control and even less on the ball.

BOB FELLER

	W–L	ERA	K/9	BB/9
1936	5–3	3.34	11.0	6.8
1937	9–7	3.38	9.0	6.4
1938	17–11	4.08	7.8	6.7
1939	**24–9**	**2.85**	**7.5**	**4.3**
1940	**27–11**	**2.62**	**7.3**	**3.3**
1941	25–13	3.15	6.8	5.1
1942	Military Service			
1943	Military Service			
1944	Military Service			
1945	5–3	2.50	7.4	4.4
1946	**26–15**	**2.18**	**8.4**	**3.7**
1947	20–11	2.68	5.9	3.8
1948	19–15	3.57	5.3	3.7

	W–L	ERA	K/9	BB/9
1949	15–14	3.75	4.6	2.7
1950	16–11	3.43	4.3	3.8
1951	**22–8**	**3.49**	**4.0**	**3.4**
1952	9–13	4.73	3.8	3.9
1953	10–7	3.58	3.1	3.1
1954	**13–3**	**3.09**	**3.8**	**2.5**

Over in the National League, a 26-year-old left-hander with a sweeping curveball announced his arrival by winning 21 games for the 1947 Boston Braves. It was the first of 13 seasons with 20 or more victories for Warren Spahn—and he did it without ever having Feller's once-overpowering stuff. As Spahn put it, he only had two pitches: "One they're looking for and one to cross 'em up."

"Low and outside, where he can't see the ball very well, and up close on the handle of the bat at the belt, where he can't get the bat around."

—Warren Spahn, on where to pitch batters. He had the control to do it.

Throughout the 1950s, walk totals began to climb, as shell-shocked pitchers nibbled around the corners of a strike zone that had been shrunk from "shoulders to knees" to "armpits to knee tops." Many batters had switched to lighter, "whippier" bats and slid their hands down to the knob in order to boost their home run totals. While before World War II a pitcher had to contend with one or two sluggers per team, now far more hitters had the ability and inclination to go deep. The pennant-winning 1951 Giants had a lineup that featured at least 10 home runs at every position—and they didn't even lead the league in homers (the Brooklyn Dodgers did). The cost of a pitching mistake was high and getting higher.

To further tip the balance of power toward the offense, most black stars being signed by major league teams in 1947 and the years soon after were hitters: Jackie Robinson, Monte Irvin, Larry Doby, Willie Mays, Hank Aaron, Roy Campanella, Ernie Banks, Frank Robinson, and Minnie Minoso, to name just a few. Only one of 16 major league teams broke their color barrier with a pitcher. Major league teams were not as aggressive in signing black pitchers, with the great Don Newcombe being one of the few stars to emerge. Unfortunately, Satchel Paige was past his prime by the time he made it to the majors—though he did go 6–1 with a save and two shutouts as a 41-year-old rookie for Bill Veeck's 1948 Indians.

While these forces were combining to keep the advantage with the hitters, bad luck short-circuited the career of a brilliant young left-hander named Herb Score. He became the first full-time starting pitcher to strike out more than a batter per inning, fanning 245 in 227 innings in 1955. He was so overpowering, he went 16–10 with a 2.85 ERA despite walking more than six men per nine innings—holding a league that hit .258 to a .194 average. No sophomore jinx here, as he won 20 games in 1956 and lowered his ERA, as his control improved without costing him any strikeouts. Then yet another brilliant season was interrupted on May 7, 1957, when Gil McDougald of the Yankees hit him in the eye with a line drive. Score pitched again, but he was never the same.

Randy Johnson

MAKING IT BREAK:
THE CURVE AND
SLIDER

As valuable as good breaking balls—curveball or hard slider—can be, you must be very careful not to fall in love with these pitches. They are not substitutes for your fastball. The fastball is still your most important pitch, the one you must establish to set up all of your other pitches. Breaking balls are more difficult to throw for strikes, very hittable up in the strike zone, and harder on your arm if not thrown properly. The slider, in particular, is believed to take several miles per hour off of your fastball if substituted too much for the fastball.

The change-up is the perfect second pitch, allowing you to throw off the timing of hitters with minimal effort and deceptive ease. But it's the breaking ball that will give you the third weapon needed to survive against stiffer competition.

No pitch, thrown properly, is any harder on your arm than any other. But throwing a breaking ball improperly at a young age is more likely to damage your elbow or shoulder. Because the best way to build arm strength is to throw fastballs, young pitchers should place a much higher priority on building arm strength than learning a breaking ball. Steve Carlton had perhaps the greatest slider the game has seen, but he didn't begin to throw it until he reached the major leagues.

"Kids are anxious to throw curveballs, and the more you throw them the better you get. But with young players, it is dangerous to throw too many. At 13 or 14 years of age, a player can start throwing a limited number of curveballs, assuming he employs proper mechanics. Studies have shown that players' tendons, ligaments, and muscles at this age are not fully developed and there's a great likelihood you can cause injury with overuse. I think age 18 is a safer age to throw a curve ball with regularity."

—Galen Cisco, Philadelphia Phillies
pitching coach

Throw It Again

A breaking ball is no substitute for a fastball. The fastball is your most important pitch, and the only way to develop the arm strength necessary for a good fastball is to throw it. Rely on your fastball and change-up through high school and you will become a much better pitcher than if you throw a steady diet of breaking balls to over-matched hitters.

MASTERING THE CURVE OR SLIDER

Many pitchers have a hard time mastering both the slider and the curveball. You will probably find that one of these pitches will be easier for you to command than the other. One you will come to rely on to help you get tough outs, while the other may never make it out of the bullpen. Or you may use it, but only as a "show" pitch—a pitch you throw early in the game just to give the batter something extra to think about.

You will need to work with both the curveball and slider on the sidelines to determine which one you want to master. Most pitching coaches will recommend that you try to learn the curveball first, since you will be less likely to injure yourself. In addition, a hanging curveball is not as bad a pitch as a hanging slider. A hanging curveball is like a high change-up, while a hanging slider is like a batting practice fastball. Two of the most famous World Series home runs in recent memory came off sliders—Kirk Gibson's off Dennis Eckersley in 1988 and Jim Leyritz's off Mark Wohlers in 1996. With the curve, you at least know that you're getting a change of speeds, even if the movement or location isn't what you want. A hanging slider is a mediocre, flat fastball over the plate. Good pitching requires velocity, movement,

and location, and a hanging slider offers none of the above.

Once you've made your choice, it will take some time before you truly get comfortable with a breaking ball. This is hard enough on its own, so don't make it any harder by trying to master both pitches until you've learned how to command the first one. Whether you go with the slider or the curve, you should know that less is often more. You may throw fewer than 20 breaking balls in a 100-pitch game. If you're in high school and have a good change-up, you may not even have to throw 10. These limited numbers of breaking balls, thrown at the right time, can be more than enough to get the outs you need.

"I know that young pitchers want to throw breaking balls because most young hitters cannot hit them. But if you have aspirations for college or professional ball you can always learn how to throw breaking balls after you're out of high school."

—Jeff Nelson, New York Yankees pitcher

It will be very tempting to throw breaking balls early and often when you're a young pitcher, especially if your fastball isn't great. At very low levels of competition, a curveball is an extremely effective pitch. But even without considering the risk of injury, it's still a bad idea to throw it too often when you're young. As you climb higher and higher in competition, you will face better and better curveball hitters and you will need a good fastball to set up all of your other pitches. If you throw too many breaking balls very early in your career, you will never develop that good fastball you'll desperately need later. As a young pitcher, the best way to improve your fastball is to throw it and rely on it.

LEARNING TO THROW THE CURVE

"If my curveball is breaking and I'm throwing it where I want, the batter is irrelevant."

—Steve Stone, Cy Young award winner

A good curveball is effective not only because it moves, but because it is a change-of-pace pitch that can throw off a hitter's timing. There are different types of curveballs, depending on whether you release the pitch from an overhand, three-quarters, or sidearm angle.

The overhand curveball—also called the "12-6" because it has a forward rotation from "twelve o'clock to six o'clock"—is the toughest to hit. It has little to no lateral movement, but very sharp downward movement. When thrown from a three-quarters motion, a right-hander's curveball will break from two o'clock to eight o'clock. Many hitters find it easier to identify a 2-8 curve as a curveball than a 12-6, so it's not as effective as a "change-up." But because there is less downward break, the 2-8 curveball is easier to throw for low strikes. You don't want a curveball that has all lateral break and *no* downward break. You will very quickly reach a level where the hitters "hang in" or wait on curveballs, and they will feast on a curve that only breaks along one plane.

"I learned to throw an overhand breaking ball when I was a kid so I could throw it without twisting my wrist. That twisting action can put strain on your elbow. My coach told me to get my arm out front and pull down like you're ringing a bell. I apply pressure to my middle finger, which sits on the seam, and I just let it fly."

—David Wells on learning his overhand breaking ball.

Bert Blyleven had one of the best curveballs ever, a real "knee-buckler." But he also holds records for home runs allowed, which shows what happens to hanging curveballs.

Don't try to force yourself to throw a 12-6 curve if you are a natural three-quarters thrower, and don't drop down to throw your curve if you are an overhand thrower. Changing your arm slot or release point will tell the hitter that a curveball is coming. In addition, your breaking pitch will come much more easily to you if you throw it like your fastball, thinking fastball until you release the ball.

The movement on your curveball comes from the topspin you create with your release. The bigger your hands and the longer your fingers, the easier to create spin. The more rotation you can get on the ball with your release, the sharper the break of your curveball. Even if you don't have long fingers, you can improve your curveball by strengthening your fingers and wrist. You can do this by simply squeezing a tennis ball, with special attention paid to your thumb and middle finger.

David Wells throws a "12-6" curveball, a pitch that is as difficult to throw as it is to hit.

CHOOSING A GRIP

The best grip for getting movement on your curveball is what is called the four-seam grip. Like the four-seam fastball, it allows you to get maximum rotation on the ball, though more rotation also means a pitch that can be more difficult to control. Regardless of the grip you use, it will be your middle finger and thumb that generate the topspin you need to make the pitch move. In many ways, the index finger is just along for the ride. Some pitchers throw their curve without their index finger even being on the ball, But if the hitter is able to see this raised finger in their delivery he'll know to expect something off-speed.

"The most important aspect to throwing a good breaking ball is getting a tight rotation. You get that rotation by putting pressure on your middle finger [which is on the seam], and then you pull down on it."

—Mel Queen, Blue Jays pitching coach

NOLAN RYAN

"The first time on a major league mound was a big learning experience for me. Hank Aaron said I had one of the best fastballs he had ever seen. But one of the best fastballs I'd ever thrown was hit for a home run by Joe Torre. I learned the hard way that it would not be possible to get by in the major leagues with just a fastball, no matter how hard it was thrown."—Nolan Ryan

Nolan Ryan made it to the majors on the strength of one pitch, an overpowering fastball. He quickly learned that he would need more than that to stay there. Later in his career he would master a change-up, but the first pitch Ryan added to his repertoire was a curveball. Along the way, he got some of his most important outs on his curveball.

Ryan got Dusty Baker to ground to third on a curveball to end his fifth no-hitter. He later said that he thought Baker was expecting the curve, but didn't think he could hit it with any authority. He passed Walter Johnson on the all-time strikeout list by fanning Brad Mills on a "backdoor curveball" in 1983. Then he got Danny Heep on a curveball for his 4,000th strikeout in 1985.

One of the most important outs Ryan got as a pitcher came before he even felt he'd learned how to pitch. Ryan struck out Paul Blair on an 0–2 curveball with the bases loaded and two outs in the ninth inning to save Game 3 of the 1969 World Series for the Mets. With Blair having crushed an 0–2 fastball against him with the bases loaded in the seventh—only to have center fielder Tommie Agee make an incredible running catch—Ryan made sure not to make the same mistake twice.

So much for being a "one-pitch" pitcher.

To throw a four-seam curve, find one of the wide gaps between the seams and place your middle finger along the inside of the right seam (for a right-hander). Simply lay your index finger alongside your middle finger. With a fastball you grip the ball with your finger pads, but with a curve you place almost the entire length of your finger on the ball. How deep you end up holding the ball in your hand will determine how good your curveball will be. Holding it too deeply is called "choking it," and it will usually get you a slower pitch that doesn't break as much and is harder to control as it rotates out of your hand.

Place your thumb underneath the ball, slightly bent and on the seam. A line drawn from your middle finger to your thumb cuts the ball exactly in half. The ball will be held steady by the inside of your ring finger, with the second joint on the wide seam, across from your thumb. Your middle finger will pull the ball toward the plate, while the thumb will push.

When you throw the curveball, your delivery is nearly identical to your fastball's. Your arm follows the same path as it does on your fastball, but as it passes your ear you turn your wrist so that the palm of your hand is facing the side of your head rather than toward home plate. The pitch will not break sharply, or "bite," if you release it before your arm passes your head.

Left-hander David Wells has one of the best overhand breaking balls in the game today. His ability to locate a pitch with such lavish break makes him effective. But deception also plays a vital role in keeping hitters off stride. Wells says, "You've got to think fastball throughout your windup. Don't start your breaking ball from behind your head. That's too early. Keep the same delivery as your fastball and then pull down on the ball out in front of you so you get a good, tight rotation. Hooking your wrist early will not only diminish the sharpness of the pitch, but it will also tip the hitter to what pitch is coming. Combine those two things and you're gonna get lit up."

Your wrist must remain straight and relaxed. Bending it, so that the palm of your hand is facing up or facing down toward your elbow ("wrap-

The standard curveball grip, with the middle finger butted against the seam for leverage.

ping" your wrist) can cause you to tip off the batter, hang the pitch, and possibly injure yourself. Keeping your wrist too rigid will minimize the power of your wrist snap, costing you rotation.

Remember: Rotation is more important than velocity when throwing a curveball. A hard curveball that doesn't move very much is a very hittable pitch. To generate the downward, tumbling topspin you need to throw a good curveball, your wrist must be straight but relaxed. The release is just as important as the grip. You snap your wrist toward home plate as you deliver the ball— pulling down with your middle finger, pushing up with your thumb. As a result, the ball is released over your fingers—unlike a fastball, which leaves your hand under your fingers.

········ **Throw It Again**
When throwing breaking balls, pay very careful attention to your mechanics. Throwing these pitches with improper mechanics is an easy way to injure yourself.

FASTBALL MECHANICS

Major league pitching coach Bob Cluck has an excellent method of teaching the proper release of a curveball. Hold the ball with the curveball grip, then think "fastball" and point your index finger toward the target as you release. You can't do this without the "turn and snap" described earlier.

As with all pitches, proper mechanics are vital. Be careful not to drop your elbow, rush your delivery, open your front shoulder too soon, or throw across your body. (For more details on proper mechanics, or if you're struggling with your curveball, see Chapter 2.) These mechanical flaws almost always lead to hanging curveballs.

Other pitchers struggle with their curveball because they're trying to throw it too hard. It's rotation, not velocity, that you want. Practice throwing the pitch 30 feet rather than 60 feet, focusing solely on rotation. You'll see that when combining the proper grip and release with good mechanics, you won't need any additional effort.

Maybe your problem isn't hanging your curveball, but bouncing it in the dirt—the so-called "55-foot curveball." This can happen when your upper body gets too far in front of your hips or when your arm comes through too quickly. Common causes of these problems are a shortened stride and a shortened arm path. Changes in your arm path can happen if you're so focused on getting your elbow up and staying on top of the pitch that you rush through your backswing or take a shortcut to the "cocked" position rather than completing the circle.

"I can't tell you how many times in my career I've seen a pitcher throw a good breaking ball for a strike, and then throw another one that gets crushed for a home run. What happens is after throwing a good breaking ball, pitchers will try to follow it with one that's even better. More often than not, your accuracy suffers or you tense up by trying to get too much break on the pitch. If you've thrown a good curveball, the next doesn't necessarily have to be better."

—Dan Plesac, veteran middle reliever

When throwing a fastball with proper mechanics, your follow-through tends to take care of itself. Not so with a curveball. Your follow-through should not bring your hand down to your ankles as it does with the fastball. You should be finishing with your elbow at your opposite knee, as you do with your fastball, *but your elbow should remain bent*. This is called "short-arming" your follow-through, and failing to do so can lead to elbow trouble. Practice the curveball grip and wrist snap without throwing the ball, and feel how much more strain is put on your elbow when you follow through with a straight arm than when it's bent.

A good curveball probably won't come to you as easily as a good fastball. As you work to master this pitch, consider the advice of Red Sox closer Tom Gordon: Work hard to develop a feel for it, then throw it with confidence. Gordon says, "It takes a lot of work. The curveball is a feel pitch. If you don't have the feel for that pitch, or the confidence to throw it behind in the count, it won't work for you."

········ **Throw It Again**
Keep your elbow up and your fingers on top of the ball to avoid hanging a breaking ball. Don't shorten your stride or take shortcuts with your arm. This can get your upper body too far out in front of your legs, which can cause you to throw your breaking balls in the dirt. Don't overthrow; let the grip and release do the work.

Fault: A closed position of the stride or plant foot inhibits the downward swing of the arm. Fix: Step straight toward the target.

"You can't be making many adjustments [on the mound]. If you feel it, throw it. If you don't feel it, you have to be able to show it but at the same time just get by with it. You don't do anything to the pitch but throw it the way you've always thrown it. More than 90 percent of the time it's going to work for you."

—Tom Gordon, on when your curveball isn't working

LEARNING TO THROW THE SLIDER

"[The slider] is the pitch that has changed the game of baseball. . . . You can see the spin, but unless you anticipate it or the pitcher hangs it, there is not much chance of your hitting it solidly."

—Lou Piniella, Seattle Mariners manager

Many of the greatest power pitchers in the game's history—Bob Feller, Nolan Ryan, Sandy Koufax, and Kerry Wood—have featured nearly unhittable, knee-buckling curveballs. But for many power pitchers, a slider proves to be the perfect breaking pitch. It's also very popular for relief pitchers.

A hitter who can catch up to your fastball may be easy prey to the slider—a pitch that comes in looking like a fastball, only to break down and away (to an opposite-hand hitter). Randy Johnson and John Smoltz, like Tom Seaver before them, make their living with this pitch. The pitch wasn't thrown by a large number of pitchers until the 1950s and wasn't mastered until the 1960s—not coincidentally, a period in the game's history when the balance of power began to shift back to the pitchers. Unlike the curveball, the slider wasn't significantly slower than the fastball, so it was much harder for hitters to tell the difference. It was also easier to throw for a strike. The combination of the two can make the slider, at times, a virtually unhittable pitch.

More good news: for many pitchers, the slider is easier to learn than a curveball. Unfortunately, it's also very easy to injure yourself with this pitch if you don't throw it properly. And a poorly thrown slider is one of the easiest pitches to hit.

CHOOSING A GRIP

There are many different types of slider grips. You can grip the ball across the seams, like a four-seam fastball, or along a seam, like a curveball. What is common to both of these grips is that the ball is held off center, deeper in the hand than a

Steve Carlton's slider was nearly unhittable from either side of the plate.

the seam. Your middle finger should be held next to the index finger. Your thumb should slide along the seam toward the middle-finger side of the ball. The ball should be held in place by a flexed ring finger, with the seam resting on the inside of the finger between the first and second joint.

"The key for me to learning the breaking ball was basically the grip, which simply relies on holding the ball off center and throwing it like a fastball. My delivery and arm angle are the same as when I throw a fastball, but the grip off center gives the pitch a tight spin and sharp break."

—Matt Anderson, Detroit Tigers

The standard slider grip.

fastball but not as deep as a curveball, with the index finger and thumb doing most of the work (unlike the curveball, where the middle finger and thumb do the work).

With the across-the-seams grip, begin with a four-seam fastball grip. The index and middle fingers cross the ball where the seams are widest, with the pads of the fingers on the seams. If you are a right-hander, the closed end of the seam should be on your right. The thumb is underneath, on a seam, along the center of the ball. Now, move your index finger to the right (for a right-hander), until it is between twelve o'clock and one o'clock. You may need to slide your index finger forward slightly, so that the pad remains on

With the along-the-seams slider, start with the curveball grip. Your middle finger is inside the wide seams and is pointing toward the closed end of the seams. Your thumb is on the seam directly underneath, centered on the ball and flexed. You are exerting pressure with the inside of your thumb and with most of your middle finger. With the slider, you will be shifting this grip so that the index finger exerts the greatest pressure, the ball is held off center and the ball is not held so deeply in your hand. Slide your index finger to the right (for a right-hander), so that both your index and middle fingers are running along the seam. Slide your index finger forward, so that the finger pad is on the closed end of the seam. At this point, the ball should be very deep in your hand. Slide your thumb down the seam, which will bring the ball out of your hand. It will cause you to hold the ball with your finger pads and not your entire fingers. Shift the thumb toward the middle-finger side of the ball, and grip it with your thumb and index finger.

Try them both and you'll see that the along-the-seams and across-the-seams grips are virtually identical. The only difference is where on the seam your index and middle fingers end up. You might want to experiment with grips on other parts of the baseball. Just remember to grip the ball slightly off center with pressure on the index finger and thumb, and not to hold the ball as deeply in the hand as you do on a curveball.

FASTBALL MECHANICS

The grip is very important to getting the proper movement on your slider, while the release is critical not just to movement but to avoiding injury. As is the case with the curveball, you need to think "fastball" as you throw this pitch. Your knee lift, stride, backswing—all of your mechanics—need to be the same as with your fastball.

Again, just like the curveball, the only changes take place as you bring your arm forward, release the ball, and follow through. As you bring your arm toward the plate, you will turn your wrist 45 degrees. You are not turning your wrist as much as you do with the curveball, which involves a 90-degree turn. Don't turn your wrist too much, because your index finger needs to remain on top of the ball to get the proper action on the pitch.

As you release the ball, do not twist your wrist or arm. Let the grip and the 45-degree turn of the wrist do all of the work. Bend your wrist when you release this pitch, but the bend must only be forward. Remember, your wrist is already turned. Avoid any twisting motion that will bend your wrist any farther to the side. This will put too much strain on your arm and will keep you from getting maximum velocity and movement on the pitch. Your index finger needs to stay on top of the ball, not on the side. The action of the index finger down the outside of the ball is what creates the

Roger Clemens in perfect position to throw a slider, elbow above his shoulder, wrist cocked slightly, and his body moving directly at the target.

slider spin. You can't get that spin if your index finger is already on the side of the ball.

Some coaches teach a stiff-wrist slider, in which you throw the pitch without snapping your wrist. This can be hard on your elbow, and you should avoid it. *The slider is just a fastball held off center and delivered with a slightly cocked wrist. You don't have to do anything more than that to make the ball move.*

As is also the case with the curveball, the slider follow-through is different than with the fastball. You can't follow through with full extension on your arm or you will injure yourself. You need to short-arm your follow-through, finishing with a bent elbow at your opposite knee.

> *"I threw my slider more like a cut fastball—fingertips coming down off the side of the ball without twisting the wrist. You can also hold it farther back in the hand for a bigger break and a slower pitch."*
>
> —Larry Andersen, who threw a very effective slider in the big leagues for 17 years and nearly 1,000 innings without a serious injury.

KEYS TO THE BREAKING BALL

As with all pitches, your mechanics have to be sound if you want to get velocity, movement, and location while avoiding injury. Many of the keys to gripping and releasing a curveball hold true for a slider as well.

- *The fingers grip, the wrist relaxes.* One of the biggest challenges you will face with the breaking ball is to grip the ball firmly while maintaining a loose wrist. When sitting in the dugout between starts, you may want to get in the habit of holding a ball with a breaking ball grip while slowly rolling your wrist in all directions. Do this until you've developed both a firm grip *and* a loose, relaxed wrist.
- *Think "fastball" throughout the delivery.* You cannot change any aspect of your delivery if you want your breaking ball to be effective. You can't slow up your motion, shorten your arm arc, or cock your wrist. Everything has to be the same as the fastball until release, except the turn of the wrist as your arm comes forward. The best way to do this is to think "fastball" until you bring your throwing arm forward.
- *Drive down with your front shoulder.* To get the spin necessary for a good breaking ball, you need more than just a snap of the wrist. To generate good hand speed, you need to drive down with your lead shoulder as you bring your throwing arm forward. If you're using your front shoulder properly, you should find yourself bending sharply at the waist so your torso is almost parallel to the ground.
- *Keep your elbow up.* Keeping your throwing elbow at least as high as your shoulder is important, regardless of the pitch you're throwing. It's absolutely critical with a breaking ball, because when your elbow drops, your pitch flattens out and stays up. Dropping your elbow will make it hard for you to stay on top of the ball, and staying on top is vital to generating the spin that makes a curveball or slider move. Your fingers will drop to the side of the ball, virtually eliminating any downward break. Don't drop your elbow or you'll be throwing "uphill." This is how to hang a breaking ball, a skill you don't want to master.
- *Keep your fingers on top of the ball.* Even if you keep your elbow up, you can still hang a breaking ball if you don't keep your fingers on top of the ball. This can happen if you don't turn your wrist properly during your delivery or if you twist your wrist as you release the ball. Remember these two simple rules: (1) turn your wrist as you begin your release, don't bend it; and (2) snap your wrist down toward home plate as you release the ball, don't twist it. Many young pitchers try to do too much to the ball when learning to throw a breaking ball. It's not as hard as it looks, provided you turn and snap rather than bend and twist.

- *Short-arm your follow-through.* It's very important that you follow through with a bent elbow. Keeping your arm straight after releasing a curveball or slider puts enormous strain on your elbow.
- *Don't overthrow.* Finally, you need to avoid overthrowing your breaking ball. Try to throw a curve too hard and you'll probably end up bouncing it five feet in front of the plate, or have it slip out of your hand and hang over the plate. An overthrown slider often ends up outside and in the dirt for a wild pitch. You need to trust your catcher to throw the breaking ball, since even a good one may end up in the dirt. Don't make it any tougher for him by trying to throw it too hard.

> *"One problem that I experience at times is that I throw everything too hard. I'm too aggressive with all of my pitches. When my off-speed pitches are all coming in around the same speed, hitters start to time me and begin to worry less about a change of speeds. You have to be able to change speeds in order to be effective."*
>
> —Roger Clemens, New York Yankees

LOCATION AND SITUATION: WHERE AND WHEN TO USE THE BREAKING BALL

> *"You have to find something you can throw behind in the count as well as early in the count and mix it both ways."*
>
> —Tom Gordon on having a complement to your fastball

There is a trade-off between the amount of movement you get on your pitch and the importance of location. If you don't have a big-breaking curveball or a sharp-breaking slider, it becomes all the more important that you put it where you want to put it. An average curveball or slider may not be a strikeout pitch for you, but it can be a groundout pitch. To get groundouts on your breaking balls, you must throw them in the strike zone or just off the plate.

As you face higher levels of competition, one of the first things the opposing hitters will look for is when and where you're throwing your change-up and breaking ball. If you can't throw strikes with your curveball or slider or change-up, hitters will simply lay off these pitches and wait to jump

Barry Bonds is out in front and over the top of an off-speed breaking pitch.

on your fastball. The same holds true if you're too predictable with your pitch patterns. First and foremost you will need to be able to throw your breaking ball for a strike—or at least for what looks enough like a strike that you can get the batter to swing. Once you've shown that you can throw it *in* the strike zone, you'll be able to be effective with it *out* of the strike zone.

ATTACKING THE HITTER

In general, a good 12-6 curve will get you swinging strikes and a good 2-8 curve will get you called strikes. A 12-6 curve thrown down in the strike zone will often end up in the dirt and be called a ball if the batter doesn't swing at it. To get called strikes with it, you will need to become comfortable throwing it higher in the strike zone. Bert Blyleven won 287 games with one of the greatest curveballs the game has seen. He also gave up more than 50 home runs in one season. If you're counting on getting a strikeout or groundout with your curve, don't leave it in the middle of the plate or break it along a flat plane.

A 2-8 curve thrown low in the strike zone will get more of the plate than a 12-6 curve will. Its downside is that because it breaks in to opposite-hand hitters, you may only be comfortable throwing it as a "backdoor" curve—starting it off the plate and breaking it over the outside corner. Clutch right-hander Orlando "El Duque" Hernandez used it to consistently get ahead of left-handers during 1998 and 1999 post-season play.

"You can't be afraid to throw a breaking ball. I never hesitate. I just get the ball out in front of me and break it off. If you hesitate, or if you're timid throwing it, I can almost guarantee the result will be a hanger."

—David Wells

Because a 12-6 curve does not break into or away from a batter, it can be effectively thrown to both left- and right-handed batters on either corner of the plate. Boston Red Sox reliever Tom

Gordon has a 12-6 curve that is considered one of the best in the American League. He credits it with allowing him to go after both lefties and righties aggressively, while a curve with lateral break requires more finesse.

Because a slider breaks down by about six inches and in by six inches (to an opposite-hand hitter), some pitchers use it to jam opposite-hand hitters. If you can throw it so it breaks off the plate, down and in, you will get a lot of swinging strikes. But get too much of the plate or get it up in the strike zone, and you'll pay the price. That's why, like the 2-8 curveball, many pitchers throw their slider almost exclusively low and away. Against an opposite-hand hitter, you can throw a backdoor slider—starting it off the plate and nicking the outside corner. Against a same-hand hitter, you can get him to chase low and away if you can start your slider on the outside corner and break it off the plate.

"It's a good pitch to use after you establish the fastball. You try to get the hitter to chase one down and away. Even if he hits it, he'll lose power."

—Jim Palmer on the slider

Unfortunately, there's no such thing as a backdoor breaking ball to a same-hand batter. So maybe you're a righty and you're thinking, why not throw a curveball or slider that breaks across the *inside* corner to a righty? This is called a backup breaking ball, and Bob Gibson called it his most effective pitch. Unfortunately, Gibson went on to say, it only happened by accident. He couldn't do it consistently. With a backup breaking ball, you need to almost aim it *behind* the batter—and this throws most pitchers off. They misfire with it, and it ends up getting too much of the plate. Hang one and it ends up in the hitter's wheelhouse. Throw it to a big swinger who starts early with his swing—and is committed to swing—and he could drive this pitch almost by accident, even if you *don't* hang it. If you had the kind of pinpoint control to throw a backup breaking ball consistently, the thinking is that you'd be better off using that control to paint the outside corner the way left-hander Steve Carlton did to lefties with his slider. Miss on a slider away and it's much less likely to be crushed.

As you progress to higher levels of competition, you'll need to throw your breaking ball more often. At the high school and youth league level, you should be getting by with your fastball and change-up and using your breaking ball sparingly for the very tough batters and the critical outs. If you have command of your breaking ball, here are some good spots for it.

Nearly all hitters look for a fastball and try to adjust to the breaking ball and change-up. Mike Schmidt said he could look for the slow stuff and still catch up to the fast stuff, but this is extremely rare even at the highest levels of competition. (You may run into some guess hitters who play a hunch and look for the breaking ball or change-up, but don't try to guess along with them. Just stay out of predictable patterns and you'll be fine.) Because so many hitters look for the fastball, you can often freeze them with a breaking ball. If you can get your breaking ball over when a hitter is sitting on a fastball—first pitch, 2–0, 3–1—you will be a very tough pitcher.

Many hitters have trouble with breaking balls, especially big swingers who start their bat early and have to commit to swinging. But there are other hitters who you don't want to throw breaking balls to, for example an opposite-hand hitter who likes balls low and in. A hitter who can't handle your fastball is also someone who shouldn't see your curve. Why speed up his bat? That pitch is wasted on him. You especially don't want to throw this type of hitter a breaking ball on 2–0 or 3–1. All you'll be doing is showing your best weapon to the better hitters in the dugout. If you can save it for when you really need it— tough hitter, men on base—you'll be an even tougher pitcher.

At the higher levels, your breaking ball might even become your best pitch. Some pitchers use what they call a "get-it-over breaking ball" rather than the fastball on strike one. They're counting on the fact that most hitters are looking for a fast-

For lefties, Jesse Orosco's three-quarter to sidearm delivery makes his slider nearly an impossible pitch to hit.

ball on the first pitch. This might not work at the lower levels, where there are especially aggressive hitters who aren't all that selective.

A good combination of pitches to throw is the breaking ball away followed by the fastball in. One or more of these outside breaking pitches could get the batter leaning over the plate— especially if you're nicking the corner with it. That makes the hitter very susceptible to a fastball on the inner third.

As you gain command of your breaking ball, you'll find there are times to purposely miss the plate with it. At 0–2 or 1–2, you can purposely miss away (just off the plate) with your breaking ball to get the hitter thinking "outside corner." When you see him leaning, come inside with a fastball on the "black" for a called strike three or a weakly struck ball on the bat handle.

Phillies ace Curt Schilling delivers a slider. The mechanics of the delivery are nearly identical to those of the

fastball, the only differences being the slight cock of the wrist and that

the elbow remains slightly flexed during the follow-through.

"Any time I have my curveball, slider, or fork-ball going good and I'm throwing them for strikes, then I have some other weapons to go with other than my fastball. Good hitters will force you to prove that you can throw a secondary pitch or breaking ball over the plate for strikes before they offer at it."

—Roger Clemens on the importance of throwing breaking pitches for strikes

Remember the 55-foot breaking ball covered earlier? There's a time and a place for that pitch, too. Get to 0–2 or 1–2 on a hitter, especially on an overanxious hitter, and chances are he'll even chase a curveball or a slider in the dirt. It's about the safest pitch you can throw in this situation because not even Junior Griffey can hit it.

LARRY ANDERSEN ON THE SLIDER

When the talk turns to great sliders, you hear the name of Hall of Famer Steve Carlton and a veteran middle reliever named Larry Andersen. Andersen may not be heading for Cooperstown, but he very quietly amassed a long record of very successful seasons. He was one of the toughest relievers to face in either league, though he broke most of the rules by being pretty much a one-pitch pitcher.

Here's what Keith Hernandez wrote about him in *Pure Baseball*: "Why not throw 75 consecutive sliders toward the outside corner? Mainly because you can't do it unless you're Steve Carlton or Larry Andersen. . . . [Andersen] lives and dies with his hard slider and throws it at least 85 percent of the time. He can do this because he has tremendous command of it, throwing it where he wants it time after time, biting hard and late on the ouside corner at the knees to right-handed batters, on the hands to left-handed batters."

You shouldn't try to emulate Larry Andersen and throw *any* pitch that often, unless it's a really good fastball. But if you're interested in learning how to attack a hitter with a slider, there's no better source. He's now a broadcaster with the Phillies, very generous with his time, and passionate about pitching. Here's what he has to say about how he used and located his slider:

I threw sliders in and away to lefties. With right-handers you're playing with fire doing that. To lefties, I never wanted sliders to end up on the inside corner, because that means it had to come across the nitro zone (the inner half of the plate). I threw it early in the count, middle of the thigh to the waist, where it looks like it's going to be a big, fat fastball. It started on the corner, then broke off the plate. Halfway to the plate, the hitter's got to make a decision about whether he's going to swing or not. The only way they can get the bat barrel on it is to hit it way out in front and hit it foul. I had (Andy) Van Slyke and (Barry) Bonds hit some mammoth shots . . . foul. And that's strike one. When I got ahead, I loved to throw the slider down at their knees. It looks like it's going to be a fastball down and in on the corner and they come unglued, but by the time they swing the ball's broken down at the ankles and they swing over the top of it.

Early in the count, mostly to lefties (opposite-hand hitters), you should start it off the plate away and bring it over the middle of the plate. Most hitters should be looking for a good pitch to hit, a fastball, first pitch. Most hitters are going to crush a ball middle in, about waisthigh. . . .

> ······ **Throw It Again**
> Where and when you throw your breaking ball will depend on the level of competition, the game situation, and your repertoire. In general, breaking balls are most successful when thrown low and away. With most pitchers, less is more. Reserve your breaking ball for the tough spots, then spring it on a good hitter when he's expecting a fastball.

Everybody hits the ball middle in, so they should be looking for one pitch when they're even in the count—and that's why I could start the slider away. They're not going to swing at something they think is going to be away.

If I'm getting a hitter out throwing sliders, I don't have to adjust. You see too many pitchers getting a hitter out two or three times, then he'll do something else and the guy will bridge him or hit a gapper. Well, he had to be looking for it. I don't care if he's looking for it. If he can't hit it, who cares? Don't adjust. You've got to force *him* to adjust. If he can't, why change? Too many pitchers make adjustments for no reason.

Tim Wakefield

6 FIELDING YOUR POSITION

Imagine you're pitching one of your finest games of the season. You're holding a 2–1 lead heading into the final inning. At the plate is the opposing team's leadoff hitter, and you're cognizant of how important it is to get that first out. You've worked the count to two balls and two strikes and have set the hitter up for a hard fastball on the inside corner. You put the pitch right under the hitter's hands and he "fists" one back to the mound. Chalk it up as out number one.

But wait. You failed to anticipate the ball being hit back to you. You're slow getting your feet into fielding position and are reduced to knocking the ball down with your glove. You scramble to pick up the ball quickly, but fail to get a good grip on it. The weight of your body is going the wrong way and you're off balance throwing to first base. The ball sails over the first baseman's head, and suddenly, what should have been out number one has transformed into a runner in scoring position with nobody out.

A pitcher who can field his position, who can make the correct plays in clutch situations, can put two or three more W's in his win column over the course of a season. As pitcher, your job does not end when you release the ball. Here are some of the tasks you will need to perform.

- guarding against line drives and ground balls up the middle
- knowing what base to throw to, when to throw there, and where to put the ball
- covering first base on ground balls to the right side
- handling bunts—whether to play the ball yourself, where to throw it, telling your catcher what to do with it, or simply getting out of the way
- directing traffic on pop-ups
- backing up throws to third base and home plate
- holding base runners close by delivering the ball to home plate quickly
- covering home plate on wild pitches and passed balls
- taking and giving signs from/to catchers and infielders

To help you better remember all of what you have to be ready to do while on the mound, try to think of your response to the following game situations before reading further. The key to responding to these situations correctly and immediately during a game situation is anticipation. Anticipating what you will do if a ball is hit to you—and what your responsibilities will be if a ball is hit to someone else—is critical for any fielder. Some may think it's especially difficult for a pitcher, since he has so much on his mind already, but no one on the field should be more aware of the game situation than you.

> "Becoming an efficient fielder off the mound comes from preparation. I think it's anticipating the play—knowing how much ground you can cover and the speed of the runners on base and at the plate."
>
> —Greg Maddux, winner of 10 National League Gold Glove Awards

Your catcher will often direct traffic for you, but don't automatically rely on that. To make the game-saving defensive gem—pouncing on a bunt and forcing the runner at third or covering home

on a passed ball—you should (or must) anticipate the play *before* it happens and react *before* your teammate tells you what to do.

BALLS IN THE INFIELD

Footwork is another key ingredient to fielding as a pitcher. It begins with your follow-through. As discussed extensively in Chapter 2, a good follow-through will have you on the balls of both feet, facing the plate. The correct follow-through requires a powerful and efficient delivery—and it *always* leaves you in position to field your position and protect yourself.

BALL HIT RIGHT AT YOU

Executing the proper follow-through is the surest way to guard against line drives and ground balls up the middle. What's proper execution? For starters, you're not falling off to either side or on your heels. Your glove is open, fingers pointing up, and the pocket faces home plate. When a pitcher robs a hitter of a base hit, it's rarely by accident. It's because he has put himself in position to make the play.

A proper follow-through will bring your throwing arm down and to the side of the knee of your stride leg. When your trail leg plants, bring your glove forward ready to field.

If you're in the habit of reaching for hard-hit balls with your bare hand, break that habit immediately—or it will be your fingers that you'll break. Hall of Famer Catfish Hunter missed part of the 1973 season when he broke his finger trying to bare-hand a ball in the All-Star Game. Use two hands to field a ball hit back to you whenever possible, but always use your glove hand to catch the ball.

A simple PFP drill (Pitcher's Fielding Practice) that develops your reflexes and improves your agility off the mound requires only you, a coach, and a first baseman. From the mound, go through your regular motion and delivery (without a ball). Just as you complete your follow-through, your coach (standing in the right- or left-hand batter's box) hits a ground ball back to the mound. Field the ball with two hands and make a crisp, accurate throw to first base. As you improve, your coach can challenge you with balls hit farther to your right and left to expand your range.

Pitchers will also benefit by playing "pepper" during pregame warm-ups. It's certainly more useful to a pitcher than shagging fly balls. Three or four players stand 20 to 30 feet away from a batter who hits the ball with a short, downward stroke. Whoever fields the ball throws it quickly to the batter, who hits the ball again. Be sure to play this at a safe distance from any spectators, bystanders, or teammates.

The PFP drill and pepper will help you flag down balls hit back up the middle. Once you glove them, what do you do with them? Following are some situations in which a ground ball is hit back to the pitcher.

> *"Bobby Shantz was my hero when I was a kid. We didn't have a lot of games on television when I was a kid, but I saw pictures of his follow-through. He used to have a little bounce step in his follow-through. I would practice that follow-through throwing tennis balls off the back of my garage door. The ball would come back to me quick, so I had to be ready to field the ball."*
>
> —Jim Kaat, winner of 16 Gold Glove Awards during his career on the mound. His hero, Bobby Shantz, won 8 Gold Gloves.

Two outs and/or no runners on. Take your time. Catch it before you try to throw it. Even the fastest base runner in the world is going to have a hard time beating out a sharply hit ball to the pitcher.

To simulate a game situation, throw a phantom (fake) pitch from the mound. As you're completing your follow-through, have a coach or teammate hit a ground ball back

to the mound. Field the ball like an infielder and make an accurate throw to first base. Never underestimate the importance of fielding your position.

Don't take the ball out of the glove until the first baseman gets near the base. Raise up, square your hips and shoulders, and step toward first, pointing your toe at the base. Use your natural throwing motion—unless you're a sidearmer or submariner, in which case you should throw three-quarters or overhand to avoid having your throw tail in to the base runner (for a righty). Grasp the ball across the seams (four-seam fastball grip). Take the ball out of your glove and straight up behind your ear. Do not drop your arm down as you would in your pitching motion. This takes too much time. Shorten your arc, which will reduce your time of delivery. Throw firmly to the first baseman's chest. Even if you have force options at other bases, go to first. He's the fielder most familiar with taking throws.

Use these basic principles—shoulder and hips in line with the target, holding the ball in the glove until ready to throw, stepping toward the

target, and throwing three-quarters or overhand with a four-seam grip—for all plays unless otherwise noted.

Runner on first, less than two out. Unlike the basic play at first, you're trying to turn a double play so you will need to react quickly. (Knowing how fast the hitter is will help you to know just how quickly you need to react.) You still need to catch the ball before you throw it, but once you do you need to turn 90 degrees to your left (for a righty) and pick up the fielder who is covering second base. (You should know who is covering prior to delivering the pitch by discussing and agreeing on coverage.) Throw the ball chest-high *to the base, not to the fielder.* If the shortstop is covering, lead him across the base. This allows him momentum to carry him toward first base so that he can get some zip on his throw. Throwing it low is a good way to get your shortstop hurt; with a base runner

---

KEEP YOUR WITS

Strange things can happen on what appear to be the simplest of plays. When he was with the San Francisco Giants, Terry Mulholland fielded a comebacker that broke his glove's webbing and got stuck between the webbing and the pocket. After trying in vain to extricate the ball, Mulholland threw his entire glove to first base and got the out.

In *Pitching in a Pinch*, Christy Mathewson writes of a bizarre play in Game 1 of the 1911 World Series. With a crucial play unfolding on a slow grounder to first base, Mathewson threw his first baseman, ball and all, at the sliding base runner to record the out:

The score was tied, with runners on second and third base with two out, when [Hall of Famer] Eddie Collins, the fast second baseman of the Athletics, and a dangerous hitter, came to the bat. . . . Collins hit a slow one down the first base line, about six feet inside the bag.

With the hit, I ran over to cover the base, and [first baseman Fred] Merkle made for the ball, but he had to get directly in my line of approach to field it. Collins, steaming down the baseline, realized that, if he could get the decision at first on this hit, his team would probably win the game, as the two other runners could score easily. In a flash, I was aware of this too. . . .

When still ten or twelve feet from the bag, he slid, hoping to take us unawares and thus avoid being touched. He could then scramble to the bag. As soon as he jumped, I realized what he hoped to do, and, fearing that Merkle would miss him, I grabbed the first baseman and hurled him at Collins. It was an old-fashioned, football shove, Merkle landing on Collins and touching him out. . . . That football shove was a brand new play to me in baseball, invented on the spur of the second, but it worked.

bearing down on him, he'll want to keep the ball and the runner in view, as he may need to leap to avoid a hard slide. If you deliver the throw too much to the left-field side of the base, the shortstop will either miss catching the throw or have to stop and reach backward. The former will retire no one and the latter will jeopardize getting the force play at second base. With practice, you will quickly learn how far from the base the shortstop needs to be before you can make your throw.

Occasionally the second baseman will be covering, such as when the shortstop is playing toward third against a right-handed batter who is an extreme pull hitter. You need to wait a bit longer to deliver the ball if the second baseman is covering. Allow him to get behind the bag as you deliver the ball to the base. If you lead the second baseman to the base, his momentum will carry him away from first base, making it difficult for him to get any strength on his throw.

On hit-and-run plays, just get the out at first base.

Runners on first and second, less than two out. When runners are on first and second with less than two out, get the force at second and possi-

> ···· **Throw It Again**
> The most important physical attribute to good fielding for a pitcher is footwork. It all begins with the proper follow-through, which will leave you facing the batter, glove up, and on the balls of your feet. Footwork is also very important for fielding slow rollers and bunts, and for executing an effective pickoff move.

bly the double play rather than trying to get the runner at third. For one thing, a 1-5-3 double play (pitcher-third-first) is much harder to get than a 1-6-3 (pitcher-short-first) or 1-4-3 (pitcher-second-first). For another, the base runner on second will have a bigger lead than the runner on first, so the force at third will be harder to get than the force at second (especially for a right-handed pitcher, who has to turn 180 degrees to make the throw). And while you can fail to get a force at second and still have time for the shortstop to retire the hitter at first, it is a lot tougher for a third baseman to pull this off. You can end up with the bases loaded very easily.

That's not to say that there aren't times when it pays to be aggressive with the lead runner. For

Remember, when attempting to get a force out at second base, field the ball first before turning toward second.

If the shortstop is covering, lead him to second base with your throw.

example, maybe your catcher has a hard time keeping your breaking balls in front of him and you're concerned that it will be difficult to keep a runner on third base from scoring. Maybe there is no one out and the next batter is a fly-ball hitter who is hard to strike out or a fast runner who is hard to double up. Smart, aggressive pitchers try to make plays the same way that smart, aggressive infielders do. The key, of course, is thinking ahead of time what you will do with the ball if it comes to you.

Finally, when the runner on second is very fast and very aggressive, you need to be aware of the possibility that he may attempt to score all the way from second on a double play. Mookie Wilson of the Mets did this more than once. Usually your catcher will be backing up first, so home plate will be unoccupied. Whether the ball is hit to you or not, break toward home as soon as the throw goes to second base. The cardinal rule for pitchers as fielders: *Don't stand there watching, get involved.*

Bases loaded, less than two out. The 1-2-3 (pitcher-catcher-first) double play is an easy one to get, and it can be back-breaking for the offense. Unless there are very fast base runners involved, or a runner on third with a huge lead, you don't need to rush to make this play. On a ball hit right back to you, throw a four-seam, chest-high fastball over home plate. Take the time to get a good grip on the ball and set your feet underneath you. The cost of a bad throw is at least a run and possibly a big inning. Make sure of the first out before worrying about getting two.

> *"Fundamentals in the National League are very important for pitchers. Bunting, moving a runner over, covering first base. Probably the thing I work hardest on in spring training is PFP drills—comebackers, fielding bunts. They are absolutely invaluable to a pitcher. They separate the 15-game winner from the 18-game winner, and the 18-game winner from the 21-game winner."*
>
> —Curt Schilling, National League All-Star

Runner on second and/or third, less than two out. When runners are in scoring position and no force play is in effect, you *must* anticipate what you will do when a ball is hit to you. Failing to do so will allow easy runs to score or bad baserunning to go unpunished. As soon as you catch the ball, check the lead runner. You should have plenty of time. Usually, a good base runner will be too close to the base to be "picked off." In this case, you "look him back," then throw firmly to first base for the out. If he's a fast runner who is a little bit too far from the base for your liking—but still too close to be nabbed—fake a throw to third, then throw hard to first for the out. This will remove any thoughts he might have of taking off as soon as you throw to first.

If the lead runner breaks and you feel you can get him, by all means, take the out. You always take a runner out of scoring position when you can.

If the lead runner has taken off at contact and finds himself halfway down the line when you field the ball, you've got him dead to rights. Take him. Run right at him until he commits to a base. Wait a second, then throw to that base, and you've got an out with one throw.

Runners on first and third, less than two out. This may be the most complicated situation you'll encounter. A runner is in scoring position, but there is also a double-play possibility. There is a good chance that the runner on first will be moving with the pitch to stay out of the double play, especially if you are facing a batter who hits down (seventh, eighth, or ninth) in the order. In this situation, it will be very important for you to anticipate. How fast are the base runners? How fast is the hitter? How good is your shortstop at turning two? Is it late in a close game or are you protecting an early lead? Will the runner on first be moving on the pitch? Is there one out or none out? Your catcher will probably call a meeting at the mound so that all of the infielders will be on the same page. Don't be afraid to call one yourself.

In this situation, there will be times when you could throw to any of the four bases. If the runner

Field the ball and check the runner at third base.

Once he moves back to third, turn to first and get the out.

baseman. You should be able to get the runner with one throw, so the runner on first won't be able to come around to third. Do it right and it's just about as easy an out to get as a force at second or a play at first—and you won't have to concede the run.

The only way to become comfortable in this situation is to work on it in practice. Put runners on first and third in practice and have a coach hit balls back to the mound. The runners should vary their strategy each time the ball is hit.

SLOW ROLLER IN FRONT OF YOU

Most of the time on slow rollers, your play will be to first base (bunts will be addressed later). Whether you go to second, third, or home will depend on the same factors as those described in the last section. You have a lot less time to work with, but you have the advantage of a catcher telling you where to go with the ball as you come in to field it. Or he may be waving you off the play, that is, calling for himself or the first or third baseman to handle the ball. If so, you need to get out of the way. Standing still and watching could block the fielder's throw. Continuing to run through the path of a slow roller can make it very hard for a fielder—usually the third baseman—to handle the ball cleanly. Usually, your best move is simply to "stop and drop." It helps if you know how much ground you can cover—something perennial Gold Glove winner Greg Maddux considers very important—so you won't need to wait for your catcher's directions.

If your catcher is calling for you to take the ball, how you field it will depend on whether the ball is still rolling or not. If it's still moving, field it with two hands; it's very easy to make an error if you try to field a slow roller with your bare hand, and you should only do it if the play is going to be extremely close. If the ball has stopped moving, pick it up with your bare hand. Push the ball into the ground and bring your arm immediately up and back. Don't waste any motion. Whether the ball is rolling or has stopped, *don't watch the base runners*. This is your catcher's job. Trying to see

is moving, or if there are no outs and you don't want to concede the run, check the runner at third then throw to first. If the runner on first is not moving with the pitch and you think you have a good chance to turn an inning-ending double play, throw to second and go after it aggressively. If the runner on third is trapped one-third of the way down the line and you have no chance for a double play, throw to third. If he's running on contact and is two-thirds of the way down the line, throw home. If you have a big lead and are playing to avoid a big inning, skip these potentially close plays and throw to second or first.

If the runner on third is halfway down the line, run right at him regardless of the score. Force him to commit to home or third, then wait for a second and throw to the catcher or third what's going on behind you is a good way to boot a fairly easy play.

One of the keys to making the play on a slow roller is quick feet. You need to get off the mound quickly and, depending on how slowly the ball is hit and how fast the runner is, you may need to set your feet to throw as you field the ball. Your footwork depends on whether you're a lefty or righty and whether the ball has been hit to your left or right.

> *"I was a little guy growing up, but I always had quickness. When I got my size, I maintained that quickness, which is crucial in fielding off the mound. Fielding for a pitcher is reaction. You've got to finish with good balance and have fast reflexes."*
>
> —Jim Kaat

Slow roller toward third. If you're a right-hander setting up for a throw to first, it is important to place your weight on your right foot as you field the ball. Plant it about two feet to the right of the ball and push off with this foot to make your throw. You may not have time to set up your throw. If so, you'll need to get your hips in a line toward first base while you're bending to field the ball.

If you're a left-hander making a play at first on a slow roller toward third, you need to field the ball with your back turned to first base. This enables you to make a quick delivery to first. The key foot is your left, on which you will be pivoting as you wheel back toward first. Pick up your target very quickly and align your hips and shoulders with the target. Lefties should practice this play a lot. Do it poorly and you can heave this ball down the right-field line. Do it well and you can keep speedy base runners from bunting their way on against you. The cat-quick Ron Guidry was a master of this play.

Slow roller toward first. If you're a right-hander, the key to making this play will be getting a clear line of sight to first base. Because the throw is much shorter than the one the left-hander has to make from the third base side, you shouldn't have to rush. Field the ball with your feet pointing toward the first-base line, so your hips will already be in line with your target. Even if your first baseman is a right-hander, you're better off making the throw to the fair side of the baseline. If you throw to the foul side, you could hit the base runner or cause a nasty collision if the ball and runner arrive at the same time. If you field the ball close to the baseline, you need to take a step back into fair territory before throwing rather than trying to throw "through" the base runner.

If you're a left-hander, this play is tougher because you have to turn your body to make the throw. Field a slow roller by "hurdling" the path of the ball with your left foot, then turning on it so that your back is toward the first-base line. You aren't actually jumping over the ball, but over the point where you expect it to be after you complete your hurdle and turn. Once you've fielded the ball, getting a clear line of sight to the first baseman is key. A step from the foul line toward the pitcher's mound may be necessary to avoid throwing through the base runner.

This is a perfect example of how *not* to throw to first base. Not only is this pitcher off balance and in danger of making an errant throw, but he's also risking injury by putting unnecessary strain on his arm.

GROUNDER HIT TO YOUR LEFT

On ground balls hit between first and second, your first instinct must be to cover first base. You shouldn't have to *think* about it. It's a timing play that requires a lot of early season practice with your first basemen. But once you've put in that practice, it should be a play that you make ten times out of ten. Here are the five steps to making it work:

1. Don't sprint directly toward first base. Sprint toward a point on the first-base line about 10 feet short of the base.
2. Slow down when you hit the foul line, then give a chest-high target in fair territory as you head up the line toward the base. Left-handers may want to head toward first base from a point a few feet farther from the foul line, so that they can give a target with their glove that's not in the base runner's path.
3. You should be receiving the ball two or three steps before you reach the base, which will give you time to adjust your strides and step on the base. Catch the ball before looking for the base. If the fielder is slow in reaching the ball, get to the base and take the throw like a first baseman.
4. Touch the inside of first base with your right foot. Avoid touching it with your left foot; this is a great way to get yourself run over and/or spiked by the base runner.
5. Don't keep running down the foul line; turn toward second base. If there are runners on base, find the lead runner and be prepared to throw. If the lead runner is on second, you'll need to wheel quickly back toward home plate to make certain that he doesn't try to score. Notice that big league pitchers turn toward second even when no one is on base, having gotten themselves into a *good* habit.

On balls hit to the first base side of the mound, the first baseman will set up a target inside the baseline.

No matter whether it's a sharp grounder or a slow roller, follow the same path to first base. On slow rollers, *you* will act as the traffic cop, not the first baseman. If you can field the ball on your path to the base, let him know that you're taking it. Yell early, loud, and often: "I got it. I got it. I got it." He'll cover first and take your throw, or you can continue to the base and take it unassisted. If it's a slow roller that you can't get to, your first baseman may be charging the ball and fielding it on the infield grass while his momentum takes him toward home. On this type of play, you need to be prepared for a throw that is behind you, since you're moving in opposite directions. Often the best way to complete this type of play is for you to get to first base as quickly as you can and turn back toward him, so you can field the throw like a first baseman rather than on the run.

> *"When covering first base, your first three steps should be giant strides. When you get close to the base, then you can shorten up to find the bag. Too many guys don't get off the mound quickly enough and they approach the bag taking big long strides and bouncing up and down, which makes it difficult to pick up the ball."*
>
> —Jim Kaat

As fielding great Jim Kaat says, your first three steps off the mound covering first base should be "giant strides."

With men on first and second or the bases loaded, with less than two out, and there's a hard-hit grounder to your left, you may find yourself part of what can be one of the game's prettier plays: a 3-6-1 (first-short-pitcher) double play. Take your standard path to the base. On most plays, you should take the throw from the shortstop while standing at first base rather than running through it.

········ Throw It Again

Timing is very important for a pitcher on many fielding plays, most notably the 3-1 (first base to pitcher) groundout. You need to automatically break for first on balls hit to your left side, direct traffic on grounders that either you or your first baseman could get to, and practice this play enough times that you can take his toss and touch first on the run without breaking a sweat.

BUNTS

Bunting is a popular strategy, especially at the high school level. At the bottom of the order in a close game with a man on and no one out, it can be an automatic. Your first order of defensive business is to make it difficult for the batter to get the bunt down. High four-seam fastballs are difficult to get on the ground. Try this pitch first. If you fall behind the batter, just throw a strike. Any time you're offered an out, take it! A sacrifice is better than a base on balls.

In a bunting situation, it's critical that all infielders know their responsibility. That includes the pitcher, who is as involved in this play as anyone else on the field. As you read further, pay attention to the directions on footwork; this is important not only in getting to the ball, but also in setting yourself up to throw as you pick up the ball.

Runner on first. With a man on first, a bunt right back to you is a great opportunity to force the runner at second. After fielding the ball, quickly align your hips and shoulders along an imaginary line to the target (second base). Keep your weight on the foot closer to home plate, then step and throw. Be aware of how fast the base runner is, know how much ground you've covered, and listen for any instructions your catcher offers. He should be telling you where to go with the ball, which in turn will tell you how to set your feet.

When going for the force at second, you don't have the luxury of time. Be aggressive about it. If you hesitate at all or if you're not certain that you can make the play, bring the ball back into your glove, shift your feet so that your hips are in line with first, and take the easy out there.

Better bunts will be laid down closer to the first-base or third-base lines. In these instances, the force at second won't even be a consideration. It will be enough work just to get the out at first. If the bunt has stopped rolling by the time you reach it, remember to "push it into the ground" before you pick it up. As described in the section on slow rollers, a left-hander will need to "hurdle" the path of a bunt to the first base side in order to be in position to throw.

Runners on first and second. If you're a right-hander, you'll need to "hurdle" when going for a force at third on a bunt to the third base side—jumping right-foot first and pivoting on that foot as you land. You usually won't have a play at third unless the bunt is very hard, the runner on second gets a bad jump, or the runner on second is slow. If the ball is bunted toward the pitcher's mound, you'll want to get across the path of the bunt and plant your back foot as quickly as possible. If you don't have a play at third, field it as you would a slow roller and make the play at first.

Keep in mind that a ball bunted in the air can affect where you have a play. Base runners are taught to hold until they see the ball on the ground. If the batter bunts the ball in the air, base runners can't break immediately, giving you more time to get the lead runner.

Plant your back foot to ensure proper balance. Poor weight distribution (caused by rushing) is the biggest reason for errant throws by pitchers.

Runner on third. If you're in a close game and there is a runner on third with less than two outs, and a weak hitter at the plate, you must be alert for the sacrifice bunt, or "squeeze." The runner on third could be taking off for home with the pitch—the "suicide squeeze"—or he could be going "on contact." If you're a right-hander and you see that the base runner is breaking for home—or if you're a left-hander and you hear one of your teammates yell "Squeeze!"—throw a fastball high and outside to a left-handed batter or high and inside to a right-handed batter. These are difficult pitches to bunt and put your catcher in position to tag out the base runner. (The squeeze is hardly ever used when the bases are loaded and there is a force play at home.)

If the batter can get a bunt down on a suicide squeeze, you probably have no chance to get the runner at the plate unless it's hit right back to you. Even then, you may need to bare-hand the ball and flip it to the catcher, or glove it and shovel it in one motion—keeping the glove open and pushing the ball forward. If the runner is waiting for the batter to make contact to break for home—the safety squeeze—you have more time to field the ball cleanly and make a good throw—low and on the third base side of home plate. Whether the runner is going with the pitch or on contact, sometimes the bunt is so good that you have no option but to take the out at first and let the run score. Don't make a great bunt even better by going for an out at the plate that you can't get.

POP-UPS

The pop-up to the pitcher is perhaps the rarest out in baseball. That's because on a pop-up in front of the bases, the pitcher's responsibility is not to make the play but to direct traffic—unless it's a very low pop-up that no other fielder can get to. On higher pop-ups, you have the best view of the ball and who has the best angle to catch it. Pick up the ball, point out its location in the air, shout your directions quickly and clearly, and, if necessary, cover the base vacated by whoever is catching the ball.

BACKING UP AND COVERING BASES

So far, the defensive responsibilities of the pitcher we've discussed have been limited to balls in the infield. A large part of a pitcher's game is spent backing up bases on balls hit to the outfield, or covering a base in the event of a wild pitch, passed ball, rundown, and so on. You need to know the ground rules of the park you're pitching in, so that you can pay special attention to any "dead-ball" areas (such as the dugout) and "play goaltender."

> *There is always a spot for the pitcher to be. He should never be standing on the mound watching the game go by. The pitcher should always be anticipating where an overthrow might be and pay attention to what the base runners are doing.*
>
> —Jim Kaat

BALL HIT TO THE OUTFIELD

There are a few simple rules to follow when a ball is hit to the outfield.

1. Don't just stand there. There is a place for you to go on every fly ball or base hit, and the pitching mound is never that place.
2. On a base hit, you need to back up the base that is two bases ahead of the lead runner.
3. Line yourself up with the base and the outfielder or cutoff man making the throw.
4. When backing up third or home, stand as far back from the base as the field allows. This gives you the best chance to keep an overthrown ball in play.
5. When crossing a baseline, be aware of base runners and don't interfere with them.

The following table summarizes where you need to go on a ball hit to the outfield.

There may be times when you're uncertain whether you should be backing up home plate or third base—such as when there is a single with runners on first and second. Run to a spot equidistant between home and third in foul territory, then move into the appropriate position as the play unfolds and the catcher shouts directions to the cutoff man.

RUNDOWNS

Most of the time, if a pitcher gets involved in a rundown it's because too many throws have been made. Regardless of how it happens, a pitcher should never be standing still watching the action. Head to the base that is covered by the fewest number of fielders and be prepared to take a throw and make a tag.

For example, let's say you pick a runner off first. You throw over as the runner breaks for second, and he gets himself caught in a rundown. At this point, second base is covered by the second baseman and the shortstop, while first is covered only by the first baseman. Run behind the first baseman and back up the play. If the first baseman runs the base runner back toward second but throws the ball to the shortstop too early, the runner will be able to head back to first. You'll be there to make the tag and keep a good pickoff move from going to waste.

When you come off the mound to make a play, make sure your feet are underneath you and you step directly at your target.

Hit	Field	Lead Runner	Responsibility	Where to Go
Single	Left	None, Third	Back up second	Between 1B and 2B
Single	Center	None, Third	Back up second	Between mound and 2B
Single	Right	None, Third	Back up second	Between 2B and 3B
Single	Left	First	Back up third	In front of 3B dugout between 3B and home
Single	Center	First	Back up third	Behind 3B along fence
Single	Right	First	Back up third	Behind 3B along fence
Single	Left	Second	Back up home	In front of backstop on 1B side of home
Single	Center	Second	Back up home	In front of backstop directly behind home
Single	Right	Second	Back up home	In front of backstop on 3B side of home
Extra Bases	Left	None, Second, Third	Back up third	In front of 3B dugout between 3B and home
Extra Bases	Center	None, Second, Third	Back up third	Behind 3B along fence
Extra Bases	Right	None, Second, Third	Back up third	Behind 3B along fence
Extra Bases	Left	First	Back up home	In front of backstop on 1B side of home
Extra Bases	Center	First	Back up home	In front of backstop directly behind home
Extra Bases	Right	First	Back up home	In front of backstop on 3B side of home
Fly Ball	Left	First	Back up second	Between 1B and 2B
Fly Ball	Center	First	Back up second	Between mound and 2B
Fly Ball	Right	First	Back up second	Between 2B and 3B
Fly Ball	Left	Second	Back up third	In front of 3B dugout between 3B and home
Fly Ball	Center	Second	Back up third	Behind 3B along fence
Fly Ball	Right	Second	Back up third	Behind 3B along fence
Fly Ball	Left	Third	Back up home	In front of backstop on 1B side of home
Fly Ball	Center	Third	Back up home	In front of backstop directly behind home
Fly Ball	Right	Third	Back up home	In front of backstop on 3B side of home

On a rundown between second and third, you'll usually be responsible for backing up third. If the rundown is between third and home, back up the plate. Never leave home plate unattended.

WILD PITCHES AND PASSED BALLS

Even at the major league level, you will see pitchers talking to themselves after wild pitches rather than getting into defensive position. A pitcher has three responsibilities on wild pitches and passed balls.

1. Tell your catcher where the ball is. Yell "First," "Back," "Third," "Front," or "Down," depending on whether the ball is: behind the catcher on the first base side, directly behind the catcher, behind the catcher on the third base side, in front of the catcher, or at the catcher's feet.
2. Tell your catcher where to throw the ball. Yell "One, one, one!" "Two, two, two!" "Three, three, three!" "Four, four, four!" or "No play, no play, no play!" depending on whether there is a play at a particular base or no play at all.
3. Cover home plate when there is a runner on third, or a very fast runner on second. Don't try to be a hero on tag plays and block the plate. Play it like a matador. Stand on the first base side of home plate, set a low target to the third base side, and make a sweep tag on the base runner. If other runners are on base, spin immediately back toward the field and get yourself in position to make a throw.

····· Throw It Again
No fielder should ever be standing still and watching the play, especially not the pitcher. On balls hit to the outfield, you need to back up the base two bases in front of the lead runner while paying special attention to any dead-ball areas.

HOLDING RUNNERS ON BASE

Pitching entails not only keeping hitters off the bases but keeping them from advancing any closer to home when they reach base. Part of that is being able to hold runners on base, which is one of the most underrated weapons in a pitcher's arsenal.

You do not need to throw over to first base a lot to limit base stealing. There are a number of techniques that a pitcher can use to discourage base stealing *without having to make a pickoff throw at all.* For starters, a quick delivery will cut back on the number of bases swiped while you're on the mound. Deliver the pitch to the plate in 1.3 seconds or less and your catcher will have an excellent chance at throwing out the runner. Here are some alternate methods.

1. Vary the length of time that you hold your set position—from the one-second minimum to three or four seconds, which will make it harder for the runner to time his jump.
2. Hold your set position for three or four seconds, then step off. This has the added benefit of allowing the offense to potentially tip their hand, perhaps by the hitter sliding his hand down the bat for a bunt or squaring around in his stance. You can also fake a throw to first after stepping off, which you cannot do from a regular pickoff move.
3. Quick-pitch. When you come to your set position and step off, most base runners walk slowly back to the base out of habit. Step back on the rubber, come to an accelerated set position, and deliver the pitch before he can reclaim his full lead. Be certain that you come set for a full second before pitching and that you don't rush your delivery.
4. Deliver a slide-step delivery. If you can maintain your timing with a slide step—skipping the knee lift and moving right into the fall phase to throw a fastball—this will do a lot to hinder base stealing.

Bret Saberhagen is one of the best in the game at keeping the runner close at first base. Here he executes a pivot move. Notice he has pivoted and released the ball

before the runner is able to make his crossover step back to first. Quick feet and a short release may result in an easy out at first base.

When Mark Leiter was moved to the bullpen, he found the need to develop a slide-step delivery. If the slide step costs you any velocity, Leiter is no evidence of it. His velocity actually went up when he pitched in relief. You must be cautious of rushing your delivery in a slide-step delivery. Pitchers often lose control and leave pitches high in the strike zone. If this is the case, leave the slide-step delivery in the bullpen.

As for making a pickoff attempt, the technique depends on the base you are throwing to and whether you are right-handed or left-handed. In addition, you should have at least three moves: a slow move, a quick move, and a pickoff move. Base runners expect you to try to set them up with a slow move followed by a quick move. Many aren't expecting slow followed by quick followed by quicker.

FIRST BASE

First, a brief review of the rules for pitching from the stretch. You must take your sign from the catcher with your back foot touching the front of the rubber, your hands apart, and your throwing hand at your side or in back of your body. You must come set with your hands together between your belt and chin, and you must hold that position for one second before delivering the ball to the plate.

BALK!

Here are some common ways that a pitcher will balk:
- Left- or Right-handers: Not coming set for a full second before delivering the ball to home plate.
- Left- or Right-handers: Beginning your move to the plate without completing it, usually by moving the front knee or the hands.
- Left- or Right-handers: Faking a throw to first base without stepping off the rubber.
- Left-handers: Bringing the front leg behind the imaginary line between first base and the pitcher's mound, then throwing to first.
- Left-handers: Stepping more than 45 degrees toward home plate while throwing to first.

When in doubt, simply step off the rubber and become a fifth infielder.

HOLDING THEM CLOSE . . . AND NOT SO CLOSE

The chart below summarizes the best and worst pitchers in the major leagues in 1998 when it came to holding runners close. Bret Saberhagen, Shane Reynolds, Rick Reed, and Aaron Sele show that you don't have to be a left-hander to discourage base stealing. As for Terry Mulholland, he has such a good move to first base that no one even *tried* to run on him all season. This is the only aspect of Greg Maddux's game that is below average—he allows nearly as many stolen bases as the rest of the Braves rotation *combined* and a much higher base-stealing success rate—but he does lend some credence to the belief that you can get out of some tough situations by concentrating hard on getting the batter rather than giving overdue attention to base runners.

Pitcher	IP	SB	CS	%
Terry Mulholland	112	0	0	—
Omar Daal	163	3	12	20%
Brian Anderson	218	4	9	31%
Aaron Sele	213	4	8	33%
Rick Reed	212	7	14	33%
Shane Reynolds	233	6	11	35%
Bret Saberhagen	175	4	7	36%
Wilson Alvarez	143	3	5	38%
Pitcher	IP	SB	CS	%
Scott Erickson	251	28	7	80%
Juan Guzman	211	31	9	78%
Mark Clark	214	28	8	78%
Roger Clemens	235	28	9	76%
Hideo Nomo	157	25	8	76%
Tim Wakefield	216	24	8	75%
Greg Maddux	251	28	11	72%

1998 statistics. Minimum 100 innings pitched.

Throwing hard does not compensate for a slow release. Against three of the hardest throwers in the game—Robb Nen, Troy Percival, and Ugueth Urbina—base runners in 1998 were a combined 34-for-36 in stolen base attempts.

You are not allowed to stop and start any movement toward the plate. If a left-hander's front leg goes behind the imaginary line from first base to the pitcher's rubber during his knee lift, he must deliver the ball to the plate. If a left-hander's front leg goes more than 45 degrees toward home plate during his stride, he must deliver the ball to the plate. As a result of these limitations, base runners will watch a right-hander's back foot and a left-hander's front leg; these reveal whether you are committing yourself to throw to the plate.

Once you know what a runner is watching, you'll know how to pick him off.

Right-handers pick runners off with quickness, left-handers with trickery.

Right-handers

You've come to the set position with your feet shoulder-width apart or slightly closer, your right foot alongside the rubber and your left foot a few inches forward of your right foot. Your knees are flexed slightly, allowing you to turn more quickly to first base. You're gripping the ball inside the glove, with your hands together at the letters. Your shoulders are on a line from second base to home plate, allowing you to take the sign from the catcher while watching the runner out of the corner of your eye. If your peripheral vision doesn't allow you to see the base runner, your catcher can give you a sign (usually a thumb pointed in the direction of first base). Don't come set in an open position in order to get a better look at first base. You'll get a slightly better view, but it will cost you both time and balance in your delivery to the plate.

You pick runners off with the quickness of your delivery to first, not the velocity with which you throw to first base. For your quick move, turn your front shoulder while pivoting on your right foot. Your left foot is moving toward first base and your feet are set as you throw.

Shorten your throwing arc. Your arm goes up to your ear like a catcher's, rather than down, back, and around. Your target is the first baseman's right knee. For your slow move, don't shorten your arm arc.

Some pitchers use a "jump" move to first. Rather than pivot on your back foot, you jump a few inches while turning toward first with your hips and shoulders. This will get the ball to first base more quickly, but a good base runner will recognize it immediately because your feet simply wouldn't move this way if you were going to deliver to the plate.

Bringing your hands above your head while coming set results in wasted effort, but it does allow for a tricky move to first. Rather than stopping at the letters or waist and then throwing to first, you execute your pivot turn and throw from above your head. This can be a very quick move, because your arm is already in throwing position. It's also an unexpected move, and it may catch a base runner napping.

Left-handers

Though a left-hander has the advantage of being able to throw directly to first base without turning, you must be careful not to let your face or eyes give you away. As you come to the set position, stare at the runner whether you intend to throw over or not. Do this every time. If he takes his eyes off of you, throw over immediately.

When you reach the set position, shift your gaze to a point between first base and home plate that allows you to see both the batter and the base runner. The runner won't be able to read your eyes, and you'll have an easier time picking up your target when you come to the plate.

A base runner watches the front leg of a left-handed pitcher for his cue that it's safe to go. When the left leg goes behind an imaginary line between first base and the rubber, the pitcher has to deliver the ball to home plate or be called for a balk. Therefore, one way to develop a great move is to break that plane enough to deceive the runner without having it called by the umpire. To make this work, you will need your knee lift when going to the plate to be right on the line between first base and the pitcher's rubber. Lift your knee with your lead leg as close to the plane as possible, then begin your fall toward home plate. Land as close to the 45-degree plane between first base and home plate as you can get. Throw the ball from your ear to the first baseman's right knee. You might even be able to get away with breaking the 45-degree plane if you land with your foot pointed toward first base rather than toward the on-deck circle. Walking toward first base after you follow through also helps.

Be careful not to change your arm path too early, or the runner will able to tell that you aren't pitching to the plate. Dipping your back shoulder is another giveaway that you're throwing to first, as is lifting your front leg with your toes up rather than down. Finally, be certain that your lead arm continues toward the plate and does not point toward first base as you throw over. You can try this same move from a slide step rather than a knee lift and have a lot of success with it. The slide step is not just for right-handers.

These are your "pickoff" moves to first base. Your quick move will feature a more direct step toward first base. Your slow move will feature an even more direct step toward first base without the shortened arm arc.

Many right-handers consider the pivot move the quickest move to first base. From the stretch position, the pitcher has a slight flex in his knees, which puts him in good athletic position.

He bends his back leg inward to start his turn toward first. His hand remains up near shoulder level.

He then quickly opens his hips and stride foot to first base to get his body into throwing position.

He brings the ball directly up to throwing position (much like an infielder) to execute a quick, crisp throw. His eyes are now focused on the target.

By the time he releases the ball, his chest is facing the target. The target point is two feet off the ground and two feet to the infield side of the bag.

During his move to first, David Wells keeps his stride foot pointed toward first base during his knee lift. This makes

it tough on the base runner, because it gives no indication whether he's throwing home or to first.

When delivering a pitch, Wells cocks his stride foot back toward the second baseman. Because he has broken the imaginary plane between the mound and first base, he

now must throw home or run the risk of a balk. An astute base runner will pick this up immediately.

A lot of time spent in front of a mirror will help you refine your pickoff moves. Most importantly, you want your lower body, upper body, and arm to look the same to the base runner whether you are going to first or the plate. It will help you if you think "pitch" while you do this, so that your rhythm or balance doesn't give anything away either.

Here is another move that a left-handed pitcher can work into his pickoff repertoire; it will be especially effective against walking leads. It's not for everyone, though, because it requires very quick feet. At your set position or as soon as your hands come together, take a short step back off the rubber at a 45-degree angle toward the second baseman while short-arming the ball to first. The 45-degree step toward the second baseman is very important, because it allows you to get some power (hip turn) into your throw.

Dave Righetti popularized a variation of this move when he was closing games for the Yankees. As he stepped off, he would sling the ball sidearm. Though throwing virtually flat-footed, he would get an extraordinarily quick release—though some coaches feared that he was putting excessive strain on his elbow and shoulder in the process. Proceed with caution, and be certain that you can control the throw before trying this in a game.

SECOND BASE

Too many pitchers don't pay enough attention to runners on second base. Even if the runner is not a base stealer, holding him close will give your outfielders a better chance to throw him out at home on a single. There are three basic moves to

second base, two from the stretch and one from the windup: the spin move, the pivot move, and the daylight move. The moves are almost identical for right-handers and left-handers, with the only difference being the direction of the turn.

Since you can't afford to keep your second baseman or shortstop anchored to the bag, timing is critical for a good pickoff attempt. Every team will have a set of plays and signals that determine the timing on these moves. Remember: Unlike throws to first base, you do not have to complete a throw to second base.

Spin Move

Reach the top of your knee lift as if going toward the plate, pause, and then quickly turn 90 degrees toward second base on your back foot. This is a two-part move. You must lift your knee as if you're throwing home in order to sell the move to the runner. Do not lift your knee and immediately spin to second base. Like the left-hander's 45-degree "balk" move to first, good balance is critical to making this work. You'll often see this move used without a throw, because the defense just wants to see if the offense has a play on (bunt, hit-and-run, etc.).

Pivot Move

With the pivot move, the footwork will turn you 180 degrees. You come set, pivot on your back foot so your toes face home plate, and use this foot to spin you counterclockwise (clockwise for a left-hander) toward second base. As you spin, bring your throwing arm up to your ear and stride directly toward second base with your lead foot. You can also use the jump turn. You can execute the jump turn not from the set position but from the first moment the hands come together. Remember: You do not have to complete your throw to second base.

Daylight Move

You can also throw to second base from the windup. The footwork is similar to that of the pivot move, in that you step back off the rubber with the right foot (for a right-hander) and turn on this foot

The spin move is a two-part move. Lift your knee straight up as if you were delivering home. Pause for a brief

moment and then spin around (clockwise for a right-hander) to second base.

toward second base. Since you're in the windup, however, you can't turn to see what's going on at second base. When your catcher sees daylight between the shortstop and the base runner, he signals you to spin and throw by dropping his glove.

You can also see daylight from the stretch position. If your shortstop gets between the runner and the base and gives a sign (such as shaking his glove hand), pivot or spin and fire to second base.

To execute the pivot move, pivot on your back foot (so your toe faces home plate)

and spin around (counterclockwise for a right-hander). Think quick, not "fast", in

order to keep your body under control and avoid an errant throw.

THIRD BASE

The benefits of pickoff throws to third base are debatable. You can nab a particularly aggressive base runner, but the timing is difficult—since the third baseman will be playing well off the bag—and the cost of a mistake is very high. For example, during the Cubs' infamous September collapse in 1969 when they were finding new ways to lose every day, an attempted pickoff play at third base cost them a game in Philadelphia. Pitcher Dick Selma shouted a signal to third baseman Ron Santo for a pickoff play they'd never used and had only briefly discussed. Santo didn't get the signal, Selma threw the ball down the left-field line, and the Cubs lost another close one.

A right-hander can use the same move to third as a left-hander's move to first—beginning the fall toward home plate, then landing within the 45-degree line. You throw to the third baseman, who has broken for the bag as soon as you lift your leg. But because the third baseman's break for the bag is giving this move away, it will only work against a base runner with a very large lead.

An aggressive base runner on third base can prove to be a big distraction for a pitcher. When you're pitching from the windup, the runner on third can get a big lead. Make sure the runner has stopped before you start your motion. Look at him until he stops moving forward. Once he does, begin your delivery and focus your attention on the ensuing pitch.

In youth leagues, runners sometimes dance down the line, hoping it will cause the pitcher to balk. If you're taking the sign with both feet on the rubber and you step off with your stride foot, that's the balk he's looking for. You can avoid this by taking the sign with your stride foot behind the rubber and to the side. Now when the runner dances down the line, you will step off the rubber with your back foot as you're supposed to do.

A left-hander can make a move to third base from the windup. You take the sign with your left foot on the rubber and right foot behind and to the side. The third baseman breaks for the bag, the

······· **Throw It Again**

There are a number of ways to discourage aggressive base runners, only one of which is by actually making a pickoff throw. Others include stepping off, altering your rhythm, quick-pitching, and slide-stepping. When it comes to pickoffs, left-handers rely on deception while right-handers require quickness. What is consistent between both types of pitchers is the importance of throwing with the quick release of a catcher, not the full backswing and extension of a pitcher.

catcher signals by dropping his mitt, and you simply step toward third with your right foot and throw (or hold). You do not need to step back with the pivot foot first.

With runners on first and third, a pickoff play might be called in which a right-handed pitcher fakes toward third, spins, and throws or fakes to first. You must keep your knee lift on the imaginary line between the rubber and third base. If you cross over that line (toward second base) and do not deliver the ball to the plate, you will be called for a balk and the run will score. At lower levels, where double steals are often used with runners on first and third, this move can help you catch an overanxious base runner.

WORKING QUICKLY

"If a pitcher takes a lot of time, or if he throws a lot of pitches that are taken for balls, his infielders start to relax. Maybe they're playing back on their heels instead of on their toes. By working quickly, I think I make my fielders more alert."

—Hall of Famer Bob Gibson

You know what to do when the ball is hit to you, where to go when the ball is in the outfield, and how to keep base runners from running at will. Your final defensive responsibility is to work quickly. If you work quickly, you'll keep your teammates alert while putting opposing hitters on the defensive. In fact, *working quickly may be the single biggest thing you can do to contribute to your team's defense.*

Pitching coach and manager Ray Miller thinks enough of fast working that he includes it when boiling his philosophy of pitching down to only six words: "Throw strikes, change speeds, work fast." When you practice these principles, you will not just be keeping your defense on its toes and opposing hitters off balance, you'll be *intimidating* the other team. Working fast puts hitters back on their heels. And working fast *while throwing strikes* is very unsettling to hitters.

Before they know it, they're down 0–2 and you're back into your delivery.

You don't need to throw hard to do this. Working fast and throwing strikes while mixing up an average fastball with off-speed stuff may not get hitters ooohing and ahhhing in the dugout, but it will get them muttering to themselves as they walk back from the batter's box with an 0-for-4. There may be times when you want to be more deliberate—when facing a particularly aggressive and impatient hitter, for example—but for the most part, you're much better off working quickly.

If you have strikeout stuff, why hesitate with it? Bring it on. And if you don't have strikeout stuff, you really need your defense to be at its best. Get into the habit of working quickly and watch how much more crisply your defense plays—maybe even the guy on the mound, too!

> *"It's tempo. Get the ball, throw the ball. Everyone wants to hit. Fielders want to hit. Even pitchers want to hit. Work fast and everybody likes you except the beer vendors."*
>
> —Control artist, Bob Tewksbury

Kevin Brown works very quickly on the mound. Hitters often walk back to the dugout wondering what happened to their turn at the plate.

Throw It Again

Working quickly will keep your fielders alert and in the game. It may be the biggest contribution you can make to your team defense.

THE GOLDEN ERA OF PITCHING II: KOUFAX, GIBSON, AND THE NASTY SLIDER

By the time Herb Score pitched his last game in 1962, baseball was on the verge of its second golden era of pitching. Few might have expected it after a 1961 season in which the Yankees' Roger Maris and Mickey Mantle feasted on expansion-diluted pitching, combining for 115 of their team's 240 home runs—overshadowing the feats of Hall of Famer Harmon Killebrew (46 home runs), Rocky Colavito (45 home runs), and the career years of Jim Gentile (46 home runs, 141 rbi, and .302 batting average) and Norm Cash (41, 132, and .361, winning the batting title and never hitting .300 again). Completely obscured were the seasons put together by four relative unknowns: Sandy Koufax, a fireballer who finally started to throw strikes; Juan Marichal, a high-kicking 23-year-old in his first full season; Bob Gibson, a fiercely competitive 25-year-old, also in his first full season; and another Cleveland prodigy, Sam McDowell, an 18-year-old lefty who was a late-season call-up.

But the return of pitchers to prominence was not an overnight sensation. Throughout the 1950s, pitchers had begun to do what crafty Braves righty Lew Burdette called "exploiting the greed of all hitters." Home runs went up steadily during the decade, but so did strikeouts. Batting averages dropped in the AL, and so did walks and—most importantly—*runs* in both leagues.

EXPLOITING HITTERS' GREED

American League	Runs	Home Runs	Walks	Strikeouts	Batting Average	Slugging Average
1950	777	121	673	566	.271	.402
1961	697	146	560	791	.256	.395

National League	Runs	Home Runs	Walks	Strikeouts	Batting Average	Slugging Average
1950	718	137	565	624	.261	.401
1961	697	149	497	824	.262	.405

Average team, 154 games.

Control artists take note: in 1950, thanks to more walks and singles, American League teams scored more runs with fewer home runs than their National League counterparts. Teams like the champion Yankees of 1996 and 1998 continue to follow this formula today.

Now look at what pitchers learned during the 1950s. While hitters fixated on home runs, pitchers focused on throwing strikes. This led to more home runs—but it also led to fewer walks and fewer runs. With each team finally establishing the relief specialist that the Senators first introduced in the 1920s, starters no longer had to pace themselves. Hitters could no longer count on capitalizing on a tired starter in the late innings. Finally, thanks to the proliferation of a pitch called the slider—a hybrid of a fastball and a curve, and considered the hardest pitch to hit according to no less of an expert than Ted Williams—major league pitchers also had their best strikeout pitch since the spitball. No doubt, the slider also contributed to the increased home runs; a hanging slider is the most hittable pitch in the game outside of a telegraphed change-up.

Having finally learned how to counterpunch against home run hitters, the daily existence of pitchers was further improved when the strike zone was restored to "shoulders to knees" in 1963. This, along with the increased amount of night games, West Coast travel, larger stadiums replacing the older bandboxes, and teams' willingness to sign and use black pitchers—such as Bob Gibson, Mudcat Grant, Al Downing, Bob Veale, Ferguson Jenkins, and Don Wilson—all combined to usher in a six-year period of pitching dominance. With high fastballs going for called strikes, sliders getting batters swinging at balls low and away, and homer-happy batters trying to pull everything, strikeouts were up and walks were down. In 1968, Bob Gibson recorded an ERA of 1.12, Luis Tiant held opposing batters to an all-time-low batting average of .168, and Carl Yastrzemski led the AL in batting at .301.

3–2 BASEBALL RETURNS

American League	Runs	Home Runs	Walks	Strikeouts	Batting Average	Slugging Average
1962	719	155	568	855	.255	.394
1968	552	110	487	962	.230	.339

National League	Runs	Home Runs	Walks	Strikeouts	Batting Average	Slugging Average
1962	726	145	525	901	.261	.393
1968	556	89	426	947	.243	.341

Average team, 162 games.

The best pitching was seen in the National League, where Sandy Koufax finally gained control of his devastating fastball and curveball, reeling off four of the greatest seasons any pitcher has ever had before retiring at 30 due to chronic arthritis in his left elbow. He was being ably supported by teammate Don Drysdale, while Bob Gibson developed into an ace in St. Louis, Juan Marichal in San Francisco, and the overpowering Jim Maloney in Cincinnati. Meanwhile, Warren Spahn, at 42, used pinpoint control to go 23–7 for the Milwaukee Braves in 1963.

But fans prefer offense. With attendance down, the major leagues moved to shift the balance of power back to the hitters. With many pitchers being accused of restoring the spitball to the pitching repertoire, a rule was put in place in 1968 that forbade them from going to their mouth on the mound (though this did little to affect pitchers who loaded balls up with K-Y jelly). The strike zone was reduced again to "armpits to knee tops," and the mound was lowered from 15 inches to 10. At the same time, pitching was diluted by expanding from 10 teams to 12 in each league.

It's impossible to isolate the effects of each of these changes, but the combined impact was surprisingly short-lived. Offense spiked in 1970, then retreated. The effect was most dramatic, and most fleeting, in the American League. By 1972, runs had nearly returned to 1968 levels, while home runs had dropped even lower and the league batting average had slipped back into the .230s. Pitchers had responded to the challenges of a smaller strike zone by bringing their walks almost into line with 1968 levels, and by finding a way to get outs without strikeouts.

PITCHERS HANG TOUGH

American League	Runs	Home Runs	Walks	Strikeouts	Batting Average	Slugging Average
1968	552	110	487	962	.230	.339
1969	663	137	585	903	.246	.369
1970	675	145	567	912	.250	.379
1971	627	124	543	873	.247	.364
1972	562	102	501	887	.239	.343

National League	Runs	Home Runs	Walks	Strikeouts	Batting Average	Slugging Average
1968	556	89	426	947	.243	.341
1969	657	122	533	968	.250	.369
1970	732	140	577	952	.258	.392
1971	633	115	505	879	.252	.366
1972	633	118	521	918	.248	.365

Average team, 162 games.

With the situation for hitters in the AL far more dire than in the NL, the American League responded by instituting the designated hitter "experiment" in 1973. It worked, and the AL has been the hitters' league ever since.

Despite the less-than-favorable environment of the 1970s, a number of pitchers established some remarkable performances. In 1970, Tom Seaver struck out 19 men in a nine-inning game, including the last 10 he faced. In 1971, Vida Blue put together one of the greatest pitching seasons in history—limiting batters to a .189 batting average while going 24–8 with eight shutouts and a 1.82 ERA, earning him both the MVP *and* the Cy Young Awards. In 1972, Steve Carlton—perhaps the greatest slider pitcher the game has seen, and a winner of four Cy Young Awards—won 27 games for a team that won only 56 all season.

But no pitcher excelled in the 1970s quite like Nolan Ryan of the California Angels. As only Herb Score before him had been able to do, Ryan had such great stuff he could dominate without very good control. From 1972 to 1977, Ryan won 102 games with control that was never better than 4.5 walks per nine innings, and for two seasons was more than six walks per game. In the process, he threw four no-hitters and rewrote the strikeout record book, including a major league record 383 in 1973. Ryan once said that "it doesn't matter how many you walk, just so long as they don't score," but he is the exception that proves the rule. Any pitchers who think they can win without throwing strikes should ask themselves if they have a high-90s fastball, a high-80s change-up, and a drop-off-the-table curveball. If you can say yes to all three, you can try to be like Nolan.

> *"He was a workhorse on a team that couldn't hit or field. Some idiots called him a .500 pitcher. He was a .500 pitcher on a .350 team."*
>
>   —Whitey Herzog, former Angels coach, on Nolan Ryan

> *"From the first pitch Nolan threw, there was no question the batters would have no chance. That game, when he wanted to hit an inside corner, he hit an inside corner. When he wanted to throw letter-high, he threw letter-high. It was the most perfect pitching I've ever seen in my life."*
>
>   —Ron Luciano, home plate umpire for Nolan Ryan's second no-hitter in 1973

With Ryan's overpowering and sometimes unpredictable stuff, most nights it meant very deep counts. In 1974, he went 12 innings against the Boston Red Sox, struck out 19 hitters, and threw *235 pitches*! And that wasn't even his all-time high. He struck out 19 in nine innings two months later, then struck out another 19 in 11 innings eight days after that. Ryan might not have been able to consistently hit his spots, but he wasn't just chucking. His catcher, Jeff Torborg—who also caught Sandy Koufax—worked very hard with him on keeping the ball down and on the outer half of the plate. When he was doing that, and getting his curve over, a two-hitter or better was usually the result.

Keeping the ball down had always been a sound strategy, but it became even more so during the 1970s as the low strike started to get called more frequently. Challenging hitters up in the zone became a lost art, as the strike zone gradually shifted downward on its journey to its current, unofficial coordinates: "belt to shins."

> *"If we called strikes up around the letters, the hitters wouldn't hit."*
>
>   —Dick Stello, NL umpire

Cleveland Indians pitching staff running

7
Preparation and Conditioning

Preparing to pitch is a formidable undertaking. The game's elite pitchers understand this. Roger Clemens would run five miles after pitching a spring training game. Dennis Eckersley pitched into his 40s, working out six hours a day, seven days a week in the off-season. The night of Nolan Ryan's seventh no-hitter, the 44-year-old "celebrated" with his standard postgame workout on a stationary bike; he didn't leave the stadium until 2:30 and was back there at 9:00 A.M. for his three-hour workout.

Yes, pitching is a lot of work. But if you are willing to do the necessary preparation, your reward will come when your catcher hands you the ball after a complete game.

To reach your maximum potential, you must realize what the "necessary preparation" requires. It entails hours in the weight room increasing your strength and improving your flexibility. It requires running long distances to build up your endurance. It means pushing yourself during wind sprints to simulate the short bursts of energy required in pitching. And above all, it takes dedication and discipline to develop the physique and stamina of an exceptional pitcher.

DEVELOPING A CONDITIONING PLAN

Some coaches will argue that pitchers should simply focus on running as *the* method of physical conditioning for a pitcher. Some feel weight training will build overall body strength and increase power in the pitcher's motion and delivery. Others stand by flexibility training, fearing muscle mass will cause tightness and result in decreased velocity and risk of injury.

The consensus among major league pitchers, coaches, and trainers is that all of these methods of exercise are integral parts of a training regimen for pitchers. The key is incorporating an appropriate blend of each into your exercise program. Weight training does not simply mean finding a gym and pumping iron. It requires concentration on specific muscle regions to strengthen (and not hinder) your throwing motion. Flexibility training can help stave off injuries and allow you to maintain fluid mechanics, but this training method alone will not necessarily enhance your ability. Distance running will increase longevity, but you need to combine that with short sprints and interval training to heighten your explosiveness.

Throwing a baseball starts from the ground up. You need strong legs to maintain balance in your motion and generate body momentum, an important element of your delivery. A strong torso, lower back, and abdominal region equips you with the force to create powerful torque during your hip rotation. Flexible yet solid shoulders, arms, and chest muscles enable your upper body to create a flowing yet powerful whipping motion to propel the baseball at maximum speed. A golden arm may signal promise, but you need to condition your entire body to attain success.

"We correlate the pitcher's body to a bullwhip. It has a thick strong base, but as it comes up it gets narrower but remains strong. It culminates with a short, quick explosive whip right at the top. That's how we try to build our pitchers. Big strong legs, strong and flexible torso, loose and flexible yet strong upper body."

—Phil Falco, Atlanta Braves minor league strength and conditioning coordinator

This chapter will take you up to game day. It will discuss the preparatory work and conditioning you'll need to execute off the field in order to perform on the field. A mediocre pitcher should be able to get that first out of the game. But it takes months of dedication in advance to record the first *and* final outs of the game.

STRETCHING

You need to stretch muscles throughout your body. Like most forms of exercise, there is a right

The Atlanta Braves pitching staff stretch out prior to their spring training workout.

> ······ **Throw It Again**
> To reach your potential as a pitcher, it is critical that you be in excellent physical condition. This begins with your legs, which you must strengthen with distance running, sprints, and intervals (a combination of jogging and sprinting).

way and a wrong way to stretch. For a pitcher, your objective is to stretch a muscle until you first feel a slight discomfort and to hold that stretch for 5 to 10 seconds—not to bounce or pull your way past this point. As you do these exercises every day, you will find yourself gradually extending your "discomfort point," without running the risk of injuring yourself by pushing your muscles too far, too soon.

The following are some good stretching exercises. Your coach or trainer may want you to emphasize some of these over others, eliminate others, or have other exercises for you to do. Remember to hold your stretch for five 5 to 10 seconds, and do not try to "force the stretch."

Groin stretch

Legs. Sit with your legs outstretched in a V position and your toes pointing forward. Turn your upper body to your left, grab your left ankle or calf, and bend your head toward your left knee as far as you can. Do the same with your right knee. Then face forward and bend forward at the waist, bringing your head as close to the ground between your knees as you can.

Hamstring. Stand with your left foot crossed over and next to your right foot. Bend forward at the waist as far as you can and hold. Switch feet.

Groin. From the seated V position, bend your knees and bring the soles of your feet together. Pull your feet as close to your groin as you can. Lean forward and place your elbows on the sides of your knees. Exert some downward force with your elbows to feel the stretch in your groin. This is also known as the "butterfly" stretch.

Calf. Stand facing a wall about four feet away. Place both hands on the wall at shoulder height and lean forward. Bring one foot forward while

V-seat stretch

Calf stretch

keeping the other leg straight with the heel flat on the ground. Get as far back from the wall as you can while keeping your back leg straight and your back heel flat on the ground. You should really feel this in the Achilles tendon area of your rear leg. Switch legs.

Quadricep. Stand on your right leg. Bend your left leg up behind you and grab your left foot. Pull the foot toward you and feel the stretch in the front of your upper leg. Hold for 5 to 10 seconds. Then bend forward at the waist, pull your foot up as high as you can go, and hold. (In addition to being a good stretch, this will help your balance.) Switch legs.

> *"Before I do anything, I have an entire stretching routine devised by [Philadelphia Phillies trainer] Jeff Cooper that I go through. I don't touch a ball until I'm properly stretched."*
>
> —Curt Schilling

Hips. Stand on your right leg, grab your left knee with your left hand, then pull up and to the side so that both your thigh and calf are parallel to the ground. Hold your right arm out for balance. It's harder than it sounds, and it's also very good for your balance. If it's hard to maintain this position for several seconds, repeat. Switch legs.

Lower Back and Abdominal Muscles. Sit on the ground with your right leg straight, your left leg bent, and your left foot on the outside of your right knee. Place your right elbow inside of your left knee and turn your upper body as far as you can to the left. Use your left arm behind you for balance. Keep your back straight. Switch legs.

Lower Back and Side. Stand with your feet more than shoulder-width apart. Lift your arms straight above your head. Bend forward and try to touch the ground to the outside of your left foot with your right hand. Switch sides.

Neck. Stand straight. Turn your head as far to the left as you can and hold, then as far to the right as you can and hold. Bring your chin to your chest and hold. Bring your left ear down to your left shoulder and hold. Do not shrug your shoulders, let your neck do the work. Switch sides.

Quadricep stretch

Lower back and abdominal muscles stretch

Lower back and side stretch

Shoulder stretch (1)

Shoulder (2). While standing straight and facing ahead, hold your right arm at shoulder level and point across your body to your left. Put your left hand on your right elbow and pull your arm toward your body to stretch the muscles around your shoulder joint. Switch sides.

Upper Back and Shoulder. Hold your left arm down at your side and lift your right arm straight above your head. Bend your right arm so that your right hand is behind your head, palm down. Bend your left arm up so that your left hand is between your shoulder blades, palm up. Clasp hands. Pull up with your right and down with your left. Switch sides. If you can't make the clasp, hold a towel in your right hand and grab it with your left hand as close to your right hand as possible. Pull up with your right and down with your left. Work with the towel for a few weeks until you're able to clasp hands behind your back.

Shoulder (1). Lift your right arm straight up above your head and bend your elbow so that your right hand is behind your right shoulder. Put your left hand on the back of your upper right arm near the elbow and exert backward force to stretch the muscles around your shoulder joint. Switch sides.

Shoulder stretch (2)

Wrist and Forearm. Hold your right arm straight out in front of you with your hand palm down. Bend your wrist down and hold it with your opposite hand, keeping your arm straight. Bend your wrist up and hold. Switch sides.

This group of exercises should take 15 minutes—longer at first when you don't know the exercises. Only when you're done stretching are you ready to start throwing. Remember: Pulled muscles in your legs, back, and groin can shut you down, so take stretching *all* parts of your body very seriously. If you do suffer a serious muscle pull, don't try to be a hero and fight through it. Injuries to the rest of your body—and not just muscle pulls—have a way of eventually affecting your arm, because you end up changing your delivery to compensate for it.

The only time Nolan Ryan was shut down for an extended period of time with a sore arm was in 1975, when a groin pull messed up his delivery. He fared better than Dizzy Dean—the National League's last 30-game winner—who blew out his arm after breaking his toe. Dean changed his delivery because of the injury and was never the same again.

Wrist and forearm stretch

> ······ **Throw It Again**
> Prior to doing any throwing, you must perform a comprehensive stretching program that loosens up the muscles in your lower body and torso as well as your arm. *This is not optional.* Injuries to other parts of the body can affect your mechanics and put excessive strain on your arm.

CONDITIONING

"I believe the biggest key to any pitcher's success is to treat the ability to pitch as though it were a gift, to treat it with respect and reverence, and to make sure that when you go out there you've got 100 percent of your ability ready to go with you. Don't shortchange your body, because it is a gift."

—Hall of Famer Don Sutton

Getting in shape to be a pitcher involves exercising and conditioning nearly all of the muscles in the body, not just your arm. You need to build the necessary strength and stamina with running and supervised weight training.

RUNNING

"You take away a pitcher's legs, you take away his power."

—Roger Clemens, New York Yankees pitcher

It's been estimated that four out of five pitching injuries take place late in games and are a direct result of fatigue. When the legs get tired, the mechanics are thrown off, and more and more of the load is being carried by your arm. Like a house, your arm needs a strong foundation to withstand the forces that batter it over the course of a game. That foundation is your legs.

Former manager and pitching coach, George Bamberger has this to say about leg fatigue: "You can lose coordination, and that leads to loss of control and sore arms. . . . There's no way you can overdo the running and throwing that pitchers do in spring training. The more work you do, the more endurance you will build."

Baltimore Orioles former manager and long-time pitching coach Ray Miller echoes those sentiments: "For a pitcher to throw a baseball hard, he must drive with his legs. If he doesn't condition his legs by running, then late in a game when his legs start to weaken, he will start throwing high and put stress on his arm."

"Pitching starts from the ground up. What your feet and legs [your core] do affect what your arm does, which affects where your pitch goes and how fast."

—Bob Apodaca, former major league pitching coach

Distance work (three to six miles) will help you get into shape—as will biking—and should be an important part of your training program. Run with a teammate and you can pass the time by talking baseball. Run with your catcher and you can get his perspective on both pitching *and* hitting.

Distance running won't do much to help you with those quick bursts of power that you need in throwing a baseball. You will need to do some interval running as well, where you jog a quarter mile then sprint a quarter mile. You can do this when running "poles" (foul pole to foul pole) at the end of practice, or you can run "wind sprints" in the outfield. Wind sprints are a part of the daily routine for Houston Astros closer Billy Wagner. He focuses on running short distances because it correlates to his role on the mound. "Because I'm a short reliever, I do mostly sprints. I run a lot of 50-yard sprints and 30-yard sprints because they require quick and explosive movements. In my role, I'm not out there for endurance. I'm out there to go all out for one inning, so I work on conditioning myself for short bursts of energy."

"It may sound strange, but I really don't run at all. I wouldn't recommend that to kids, but I've had some problems with my knees and running really aggravates them. So to make sure I get my leg work and cardiovascular training in, I use the Stairmaster machine a lot and also ride the stationary bike."

—Curt Schilling

One method of conditioning is running from foul pole to foul pole along the outfield warning track.

Run sprints with a partner to help intensify your workout.

WEIGHTS

"Don't get bulky. Stay flexible."

—Dave Steib, former Blue Jays ace, on
weight training

Recommending a specific weight-training program is a delicate topic when dealing with young athletes. Every player has a distinct body type, physically develops and matures at different stages of life, and maintains a particular muscle structure. Add in the fact that pitchers must beware of building too much mass in certain muscle regions (such as the chest and biceps), and it becomes very difficult to suggest a general workout program.

This does not mean, however, that lifting weights should be ignored. A stronger body is a better body, and every pitcher can enhance his ability through weight training. Muscle strength can also help to avoid injuries. It protects you

---

PRINCIPLES OF WEIGHT TRAINING

Stay focused on what you're setting out to accomplish in the gym. The purpose of weight training is to develop and improve your body for *pitching*. This is only achieved when you build strength without sacrificing flexibility. According to Atlanta Braves minor league strength and conditioning coordinator Phil Falco, young pitchers often lose sight of their goals and fall victim to concerning themselves with what they look like in front of a mirror rather than on the mound.

Falco says this about young pitchers: "What young pitchers have to be careful of is building up muscle mass in the 'beach muscles': big chest, big biceps, big shoulders and upper back. Young pitchers often get caught up in that whole mentality. It's OK to work those areas, but simply to strengthen them without adding a whole lot of muscle mass. When you get too big in those muscle regions, your flexibility suffers, which can hinder your arm speed and in the end decrease the velocity on your fastball. When adding muscle mass, focus on the legs, lower back, and abdominal regions."

Here are some general principles you should know so you don't hinder your pitching development.

- *Use weights to build strength and flexibility, not muscle mass.* You're working out to get flexible, "whippy" muscles, not to look good on the beach. Think Mariano Rivera, not Mark McGwire.
- *Repetitions are more important than weight.* Depending on the program your coach or trainer prescribes for you, you may be working with weights of 10 pounds or less. You don't need to work with heavy weights to feel your arms getting a workout. Doing a lot of repetitions with low weights will build strength without bulking up your body.
- *Work your opposite arm as well as your throwing arm.* When your throwing arm is significantly stronger than your lead arm, your delivery will not be as efficient as it should be. A drill in which you throw on your knees from increasing distances will show you very quickly how important the front arm is. You need to do just as much work on your opposite arm and shoulder as you do on your throwing arm.
- *Work your legs and torso, not just your arms.* As you saw in Chapter 2, the power in your delivery comes from your legs and hips, which then must be transferred through your torso to your arm. If the leg and/or torso muscles aren't in shape, you won't generate as much energy and some of what you do generate will be lost before it reaches your arm. Proper weight training can help add efficiency to your delivery, while protecting all parts of your body from breaking down, not just your arm.

from slight tears in muscle tissue that can lead to tendon and ligament injuries. Suffering ligament and/or tendon damage can initiate more serious injuries such as stress fractures, bone chips, and even structural damage.

All of that said, you must educate yourself first and understand your personal limitations before lifting a single dumbbell. Meet with your baseball coach, a certified trainer, or a health and fitness instructor. Allow them to assess your body type, evaluate your strengths and weaknesses, and recommend a training program. Let your instructor know that you're a pitcher and alert them to when your season begins and ends.

Listed below are some basic weight-training exercises commonly used by pitchers. These exercises concentrate on strengthening muscle regions used in the pitching motion. They include the legs, gluteus maximus, lower back, torso, abdominal region, *latissimus dersi* (middle back) *pectoralis minor* (upper chest), and deltoids (front shoulder). Again, before doing *any* work with weights, consult your trainer, coach, or family physician for a specific set of exercises and the amount of weight appropriate to your development.

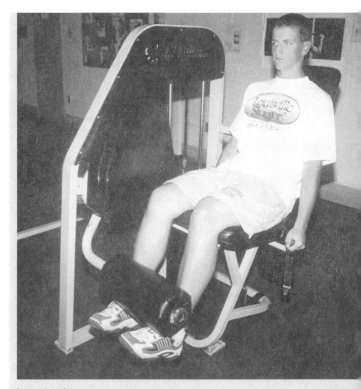
Leg extensions

LEGS

Leg extensions (works quadricep muscles). Seated on a leg-extension machine, hook the tops of your feet under the pads. Lock your ankles, but don't point your toes. Reach down by your waist and hold the bench or handles with your hands. Extend your legs up so your thighs are flexed and your toes are pointed toward the sky. Slowly lower the weight back down until you're just short of the starting position. This keeps the pressure on your legs throughout the exercise. Continue for 10 to 15 repetitions.

Leg curls (works hamstrings). Lying face down on your stomach, lock your heels under the pads of the machine. Point your toes to the ground. Contract your glutes and then curl your legs up as far as you can. The soles of your shoes should face the ceiling. (Note: If your hips rise you're using too

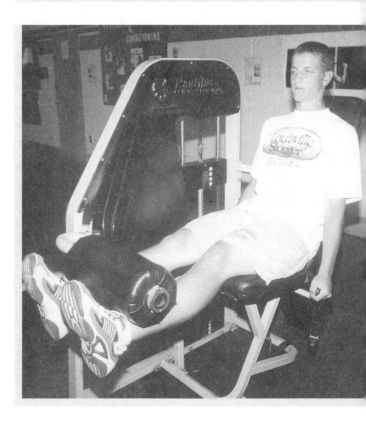

Leg curls

stride with your left leg approximately three to four feet in distance. As your stride lands, bend your lead knee and lower your rear knee almost to the floor. Push yourself back up to the starting position and repeat with your right leg.

Position your feet about shoulder-width apart. Bend your knees, keeping your back straight, and lower your body as if you were sitting down. You should feel pressure in your thigh muscles. Once your thighs are parallel to the ground, flatten your heels to the ground, contract your abdominal muscles, and push back up to the starting position. Continue for 10 to 15 repetitions.

Leg press (works quadriceps, hip flexors, and buttocks). Sit on a leg-press machine with the soles of your feet flat against the foot plate. Slowly lower the weight down until the top of your calves touch the bottom of your hamstrings. Slowly push back up and stop just before your knees lock. Continue for 10 to 15 repetitions.

much weight.) Isolate the hamstrings by keeping your hips and chest down on the bench. Lower the weight slowly just short of the starting position. Continue for 10 to 15 repetitions.

Lunges (works gluteus maximus). Holding either a barbell across the back of your shoulders or a dumbbell in each hand down by your sides, stand upright with your feet together. Take a forward

"We do a lot of leg work. We focus on exercises that develop explosive, powerful legs. We also concentrate on exercises for the lower abs, hip flexors, and lower-back stabilization exercises. We want to make sure the entire trunk area is strong."

—Phil Falco

Lunges

Leg press

ABDOMINAL MUSCLES

Bent-leg sit-ups. Lying on your back, bend your knees in and place the soles of your feet flat on the ground. Place your hands behind your head and curl up by bringing your rib cage up to your pelvis.

Bent-leg twisting sit-ups. Lie flat in the bent-leg sit-up position. As you curl up bringing your rib cage up to your pelvis, twist so your left elbow touches your right knee. Lower yourself back down and alternate by touching your right elbow to your left knee.

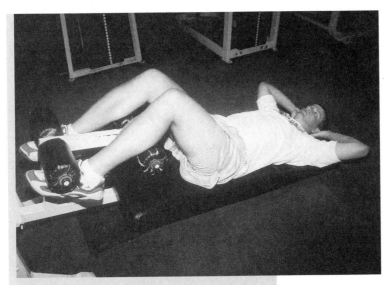

Bent-leg sit-ups

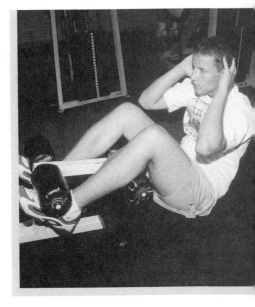

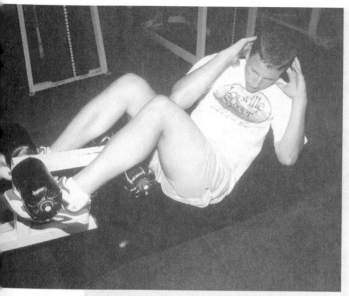
Pump sit-ups

Leg lifts. Lying flat on your back, extend your legs out in front of you with your heels touching the ground. Place your arms and hands down by your side, palms facing the ground. Lift both legs straight up and slowly lower them back down until they're about six inches off the ground. Repeat 15 to 20 times and relax.

UPPER BODY

Bench press (works pectoral muscles). Lie flat on a weight bench with your feet flat on the ground. Grip the bar so your middle knuckles are pointed up to the ceiling. Each hand should be approximately three to four inches outside your shoulder. Lift the bar off the rack and hold it over your chest. Slowly lower the bar until it touches your upper chest. Keep your elbows under the bar. (Do not bring them forward.) Press the bar back up until your arms almost lock. Continue for 10 to 15 repetitions.

Pump sit-up. Lie flat in the bent-leg sit-up position. Lift your head up so your chin touches your chest. Bring your right knee back and your left elbow forward until they touch. As they return to their starting position, bring your left knee back and your right elbow forward. Alternate touching opposite elbow to opposite knee at a quick pace.

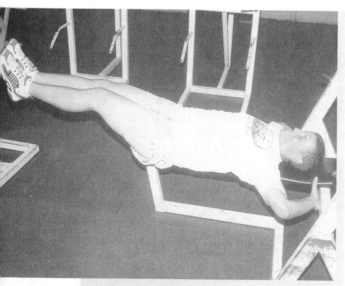
Leg lifts

Bench press

Lat pull-downs (works upper back). Seated on a pull-down machine, grasp the bar with a wide grip. Tilt your head forward slightly and pull the bar down behind your head until it touches your neck. Allow the bar to slowly raise back up to the starting position and repeat 10 to 15 times.

Lat pull-downs

V-seat pull-ins (works lower back). Seated on the floor, extend your legs out in front of you and place the soles of your feet up against the foot plates on the pull-down machine. Lean forward with your upper body to grab the handle grips with both hands. Return to the seated position and allow your knees to flex slightly. Pull the grips in to your midsection and stick your chest out as your arms come in. Slowly allow the weight to return to the starting position and repeat 10 to 15 times.

Bicep curls (works biceps). Seated on the edge of a bench, hold a dumbbell in each hand. Rotate your wrists outward so your palms face forward. While keeping a stable posture, slowly curl the dumbbell up near your collarbone. Lower the dumbbell back down and repeat the movement with your opposite arm. Repeat this 10 to 15 times with each arm.

V-seat pull-ins

Bicep curls

Tricep pull-downs (works triceps). Standing at a pull-down machine, grasp the bar with both hands a bit narrower than shoulder-width apart. Use a forward grip so the backs of your hands face you. Pull straight down on the bar until your arms almost lock. Slowly allow the bar to raise back up to the starting position and continue for 10 to 15 repetitions.

LIGHT DUMBBELL EXERCISES

Side shoulder raise. Stand erect with your arms hanging down by your sides. Holding a light dumbbell in each hand, raise your arms out to shoulder level until they are parallel to the ground. When the dumbbells are at shoulder height, your palms should face the ground.

Tricep pull-downs

Side shoulder raise

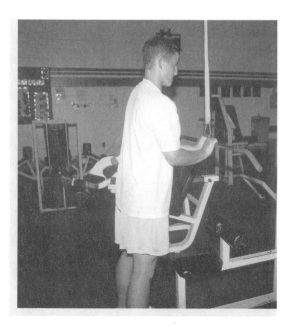

Turned-in shoulder raise. Stand erect with your arms hanging down by your sides. Grip a light dumbbell in each hand and turn your wrists inward so the backs of your hands face forward. Raise your arms out to shoulder level until they are parallel to the ground. The position of the dumbbells should look as if you are emptying a can of soda.

External shoulder rotation. Lie on a flat bench on your left side. Grip a light dumbbell in your right hand. With your right elbow pressed against your right hip, hold your arm perpendicular to the ground so your knuckles point to the ceiling. Lower your arm to the left (in toward your body) until it's parallel to the ground. Slowly raise it back up to the starting point. Repeat this 15 times and then alternate to your left hand.

Turned-in shoulder raise

External shoulder rotation

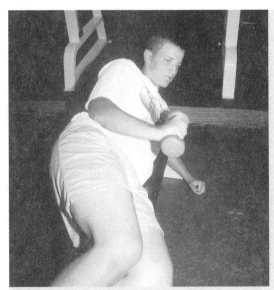

Internal shoulder rotation. Lie on your back on a flat bench. Holding a light dumbbell in your right hand, start with your right arm held off the bench and parallel to the floor. Raise the dumbbell up and inward until it's perpendicular to the floor. Repeat this 15 times and then alternate to your left hand.

Front wrist curl. Gripping a light dumbbell, hold your right wrist over a flat bench with your palm facing the ceiling. Without moving your arm, curl the dumbbell up from below to above bench level.

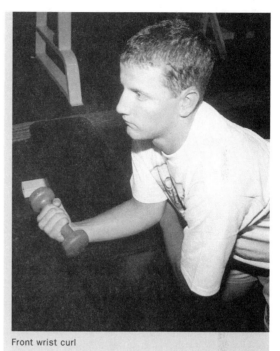

Front wrist curl

Internal shoulder rotation

······ **Throw It Again**

There is a place for weight training in a pitcher's conditioning program, with attention paid to all parts of the body and not just the throwing arm. You need to concentrate on flexibility, not muscle mass, by doing more repetitions with smaller weights. You should be certain to consult with your trainer, coach, or physician before doing any work with weights, so that a program can be established that is appropriate for your age and development.

THROWING

> *"Weights without throwing won't do you any good."*
>
> —Leo Mazzone, Atlanta Braves
> pitching coach

Weight training is no substitute for throwing. The best way to build arm strength is to throw—with the proper mechanics, of course. Don't look for your fastball in the weight room, because you won't find it there. Weight training will keep your arm healthy by building flexibility, but don't expect it to turn you into Kerry Wood.

Throwing doesn't always mean pitching full-strength from 60 feet, 6 inches. Later in this chapter, you will find a number of different throwing exercises along with a description of what they will help you accomplish.

BUILDING ARM STRENGTH

> *"Basically, I always say there's two things that a young boy playing high school ball should do. He should extend his arm every day and his legs every day. If you don't extend your arm every day, it's not going to get stronger."*
>
> —Whitey Herzog, former major
> league manager

There are three basic types of throwing work that you will do, and each has a different purpose. Regardless of the type of throwing you do, *always throw like a pitcher.* Even when you're just playing catch, throw with the lift, stride, and pull of your pitching motion. Your motion will be much slower, of course, but you must use all of your muscles the same way that you do when you're on the mound. Do this every time you throw a ball, and it will begin to feel unnatural to do it any other way.

Soft Tossing

Just because you've stretched doesn't mean that you can immediately take the mound and air it out. You need to get loose before you do any long tossing or mound work. Play catch with a teammate, starting out at a shorter distance and gradually working your way back to 60 feet.

Use 10 or 15 minutes of soft tossing to work out any mechanical issues you might be having. You're loosening up, but you're also conducting a slow-motion analysis of your pitching delivery. Sometimes it's hard for a pitcher to see whether he's doing something properly, so ask the person you're playing catch with about *specific* aspects of your delivery (e.g., "When I lift my leg, is my foot inside or outside of my knee?"). Don't just ask, "How do I look?"

You may use soft tossing as warm-up for long toss or a bullpen, or just to keep your arm loose.

As part of your warm-up routine, play catch with a teammate from a short distance and gradually stretch it to 60 feet.

Long Tossing

"Pitchers should run and use their legs every day, but they also have to keep their arm in shape on the days they're not scheduled to pitch. The day after one of our starters pitches, he plays long toss. It helps strengthen those muscles and keeps them stretched out. If you don't throw between starts, those muscles will shrink up. The bottom line is, if you don't throw, you won't build arm strength."

—Mel Queen, Blue Jays pitching coach

After developing proper mechanics, long tossing may be the best thing you can do to add miles per hour to your fastball. At the little league level, you should be maxing out at 120 feet. At the high school level, you should throw up to 180 feet. Proceed from your warm-up distance to your long-toss distance gradually—10 feet every five throws.

As with your warm-up tosses, it is very important that you throw with your pitching motion. Throw hard, though not at full strength. To build strength, you need to throw until your arm is tired and then push yourself for a few more tosses. This should help you recognize the difference between fatigue and pain. You can get a few more throws out of a fatigued arm. If you're in pain, you need to shut it down immediately.

If you do long tossing every day, you run the risk of injury. Starting pitchers should long toss twice between starts during the season, and every other day during the off-season. Relief pitchers need to do the off-season work, but are usually getting in enough throwing on a daily basis that they shouldn't be overloading their arms during the season.

Maintain proper mechanics when long tossing. Do not dip your back shoulder in an attempt to throw the ball longer, and don't fly open with your front side. Stay smooth and fluid. This drill is performed to strengthen and stretch your arm out. It's not a distance contest.

Bullpen

When you pitch from the mound during the off-season, preseason, or in between starts, it's called "throwing a bullpen." Rather than simply play catch, you should be trying to make the conditions as realistic as possible. The catcher should call pitches and establish game situations. Half of your throws should come from the stretch. And whenever possible, a batter should stand in. This is a great time to work on your concentration. Try to get so into this drill that you can forget it's not a real game.

There will be times when you don't have a mound to throw off of to do your bullpen work. Don't panic. Throwing a bullpen off flat ground actually simplifies your throwing motion and can be useful if you're struggling with your mechanics. It's easier to control your body and stay balanced. It also can force you to exaggerate throwing on a downward plane. Throwing a bullpen off the mound has more of a gamelike feel, but flat-ground work has its benefits as well.

When you finish throwing, towel off, stretch, put on your jacket, and run. Do not ice your arm. You should only ice your arm if you've thrown more than 75 pitches at full speed. You treat injuries with ice—such as those caused by throwing 75 pitches at full speed. You treat fatigue with warm-downs, which is why you need to have your jacket close at hand.

Long tossing is a terrific exercise for building arm strength.

SO WHY DO THEY CALL THEM OFF DAYS?

Many have looked to Nolan Ryan's conditioning program for the source of his amazing longevity. No program will guarantee a long, successful, injury-free career. If nothing else, though, Ryan's regimen shows just how hard pitchers could and should be working on their so-called "off" days.

The day after he pitched, Ryan would lift weights for an hour, do 20 wind sprints, spend 25 minutes on the stationary bike, work his arms and shoulders with dumbbells, and finish up with sit-ups. On Day 2, there would be no weights or sit-ups, but everything else would remain the same and he would spend 15 minutes throwing on the mound to loosen up. He would repeat his Day 1 routine on Day 3. The day before he was to pitch, he would focus on stretching and loosening up. On the rare times when an injury to his back or legs kept him from running, he would tread water in a pool instead. Swimming was also a big part of his off-season workouts.

Ryan was ahead of his time when it came to weight training. In the early 1970s, weights of any kind were forbidden for pitchers. He's shown that working with weights properly can help rather than hurt a pitcher's durability and performance.

"Throw as often as possible without overexerting. Make the ball do something without going to max effort. Don't just throw once a day. Throwing a lot will help you build up arm strength and increase velocity better than any weight you could lift."

—Leo Mazzone, Atlanta Braves
pitching coach

CONDITIONING AND THROWING PROGRAMS

"People who write about spring training not being necessary have never tried to throw a baseball."

—Sandy Koufax, Hall of Fame pitcher

Your physical needs will differ depending on whether you are working to build strength (off-season), get into pitching shape (preseason), or maintain your strength and pitching shape (in-season). Everyone is different, so there is no one *right* program. Use the following as a guideline, then modify it as you get to know your body better. Note: high reps equals 15 times; low reps equals 6 times.

OFF-SEASON (BUILDING STRENGTH)

You should work out at least three times a week in the off-season, with an off day in between. Here's a schedule for your off-season conditioning program for a high school pitcher:

1. Stretching every day.
2. Distance running (three to six miles) three days per week.
3. Weight training: two days per week heavy weights (low reps), one day light-weight circuits (high reps). Have your coach, trainer, or medical expert recommend an appropriate regimen for your age and development.
4. Flat-ground long toss (every other day).

For advanced pitchers, the off-season workout schedule should be more intense. Here's a sample schedule for the advanced-level pitcher.

1. Stretching every day.
2. Distance running (three to six miles) five days per week. Sprint work three days per week.
3. Weight training: three days per week heavy weights (low reps), two days light-weight circuits (high reps). Have an

expert recommend an appropriate regimen for your age and development.

4. Flat-ground long toss (two days per week). Form throwing drills (one day).

PRESEASON (GETTING INTO PITCHING SHAPE)

Starting on February 1, you should begin to work out at least five times per week if not every day to get ready for the season. Increase your sprint work and begin to throw from the mound. Your weight training should continue, but incorporate lower weights and higher repetitions with your upper body.

High School Pitchers

1. Stretching every day.
2. Distance running or intervals/wind sprints (alternate days).
3. Weight training: three days per week light weights, high repetitions. Have your coach, trainer, or medical expert recommend an appropriate regimen for your age and development.
4. Work with your coach to establish a throwing schedule that incorporates both long toss and throwing from a mound. Do not long toss on consecutive days.

Advanced Pitchers

1. Stretching every day.
2. Distance running four days per week, sprint work and explosion training five days.
3. Weight training: Monday and Wednesday upper-body mainenance, Tuesday and Friday lower-body maintenance.
4. Long toss two days per week, form throwing drills two days, mound work two days.
5. Pitcher's Fielding Practice (PFP) drills: 30 minutes twice per week. Work on fielding balls off the mound, covering bases, bunt plays, and pickoff moves.

Under the watchful eye of pitching coach Leo Mazzone, many of the Atlanta Braves' starting pitchers throw twice off the mound between starts.

"We do a lot of stop-and-go type drills with the pitchers. If you think about it, during the game pitchers explode for two seconds and then relax. If they give up a hit, they have to sprint to back up a base. If they have to cover first, they have to sprint to the bag. Everything they do requires a short burst of energy."

—Phil Falco

IN SEASON (MAINTENANCE)

During the season, you want to get into a routine that enables you to prepare consistently from one start to the next week. Depending on your team and level of play, you will pitch every fifth day or every sixth day. Below are four routines; two for a pitcher who throws every fifth day, and two for every sixth day.

Pitching Every Fifth Day—Routine 1

Game Day: Stretching, light jog, a few sprints, warm-up throwing from a mound, game.

Day 1: Stretching, jogging, intervals/wind sprints, very light weights.

Day 2: Stretching, distance running, bullpen.

Day 3: Stretching, intervals/wind sprints, long tossing, weight training.

Day 4: Extended stretching, soft tossing.

Routine 2

Game Day: Stretching, light jog, a few sprints, warm-up throwing from a mound, game.

Day 1: Stretching, jogging, five minutes of tossing, light weights.

Day 2: Stretching, wind sprints, long toss.

Day 3: Stretching, jogging, bullpen, light weights.

Day 4: Extended stretching, soft toss.

Pitching Every Sixth Day—Routine 1

Game Day: Stretching, light jog, a few sprints, warm-up throwing from a mound, game.

Day 1: Stretching, jogging, weight training.

Day 2: Stretching, wind sprints, bullpen.

Day 3: Stretching, distance running, light weights, long toss.

Day 4: Stretching, wind sprints, bullpen.

Day 5: Extended stretching, light jog, soft toss.

Routine 2

Game Day: Stretching, light jog, a few sprints, warm-up throwing from a mound, game.

Day 1: Stretching, distance running, soft toss.

Day 2: Stretching, jogging, long toss, weight training.

Day 3: Stretching, wind sprints, bullpen.

Day 4: Stretching, distance running, long toss, light weights.

Day 5: Extended stretching, light jog, soft toss.

When the prevailing wisdom in baseball was for starters to throw from a mound no more than once between starts, the Atlanta Braves of the 1990s had their pitchers throw twice. They threw 50- to 60-pitch "bullpens," with their emphasis on location and changing speeds. Other pitchers do less mound work than the Braves staff but throw every day—even if it's just soft tossing. There is no right or wrong way to do things, but don't think that throwing a baseball makes an injury inevitable. If your mechanics are good and you do the proper preventive work—stretching, toweling off, keeping warm, icing after extended full-strength pitching—you won't hurt yourself by throwing. But if your mechanics are bad, even babying your arm won't keep you from breaking down eventually.

"Resting between starts helped me. Over the length of a season, once you get in shape, you're not going to get out of shape. I only threw between starts when I had something specific to work on. If I struggled and had a short outing, I'd find something to work on and go throw. Mostly I'd just go play catch in the outfield. I'm a firm believer in long toss, and I also believe in weight training, too."

—Hall of Famer Don Sutton

"You have to try things. Go ahead and throw once or twice between starts, then see how you feel when it's your turn to pitch again. You need to find out what works best for your body. There's a lot of ways to pitch. Don't be afraid to try some different things. Don't think you're going to get hurt just by throwing between starts. You're young. You have to find out what works best for you."

—Greg Maddux, Atlanta Braves

There are famous examples of pitchers who had their own way of doing things. Steve Carlton built strength with martial arts training, which included pushing his arm down into a large bucket of uncooked rice—sounds easy until you try it. Nolan Ryan ran with heavy leg weights on his feet. Ferguson Jenkins swung a sledgehammer. Other pitchers have used javelins and shot puts. You need to start with the standard base of knowledge presented in this chapter and build

Distance running is certainly no cure for boredom, so pair up with a friend or teammate to pass the time.

upon it as you get to know your body better. How you choose to exercise will become a very personalized process.

WHAT ABOUT RELIEF PITCHERS?

During the season, relief pitchers don't have the luxury of a fixed schedule. They need to throw enough to stay loose, but not so much that they've got nothing left should they be needed in that day's game. If you're placed in this role, it will take some experimentation for you to figure out what works best for you.

Mark Leiter made the transition from starter to reliever very effectively in 1998. Having done both, here's his advice on how to prepare your arm for daily use.

I did a lot of long toss and throwing on the side between games as a starter. As a reliever I just throw 15 balls against the wall. After a few days without getting in the game, then I might get in the outfield to play catch and make up for it. But if I'm getting into a lot of games, I don't see why I should be going out before a game to play long toss and fatigue my arm when I might be pitching in three hours. I keep it nice and easy, just enough to keep my muscles loose. Around the

sixth inning I might go into the tunnel to play catch for literally a minute just to know I can get loose when the time comes.

It's difficult to set rules in stone when it comes to conditioning the body because of the diversity in many factors such as age, body type, size, strength, and delivery. As Greg Maddux stated earlier, you have to experiment a little to find out what routines work best for you. But if there are three absolutes you can take from this chapter, they are as follows:

1. *Pitchers must maintain flexibility to maximize their effectiveness on the mound.*
2. *Strength and endurance will improve your ability and longevity on the mound.*
3. *The only way to build up arm strength is to throw the baseball.*

Darren Dreifort

8 GAME DAY

You've done the stretching, the running, the weight training, and the throwing. Now it's game day. How you prepare for the game can have as much effect on your performance as anything you do *during* the game. This is more than simply making certain that you have your uniform, hat, spikes, glove, jacket, towel, water, and change of undershirt—though that checklist is very important. Here is a step-by-step process for getting physically and mentally ready to start a game.

PREGAME

SCOUTING THE OPPOSITION

Depending on your level of competition, you may have spent yesterday's game charting the pitches. This will have given you an opportunity to have observed the tendencies of the hitters you'll be facing. At lower levels, where scouting reports are limited—and where you weren't charting the pitches the day before because you were playing right field—your game plan will be more specific to your strengths rather than the weaknesses of the opposing lineup.

Think about your game plan the night before you start. It may be very similar from game to game—fastballs on the inner and outer half, down in the strike zone, mixing in the occasional change-up against the hitters with quick bats—but there should always be some learning you can incorporate from your last outing. The important thing is that you take the mound with some idea of what you're trying to accomplish. Don't go into a game chucking and ducking.

> *"Everybody talks about Schilling's arm and great control, but nobody prepares for a start like he does. He studies the opposition's hitters like he's preparing for a test. He knows their strengths, weaknesses, the type of success they've had against him, and whether they're currently on a hot streak or slumping. He even knows who is going to be umpiring behind the plate and what his tendencies are. When I give the ball to Schill, I know I'm giving it to someone who is giving our team its best chance to win."*
>
> —Terry Francona, Philadelphia
> Phillies manager

Kevin Brown may be a great guy off the field, but between the white lines, he's a hitter's worst nightmare.

VISUALIZATION

To get mentally prepared for the task at hand, many pitchers go off by themselves in the locker room and practice "visualization"—going through the opposing lineup in their head, imagining themselves delivering their best pitches and seeing strikeouts, pop-ups, and groundouts result. This is not fantasizing about throwing 120 miles per hour, but anticipating or rehearsing how you actually will approach these hitters and seeing yourself executing at your best. If you don't have a locker room, think about this wherever you get dressed for the game. You can also do this the night before your start, since it's a good way to formulate your game plan.

> *"Images of future action pass in and out of awareness without our willing them—sometimes showing us performing to perfection, sometimes anticipating defeat. Our imagination can be either helpful or discouraging when it begins to anticipate a course of action. It is a force that can encourage or defeat us. . . . Research has shown that by picturing the successful completion of moves they want to make, athletes can improve their performance, especially if the mental picture is accompanied by physical practice."*
>
> —Michael Murphy and Rhea White, *In the
> Zone: Transcendent Experience in Sports*

THE GAME FACE

Wherever you get dressed for the game, take some time to get emotionally prepared. This is called getting your "game face" on, because many pitchers will change visibly before a game. Talkative ones may get quiet, funny ones may get serious, and friendly ones may get downright mean. After all, most athletes don't compete at their best when talkative, funny, or friendly. Still others get so fired up that they can't execute or they burn themselves out halfway through the game. Find yourself a place somewhere in between. Treat your performance as serious business, take base hits gotten off you personally, and do your best to help your team win.

> *"I never saw a guy more psyched up—or more mad—in my life than [Don] Wilson was that night. He pitched like he had a personal grudge with every member of the Cincinnati team. He wouldn't talk to anybody on the bench. The guys were afraid to go near him. They left him alone."*
>
> —Harry Walker, Astros manager, on Don Wilson the night he threw a no-hitter against the Cincinnati Reds. Wilson had been pummeled by the Reds in his previous start in a game in which he felt the Big Red Machine had been trying to embarrass the Astros.

FIELD CONDITIONS

On your way to the field, notice the weather, the condition of the mound and infield, and the dimensions of the park. Note the dead-ball areas, as you will need to guard these when backing up the bases (if you're not certain where they are, ask your coach to find out from the umpires). All of this will have an impact on how long it will take you to warm up and whether there are any changes you want to make to your game plan. For example:

- If it's a cold day, be especially certain that you have stretched sufficiently. You'll need to take it easy in the bullpen at first, and you may need to throw more pitches to be certain that you're sufficiently warm.
- If it's a hot or humid day, look for some shade to rest in before the game and between innings. Drink plenty of liquids and have some wet towels with you to keep cool.
- Pay special attention to the wind conditions. If it's blowing out, you've got to concentrate on keeping the ball down in the strike zone. If it's blowing to left field or right field, try not to give hitters anything to pull. If the wind is blowing in, you can get away with more

pitches up in the strike zone. Also, the wind can affect your pitches. With the wind blowing at your back, you'll have a little more zip on your fastball but less break on your breaking pitches. Throwing into the wind may slightly reduce the velocity of your fastball, but you'll notice increased movement on all of your pitches.

- If the park has very short outfield dimensions, don't let this intimidate you. Hitters will be thinking home runs, and you can use this to your advantage. If there is a short porch in left, keep the ball away to righties and in to lefties. If the park is short all the way around, keep the ball down in the strike zone, throw pitches with a downward break, and change speeds; they will be on top of the ball all day. This may not be the day to challenge hitters up in the strike zone with your fastball. In small parks, don't think you have to throw perfect pitch after perfect pitch, otherwise you'll start issuing walks and falling behind in the count with runners on base.

Batting practice is a great opportunity to observe how and where the ball is carrying. You can also get a more accurate gauge in calculating the park's dimensions. In addition to watching ball flight, take notice of the opposing team's hitters. Recognize pitch locations they hit with authority and locations they tend to struggle handling. Examine their bat speed and length of their swing. They may show a weakness that you can exploit later in the game.

······· Throw It Again

Getting prepared for "game day" is just as much an emotional and mental exercise as a physical one. You need to think about your opposition and how you will approach them. You need to get yourself into an emotional state of controlled aggression. You need to factor field and weather conditions into your game plan. *Then* you go to the bullpen mound to warm up.

WARMING UP

Warming up means more than just heading down to the bullpen. You should establish a specific program and stick with it. This will help you get both physically and mentally prepared to pitch. Here is a routine to follow. Use it and adjust it to your particular needs.

1. Jog the perimeter of the field. Take the time to notice the field conditions, foul territory (or lack thereof), and any other peculiarities of the park.
2. Go through your stretching regimen.
3. Run three or four sprints to get your blood pumping.
4. Head to the bullpen with your jacket and towel.
5. Soft toss with your catcher from about 40 feet for 15 to 20 throws.
6. At 75 percent speed, throw fastballs from the mound, half from the windup, half from the stretch. Throw three to each of the four corners (down/away, down/in, up/in, up/away). Throw 10 more with the catcher moving the target on each pitch.
7. Throw change-ups to the lower half of the zone, alternating inside and outside—half from the windup, half from the stretch.
8. At 75 percent effort, throw breaking balls to the lower half of the zone, alternating inside and outside—half from the windup, half from the stretch.
9. Finish with 15 pitches in a simulated inning, mixing in all three pitches. Throw the final eight at full speed/effort.
10. Towel off, put on your jacket, and head to the dugout.

Watching pregame batting practice can provide you with valuable information. Unfortunately, watching Mike Piazza take BP may provide you with an impending sense of doom.

"I don't have any set formula before a start, because every day I feel different. The weather conditions are a factor as well as the time of day the game starts. Usually I'll run a few sprints to get my legs loose, and then I stretch out real good. I'll play a soft game of catch for 5 or 10 minutes and then get on the mound and throw until I think I'm ready. Once I'm loose and hitting the spots I want to hit, then I take the mound."

—Darren Dreifort, Los Angeles Dodgers

The order of the pitches thrown during your warm-up is important. Just as you want to establish your fastball in the game, you need to do so in the bullpen as well. The number of pitches thrown in the bullpen will vary from pitcher to pitcher. Try throwing 60 pitches—which should take about 12 minutes—and add or subtract as necessary. When warming up between innings, mix up your pitches and only throw the final one or two at full speed/effort.

"Pitchers should concentrate more on locating pitches during their bullpens. First of all, I throw 99 percent fastballs in the bullpen because from John Tudor to Bob Feller, no

one has ever had success without command of their fastball in the big leagues. Knuckleball pitchers may be an exception, but even they have to go to their fastball when they fall behind in the count."

—Curt Schilling

If you're a relief pitcher, you may not have as much time to warm up, so you need to anticipate "the call." Try to stretch during the game and remain loose as it goes on. Keep your glove and a ball close by at all times. Even though you need to get ready in a hurry, this does not mean that you should throw at full speed from the bullpen mound with your first pitch. Throw about a dozen pitches at half speed before going to three-quarters and full. Unlike starting pitchers, you'll need to establish control of your breaking balls sooner in your warm-up and do more throwing from the stretch position.

"Early in my career, if I wasn't throwing a particular pitch very well in the bullpen, I would allow it to affect my frame of mind when I entered the game. Through the years, I've learned that what I warm up with isn't necessarily what I'm going to take out with me for the game. You have to trust your stuff will be fine once you get out there."

—Dan Plesac, Arizona
Diamondbacks reliever

GAME TIME

The first thing you should do when you take the mound is find your spot on the rubber and take a few trial throws and foot plants. Make sure your plant foot comes down comfortably, that is, it doesn't alter your delivery. If necessary, dig out or fill up the hole where your plant foot or stride foot strikes the ground. If it's an opposing team's home field, make certain that you feel comfortable with the mound by the time you've completed your eight warm-up tosses. Stop between tosses and do some more dirt rearranging if you need to. If

Establishing a pregame bullpen routine is a personal matter. A knuckleballer like Tim Wakefield may have a significantly different routine than a power pitcher like Bartolo Colon.

the mound is in especially bad shape, summon your manager and tell him.

In the dugout and on the bases, you will need to keep your arm and back warm. Wear your jacket unless it's an extremely warm day. If it's a cool day, you may need to change your undershirt between innings. And if you're not pitching as well as you'd like, you need to relax and try to figure out whether you're not executing or the other team is just doing some good hitting. If you're not executing, ask yourself why. Think about how you might alter your game plan. Talk to your catcher or coach—someone you trust. Don't ask everyone or you'll simply inundate yourself with questionable advice.

KEY OUTS

"Only three or four outs directly affect the outcome of any given game."

—Hall of Famer Tom Seaver

When you're on the mound, you need to be constantly aware of the game situation. One of those three or four key outs that Tom Seaver refers to could come in the first inning or the fifteenth. The key outs depend on the score, the base runners, the batter, the on-deck batter, the number of outs—just about anything. Recognizing them is the first step in getting them, and getting them often saves not just one but several runs.

Test yourself—during games in which you pitch, but also in games that you watch—and check the scorecard later to see how good you are at identifying when you think one of these key at bats is taking place. To do so, try to imagine how much differently an inning will proceed should a certain batter be retired—an at bat that will probably turn on one single pitch. If you know a key situation is happening, you've got a better chance of getting the out because you will be concentrating harder.

Think back on some games you've pitched and how you went about getting a key out. Ask yourself why you succeeded or what you could have done better—whether you made mistakes and got away with them, or whether you made a good pitch and got beat. Always check to see the results of hitters you walked. You'll be surprised to see how many of those runners come around to score. The more you reflect, the more you will learn. If you think about what happened and *why*, you will always take the mound a smarter pitcher than you were the time before.

> *"In critical situations, I want our pitcher to go with his best pitch. Why would you want to get beat with your second-best pitch?"*
>
> —Davey Johnson, Los Angeles Dodgers manager

IN-GAME ADJUSTMENTS

There is no reason why you can't be your own pitching coach when you're out on the mound. It's very important to be able to make the necessary mechanical adjustments immediately—it will save you from some long innings and keep your catcher

or coach from wearing out a path to the mound. Here are some things to look for when your fastball, change-up, and breaking ball aren't working. By now, this advice should be familiar; refer to Chapter 2 for a more detailed discussion of mechanics.

Fastball

- *Wild high.* You could be rushing; keep your weight back. If you're landing on the heel of your stride foot, shorten your stride. You may be dropping your elbow; get it above your shoulder.
- *Wild low.* You could be understriding; try lengthening your stride. You could be shortening your arm path; drop your arm down and out when it breaks from your glove to create a greater arm swing.
- *Wild inside (to same-hand hitters).* You may be landing too closed and not opening your hips. Land slightly closed with your stride foot at one o'clock and drive through with your front shoulder and hips. You also may be opening your front shoulder too soon. Drive your front shoulder at the target.

Pitchers often dip or drop their back shoulder in an effort to put something extra on their pitches. Not only will you lose velocity by doing this, but your pitches will be wild high.

- *Wild outside (to same-hand hitters).* You may be landing on a stiff front leg and/or falling off to the side in your follow-through. Outside (and inside) wildness can also be caused by an imbalance in your grip. Be certain that you center your fingers on the ball.
- *Lack of velocity.* You may be choking the ball too deeply in your hand or gripping it too tightly. Other things to look for: rushing, not getting good hip and shoulder rotation, having too much give in your front leg, not finishing your pitches or following through, aiming the pitch instead of throwing it to the target.

Change-up
- *Wild high.* You could be dropping your elbow and/or slowing down your arm. Keep your elbow above your shoulder and throw with your normal fastball path and arm speed.
- *Wild low.* It's likely you're trying to guide the ball down in the strike zone and holding onto the ball too long. The grip will reduce the velocity of the pitch and your natural mechanics will take care of the location.
- *Wild inside (to same-hand hitters).* You may not be getting your hips into your delivery. Remember: Think fastball, let the grip take the velocity off. You could also be wild inside if your arm is too wide; stay on your fastball path and keep your fingers on top of the ball.
- *Too much velocity.* Chances are that you're gripping the ball too loosely. A firm grip will decrease the velocity. Keep in mind that sometimes what appears to you to be too much velocity on your change-up is actually a perfect pitch. You don't want there to be so much difference between your fastball and change-up that the batter has time to adjust.

Curveball or Slider
- *Wild high.* Hanging breaking balls are usually caused by dropping your elbow. You could also be having problems if your release is wrong; keep your fingers on top of the ball. For a curveball, release the ball in front of

This pitcher is collapsing on his back leg, a serious mechanical flaw.

your head and pull down on it (like you're ringing a bell).
- *Wild low.* You could be shortening your arm arc; think fastball until your throwing hand has reached your ear. You could have your hand too close to your head; stay on your fastball arm path. You could be rushing; keep your weight back.
- *Slow break.* You may be trying to start your breaking ball too early in your delivery. This is

······ **Throw It Again**
You need to know yourself well enough that you can be your own pitching coach on the mound. When you miss with a pitch or have less on it than you should, you need to be able to know why and to make the usually minor mechanical adjustment immediately. Seek any in-game advice from a limited number of sources who you trust.

called "wrapping" it. Your motion should be the same as if you were throwing your fastball until your arm gets alongside your ear. Your wrist snap occurs out in front of you.

- *Not breaking.* The biggest enemy of the breaking ball is muscle tension; relax your wrist and forearm while maintaining a firm grip with your fingers. You could have your fingers on the side of the ball when you release; turn your wrist so that your fingers are on top of the ball. For a curveball, beware of choking the ball too deeply in your hand. For a slider, be certain that you are holding the ball off center so that your fingers come down on the *outside* of the ball as you release it.

> *"When in you're in the game, there is no time to consult with your pitching coach over what you may be doing wrong. You've got to realize the mistake you're making, make the adjustment, and get the hitter."*
>
> —David Wells

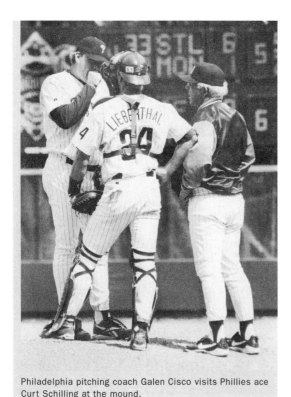

Philadelphia pitching coach Galen Cisco visits Phillies ace Curt Schilling at the mound.

KNOWING YOUR LIMITS

Every competitor wants to be out there. Think of some of the gutty performances in recent postseason: Orel Hershiser pitching in relief in the 1988 NLCS against the Mets; Jack Morris talking Twins manager Tom Kelly into sending him out for the 10th inning of a 0–0 Game 7 against the Braves in 1991; Kevin Brown practically demanding that Marlins manager Jim Leyland leave him in during Game 6 against the Braves in the 1997 NLCS. These pitchers had earned the right to ask this of their managers—and they rewarded them with a save and two wins.

Those stories are famous. No one talks as much about the Braves' Tom Glavine telling manager Bobby Cox that he was done after pitching eight one-hit innings against the Indians in the final game of the 1995 World Series. No doubt he would have loved to be the one on the mound to wrap up a championship with a complete-game shutout, but he listened to his body and knew his limits. You should, too. Trying to push yourself too far can cost your team the game and, more importantly, can lead to a serious arm injury.

> *"The first thing we look for is a pitcher using his legs less. His delivery relies more on his arm. We notice more erratic location both in and out of the strike zone. Often, the pitches are higher."*
>
> —Galen Cisco, Philadelphia Phillies pitching coach

Here are the telltale signs that you're out of gas:

- You're rushing your motion in an attempt to get more on your pitches.
- Your location is poor, never near the intended target.
- You're dropping your elbow.
- You're not following through with your pitches.
- Your pitches are up in the strike zone.
- Your breaking pitches have less bite.

Wear your jacket between innings to keep your arm warm and loose.

• Your pitching hand is shaking.
• You're not working as quickly.

Your coach should be looking for these signs, too. When you know you're tired and your coach doesn't, this can put you in a tough spot. There's a stigma about "asking out" of games. If you continually "get tired" when the game is close and late, your teammates and coaches may wonder whether you really want to be out there. You will have to gut it out to close out a few tough games. But if you are truly fatigued and you've "got nothing on the ball but your fingers," you aren't doing your team any good by staying out there. If you aren't comfortable telling your coach that, let your catcher know and *he* can tell the coach that *he* thinks you're out of gas. If you've thrown at least five innings or 75 pitches, you'll need to ice your arm for 20 minutes after the game to reduce the swelling.

It's important that you know the difference between being tired and being hurt. When you're tired, you feel a dull ache throughout your arm.

> **Throw It Again**
> The vast majority of injuries are suffered by tired pitchers. Know your limits. Push yourself if you can, but shut yourself down when there's nothing left in the tank. Know the difference between the dull ache of fatigue and the sharp pain of injury. Use ice for injuries and/or extended outings of at least five innings or 75 pitches; use warmth for fatigue.

When you're hurt, you feel a sharp pain focused in one spot or a severe tightness. When you're tired, you shut it down for the day and get back on your normal daily routine the next. When you're hurt, you tell your coach or trainer, have it checked out, and follow their advice.

> *"I've been hurt twice; my elbow in 1994 and my shoulder in 1995. To me, it's very simple. When you're sore, you can pitch. When you're hurt, you can not throw at all. A lot of guys confuse soreness with injury. The days of throwing without soreness are over when you turn about 15 years old."*
>
> —Curt Schilling

PITCHING IN RELIEF

When you're only pitching one or two innings per game, you can approach the game a little bit differently than you do as a starter. You can get by with one or two pitches, since you'll only be going through the opposing lineup once. That makes warming up a lot easier. If you've had trouble developing a second or third pitch, you might love short relief.

Other pitchers move to relief roles less because of repertoire and more because of emotions. When starting, you need to sustain a controlled aggressiveness for a long period of time. You can't afford to blow off any steam. Some pitchers have a hard time with this. They're excitable, fiery individuals who can let it all hang out for one or two innings and be unhittable. But ask someone like Al "the Mad Hungarian" Hrabosky or Rob Dibble to do this for five innings or more and they can't sustain it.

> *"For me, it was always a matter of keying down rather than getting up for a game."*
>
> —Dennis Eckersley, who had a good career as a starter and a great one as a reliever (a role to which his personality was probably better suited).

If you need to be a creature of routine, you're probably better suited to being a starting pitcher. You know exactly what's expected of you every day. A relief pitcher may not see the field for a week, then pitch in four consecutive games. Relievers need to be comfortable with this kind of uncertainty.

Relief pitchers also need to be able to shake off failure almost immediately, especially if you are the team's closer. You may give up the game-winning hit today, and you could find yourself in the same situation tomorrow. If you like to over-analyze things, you probably won't be comfortable as a short reliever.

"My mentality is that I'm gonna beat you. I'm gonna come after you, so here it comes. I attack the hitter. If you want to try and sit on a fastball, go ahead, because I'm gonna blow it by you."

—Billy Wagner, Houston Astros closer

When entering a game in relief, you must be prepared mentally as well as physically.

Being able to keep yourself from riding an emotional roller coaster is especially important for a closer, who spends the vast majority of his time working with the game hanging in the balance. To do this, a pitcher must be able to shake off a bad game and put it behind him almost immediately. As former Mets and Phillies closer Tug McGraw put it: "Sometimes you're gonna get lit up. That's it. You just gotta admit the batter did his job and forget it."

STARTER TO CLOSER

In 1998, a number of former starters found themselves in the closer's role. Mark Leiter, Bob Wickman (who had already made the transition from starter to middle relief), and Tom Gordon all had different things to say about how their approach to the game changed when they went from starting to relieving.

Mark Leiter: "They say [closers] can go at hitters with everything they've got, but I think starters do that, too. You have to do that to get major league hitters out. The difference is more in the mental approach. As a reliever, set-up guy, or closer, you come to the park every day expecting to pitch. Always prepared, ready to go. You have to learn how to warm up quicker. You have to do things between innings to stay loose. A lot of stretching."

Leiter credited his dramatic increase in strikeouts not to being able to air it out, but simply by only having to go through the lineup once: "They don't know what to expect, and that's where you can get guys."

Bob Wickman: "Long relief, set-up man, closer, you gotta get outs. Any out is important. The guys in the seventh and eighth are just as important as those in the ninth." To get those outs, Wickman will go to his out pitches more than he did when he was a starter. "If I've got to throw 10 sliders in a row to get out of a game, I'll do it. I don't think you'll see a starter do that."

Tom Gordon: "My fastball has come back to life because I've gotten to go back to throwing hard, relying more on my fastball and curveball

RICH GOSSAGE: THE CLOSER'S TEMPERAMENT

"With two out and two on, I'm facing Yaz and the blood was pumping in my ears and I could barely breathe. I had to back off the mound. I said to myself, this is silly. The worst thing that can happen is I'll be home in Colorado tomorrow."—Rich Gossage on getting the final out of the 1978 Red Sox–Yankees playoff game

When many people think of relief aces, "Goose" Gossage comes to mind. In his prime he threw nearly 100 miles per hour, only rarely mixed in a slider, and was absolutely fearless. When asked what was on his mind when facing Carl Yastrzemski with a one-run lead, two outs, and the winning runs on base in the bottom of the ninth inning of arguably the greatest game ever played—the 1978 one-game playoff between the Yankees and Red Sox— Gossage replied that he was thinking that tomorrow he was either going to the playoffs or fishing in Colorado. The Goose, already into his third inning of work, threw high fastballs and Yaz popped up to third base to end the game.

and not so much on changing speeds. I talked to pitching coach Joe Kerrigan and he agreed: 'Let's go with the pitches that got you to the big leagues. Let's have fun with it.'"

Boston Red Sox reliever Tom Gordon rears back to deliver a pitch.

Dennis Eckersley, another starter who made the transition to closer in the late 1980s, also emphasizes that the change is much more in the head than anywhere else: "It's more a mental thing. Being prepared every day." Part of being prepared every day is the ability not only to shake off a bad outing immediately, but to continue to present a confident—almost defiant—demeanor to hitters. If you got lit up the day before because your stuff wasn't very sharp, and you're back out there today after your stuff wasn't very sharp in the bullpen, you can't let the batter know it. The stakes are too high. Eckersley says, "You maybe can fake your way through it, act like you've got it going. But you can only fake it for so long."

Throw It Again

Pitching in relief requires a different approach than starting. You need to be comfortable with uncertainty, as your daily routine won't be as fixed as a starter's. You will need to be able to warm up and establish command of your breaking pitches quickly when called. You can get away with being more emotional on the mound because you're out there for only a few innings at a time, but you will need to be able to shake off a bad outing almost immediately.

Curt Schilling

ADVANCED PITCHING: MASTERING THE MENTAL GAME

Why is Michael Jordan the greatest basketball player who ever lived? There were other players in the league who could jump higher and run faster. What separates Jordan from the rest in basketball is the same thing that separates Joe Montana from other quarterbacks and Tiger Woods from other golfers: an intense competitive drive harnessed by extraordinary powers of concentration and a commitment to being prepared. In other words, the mental in addition to the physical. The same can be said for baseball's best pitchers.

Many pitchers with tremendous raw talent have failed to fulfill their potential—at all levels from the major leagues to youth league—while others with average fastballs used their brains to the fullest to fashion long, successful careers. Don't underestimate the importance of the mental game of pitching. If you think you can pitch successfully on your athletic ability alone, forget it.

This chapter will cover a number of techniques for your "mental game" that will help you reach your full potential as a pitcher—from dealing with adversity and concentrating to choosing a pitching style and selecting pitches. The keys to making it all work for you are being calm, being aware, and being prepared.

PROFESSOR MADDUX

Greg Maddux, like many other pitchers, improved with age. He became a *smarter* pitcher who learned how to keep batters off balance by throwing difficult-to-hit pitches *in* the strike zone.

The prime years often come for major league pitchers around age 29, when the mental game finally catches up to the physical. Then, though the physical tools begin to erode, success declines more slowly—as the mental game picks up the slack. It becomes more about mastering the art of sequencing pitches, hitting spots, and understanding batters' weaknesses than it is about velocity or movement. For every rookie phenom like Dwight Gooden who peaks early on the strength of one or two pitches, there are at least a dozen crafty veterans who get better with age. Brains can carry many a pitcher long after his fastball has lost its zip. Orel Hershiser has now won more games after blowing out his arm than he did when he was young and had overpowering stuff.

So the career path of a major league pitcher committed to mastering the mental game typically progresses in the manner that Greg Maddux's has—though his highs are much higher than most pitchers attain and his transition from learning to success was much more rapid. *Brains and precision drive the development of this type of pitcher.*

Hard Knocks

While learning on the job, Maddux is hit hard and goes 8–18 in his first two seasons. Is it possible? Control problems for one of the greatest control pitchers in the history of the game? Control is not about throwing *strikes* but hitting *spots*, and it's a function not just of mechanics but of knowing *how* to get batters out and developing confidence in your abilities to do it.

Maddux is getting hit, and it's making him uncomfortable about throwing the ball in the strike zone. He's focusing more on tricking batters into swinging at balls than getting them to hit *his* strikes.

Year	Age	W–L	ERA	BA	K/9	BB/9
1986	20	2–4	5.52	.336	5.8	3.2
1987	21	6–14	5.61	.294	5.8	4.3

Inconsistent Success

Maddux adapts quickly and decides he needs to throw his change-up more. He goes 52–35 in his next three seasons as he holds hitters to a batting average around .250 and cuts his walks down to about three per game. But notice that he made the first step toward Cooperstown by becoming more hittable, his strikeouts per game dropping *below* the level of his first two seasons. He's challenging more hitters *in* the strike zone.

HANDLING ADVERSITY

Pitching requires controlled aggressiveness. You need to have a competitive fire, but you must be able to harness that energy and put it to productive use. Those who do are often accused of being emotionless, but they're not. They have a fierce desire to win, but they keep it from showing on their face. They don't waste their energy by pumping their fists after strikeouts. They don't motivate their opponents by pointing fingers. They don't melt down when things aren't going their way. In a word, they're "calm."

When you make a good pitch and the batter hits it in the gap, all you can do is give him the nod. Your best against his best, and this time he got you.

PROFESSOR MADDUX (continued)

Year	Age	W–L	ERA	BA	K/9	BB/9
1988	22	18–8	3.18	.244	5.1	2.9
1989	23	19–12	2.95	.249	5.1	3.1
1990	24	15–15	3.46	.265	5.5	2.7

Consistent Success

At age 25, Maddux takes it to the next level; his strikeouts go up, his walks are down around two per game, he's tougher to hit, and his ERA drops below 2.50 as he wins his first two Cy Young Awards. He has refined his change-up and has become familiar with hitters. He has learned *how* to pitch. Not only is he challenging hitters in the strike zone, he's thinking along with them as he does it—knowing what they're looking for and giving them a strike they're not expecting.

Year	Age	W–L	ERA	BA	K/9	BB/9
1991	25	15–11	3.35	.237	6.8	2.3
1992	26	20–11	2.18	.210	6.7	2.4
1993	27	20–10	2.36	.232	6.6	1.8

Prime Years

In his late 20s, Maddux peaks, going 35–8 in 1994–95 with a ridiculously low ERA for his era and impeccable control. Here he has shown the difference between control and command. Maddux is hitting spots unlike just about any other pitcher in history; his more than 7:1 ratio of strikeouts to walks in 1995 is phenomenal, accomplished over 200 innings by only Ferguson Jenkins. The key for Jenkins and Maddux to being able to throw unhittable strikes was the same: outstanding ability to change speeds.

Year	Age	W–L	ERA	BA	K/9	BB/9
1994	28	16–6	1.56	.207	7.0	1.4
1995	29	19–2	1.63	.197	7.8	1.0

Was Greg Maddux more *physically* able to throw strikes as he got older? Yes, to some extent. His precision certainly came in part from honing his mechanics on a daily basis. Did he learn some magical new pitch? No, but with practice he did master his change-up—a pitch that many don't even try to start throwing until they're past their prime. Did he throw harder? Hardly.

Brains and precision. They don't call Maddux "the Professor" for nothing.

You care, but you don't show it. You can't wait for next time and your chance to get him. But if your pitch gets driven because you didn't put it where you wanted to, you need to recognize the mistake, learn from it, then immediately put it behind you. A one-run inning can become a five-run inning very quickly if you're still thinking about the *last* hitter instead of the man you're facing now.

"Your most important pitch is the next one."

—Jim Fregosi, Toronto Blue Jays manager

You must be able to deal with luck, too. Sometimes you'll get in a hitter's kitchen (get a pitch close to the batter's body and on the handle of his bat) on a great pitch only to watch it drop

Pitching is not a perfect science. There will be times your pitches leave the yard and times when they'll get by the catcher (shown here). What's important is to maintain focus and not allow your emotions to adversely affect your performance.

One of the best young pitchers in the 1997 amateur draft was Rice University star Matt Anderson. In his second inning of professional baseball during spring training in 1998, Anderson did anything but dominate. But he did get through it. Later, he offered these words of wisdom: "Anybody can pitch when they are throwing 98 miles per hour on the black of the plate. What separates pitchers is when they have to go out there without their best stuff. I didn't have it that day, but I got by. I was really happy about that."

"You're supposed to win when you have all your pitches going for you. You haven't become a good pitcher until you can win when you don't have anything."

—Sandy Koufax

just out of reach of your shortstop, or coax a ground ball thats slips between the outstretched gloves of your third baseman and shortstop. Those are the breaks. Keep making good pitches and the breaks will start going your way. That's called dealing with adversity.

Many scouts feel they can learn more about a young pitcher in a game in which he faces some adversity than one in which he throws a no-hitter and fans 18. When scouting, Bill Werle wanted to see "tenacity, thinking, and presence on the mound. An ideal game for my scouting is when a boy takes a one-run lead into the last inning, and then the first hitter reaches base on an error. Does the pitcher bear down? Or does he lose his composure and then beat himself?"

"When your infielders boot a couple of balls, you have to keep your concentration and not give up. Say to yourself, 'Let me pick up my teammate.' You know he feels bad enough already that he added another out to the inning. Work even harder to keep that runner from scoring. That way, you help out your teammate and make yourself a better pitcher."

—Jeff Nelson, New York Yankees reliever

CONTROLLING YOUR EMOTIONS

When you're standing in the middle of the diamond all alone—and without your best stuff—emotional control is vital if you're to have any chance of working through it. Tom Seaver said that one of the keys for him when he was in a long inning was to figure out *why* it was happening. Was it good hitting, or bad pitching? If you're throwing good pitches but they're getting hit, so be it. Don't panic. If you're throwing bad pitches, chances are you need to make a mechanical adjustment, and a *small* one at that. (See Chapter 8 for how to be your own in-game pitching coach.)

Bear in mind that with these line shots coming back at you, you'll also be hearing a few things

Throw It Again
The ability to handle adversity is critical for a pitcher, and it will mean the difference between one-run and five-run innings. Even if you are churning on the inside, you will need to appear calm, cool, and collected on the mound. This will help you to stay focused and will rub off on your teammates.

from the crowd and the opposing bench. Christy Mathewson had to deal with plenty of that during the roguish deadball era. His advice was to ignore it. Mathewson said, "When a pitcher starts to talk back, it is a cinch that he is irritated."

Toronto Blue Jays pitcher David Wells can be a target of abuse by fans because he's had some colorful off-the-field incidents. Wells acknowledged being shaken by some particularly vile things being said to him by some Cleveland Indians fans early in Game 5 of the 1998 ALCS, when he was with the Yankees. Wells struggled at first, but eventually used the abuse to his advantage—letting it motivate him, refusing to lose. He won his second game of the series and, when he was pulled for a reliever late in the game, he smiled and tipped his cap to the jeering crowd.

At the end of the day, you want to be respected as a competitor. You earn that respect not just with your performance, but with how you treat your coaches, teammates, competitors, and umpires. In short, how you conduct yourself on the mound. You'll find that how you control your emotions will have a direct effect on how you control your pitches.

CONCENTRATION

"When I'm staring in at the target, I'm not concentrating on simply hitting the catcher's glove. I imagine there is a dime inside the catcher's mitt and try to hit that."

—Sean Bergman, Minnesota Twins pitcher

Along with proper mechanics, focus (or concentration) is the key to throwing any pitch where you want it. If you've worked on your mechanics enough that they're now second nature to you, you can free your mind to think about nothing except the catcher's glove.

There is no one way to develop and maintain concentration. Pitchers as different in temperament as the fierce Bob Gibson and the goofy Mark Fidrych did a lot of talking—to themselves, or in Fidrych's case, the ball—to help them concentrate on hitting their spots. Hall of Famer Steve Carlton did not. His personal catcher, Tim McCarver, said, "Carlton does not pitch to the hitter, he pitches through him. The batter hardly exists for Steve." When Carlton was pitching, he let nothing and no one distract him. Carlton wore earplugs on the

CHRISTY MATHEWSON AND DENNIS ECKERSLEY: EMOTIONAL TOUGHNESS

"The Eck" had long black hair, a language all his own, and was known to talk trash to hitters. "The Christian Gentleman" was a blond-haired, blue-eyed, Bucknell grad who went about his business with a regal, dignified bearing and always said the right thing. Despite their differing personalities, both Dennis Eckersley and Christy Mathewson shared a mental toughness and self-confident attitude that carried them through countless tough situations—including two in particular that might have ruined other pitchers.

Mathewson blew a lead to the Cubs in one of the most pressure-packed games in big league history—the final game of the turbulent 1908 season, in which Chicago snagged a pennant that Mathewson's Giants had already thought they'd won. He returned the next season to win 25 games with a 1.14 ERA.

Eckersley hung a slider and yielded a game-winning, series-turning home run to Kirk Gibson in Game 1 of the 1988 World Series. He came back the next season to post a 1.56 ERA with three walks in 58 innings. He recorded four saves in the 1989 postseason, including the Game 4 clincher in San Francisco.

Both Eckersley and Mathewson hated losing and failure. Having to taste it did not mean that they began to expect it.

mound to block out crowd noise, and he didn't speak to the media (or the ball).

You need to find a way to block things out. How you do that is often a matter of personality. You may keep your mind from wandering to other things by constantly thinking about the batters you are facing and how you must pitch to them. Or you may do better by turning off your mind completely, the way Carlton seemed to do, thinking about nothing except the next pitch and the catcher's glove. Only you will know what's best for you. Try out different approaches when you're throwing to a catcher on the side, or simply throwing against a chalk outline on the wall, so you'll know what works for you during a game.

You'll find that the ability to concentrate will have a calming effect on you—which can have the same effect on your teammates. Your mind is not filled with all sorts of negative outcomes. You're only thinking about the pitch you need to make to the batter you're facing now. If you find your mind being filled with negative thoughts, step off the rubber, take a deep breath, close your eyes, and visualize yourself delivering the pitch you need to make. Let your body relax as you see yourself do it.

One of the best pitching matchups during the 1999 season featured the Dodgers' Kevin Brown and Phillies ace Curt Schilling at Veterans Stadium. Pitching under very windy conditions, both Brown and Schilling had difficulty throwing strikes. Holding a 3–2 lead in the top of the sixth inning, Schilling walked Gary Sheffield on four pitches, gave up a single to Raul Mondesi, and then walked Dave Hansen on four fastballs to load the bases with nobody out. Up stepped Todd Hundley, who had hit a two-run homer in the fourth inning. Schilling threw three straight fastballs out of the strike zone to run the count to 3–0. With no place left to put anyone, Schilling stepped off the mound, bent to one knee, and retied his shoelaces.

Schilling reflected on that moment: "It's so easy to concede things, and I'm a person who refuses to concede things until the final result is there. You get caught up at times on the good side

During his career, Hall of Famer Steve Carlton approached pitching as nothing more than an elevated game of catch.

of the fence and the bad side of the fence. When you're on the bad side, sometimes you need to tell yourself to relax. Tying my shoe was just a way to collect my thoughts. I knew there was only one way out of the jam and that was to throw the ball over the plate with something on it. I got the count back to full, the crowd was into it, and fortunately I was able to reach back and put something extra on the ball and I struck him out."

Curt Schilling collects his thoughts before going back on the hill to battle Todd Hundley.

Schilling went on to strike out Todd Hollandsworth and then induced Adrian Beltre to ground out to second baseman Marlon Anderson. He escaped the inning without surrendering a run and went on to win the game.

Though working quickly is very important, that's not necessarily the case when you're trying to get a crucial out. Don't be afraid to take a few extra seconds to gather yourself, rather than rush yourself through it. Rushing can lead to lapses in concentration and poor mechanics. Jeff Bagwell attributed slowing down to helping teammate Darryl Kile emerge as an ace in 1997. On Kile, Bagwell said, "He used to get in jams and couldn't wait to throw the next pitch. Now he'll walk around the mound, step off, think about it, and then execute instead of just rushing through it."

"I see, I actually seem to see, a lot of little points of light, inside, outside, waist high, down around the knees, somewhere there in the strike zone. Each light represents the exact spot where I've thrown a ball to get that batter out some time before."

—Hall of Famer Allie Reynolds

NOLAN RYAN: CONCENTRATION

Steve Carlton is not alone among pitchers who claim to not even hear the crowd or notice the batter when they are really focused. Over time, Nolan Ryan developed powers of concentration almost on a par with the velocity of his fastball. He says it simply came through experience.

Ryan says, "I have tunnel vision. It was something I didn't always have. It took several years to develop the ability to block out everything that goes on at the ballpark, to concentrate totally on what I am doing on the mound. Some days this is easier said than done. There's a zone, a tunnel, that goes from me in a straight line to my catcher. I know the hitter is there, but I hardly notice him at all. I am throwing to my catcher, who I have set up on the corners of the plate. If I paid attention to what the hitter is doing, it would break my concentration. I just zone in on the catcher."

Perhaps this tunnel vision can help explain how Ryan could maintain his concentration during his second no-hitter of 1973, when Tigers first baseman Norm Cash came to the plate with a paddle in the fifth inning and a table leg in the ninth.

PITCHING STYLE

Good pitching is all about getting outs—strike-outs, fly outs, groundouts, any outs. The type of outs you will get depends on the location, movement, and velocity of your pitches. If you throw hard or have a nasty breaking ball, you'll probably be recording your share of strikeouts. If you don't throw hard, but have good movement and location on a sinking fastball or change-up, you'll probably be getting groundouts.

Choose a style that fits your personality and the pitches you've mastered. Don't try to be tricky if you have the ability to overpower hitters. And don't try to be a strikeout pitcher if you have ground-ball stuff. You can win without strikeouts. *No-hitters have been thrown when 27 balls were put in play.*

Cy Young Award winner John Smoltz was blessed with a "live arm." But he supplements his velocity with accuracy, intelligence, and competitive fire.

POWER PITCHERS

> *"If you can get an out with one pitch, take it. . . . Winning is the big thing."*
>
> —Dwight Gooden, 1985 National League Cy Young Award winner

Do you throw harder than most pitchers at your level? Are you able to rear back and throw pitches past batters? Do you record a lot of strikeouts? If so, chances are you have at least half of the "power pitcher" equation. But having "strikeout stuff" can be a mixed blessing. Many strikeout pitchers end up walking a lot of batters, because as velocity and movement increase, location often becomes harder to predict. Even for those who keep their walks to a reasonable level, higher-than-average pitch counts nearly always result.

Strikeout pitchers often work higher in the strike zone. High fastballs are tougher to hit, but when they are hit they produce fly balls—which means fewer ground balls and fewer double plays. In 1998, high-heat-throwback Kerry Wood generated only *three* double-play ground balls all season. The pitcher's best friend—the ground-ball double play— was coming his way about 2 percent of the time he could have used it, com-pared to more than 20 percent for the league leaders.

More fly balls also tend to mean more home runs. Hitters with quick bats will tell you that they don't mind facing hard throwers who get the ball up. Todd Hundley was once asked about facing Randy Johnson: "Close your eyes and swing hard in case you hit it. With hard throwers, they supply the power for you." There is truth to that, and when high heat gets turned around, it leaves the yard in a hurry.

Most fans and many pitchers just can't get the same rush of satisfaction from a ground ball to second that they can get from a big swing and a miss at a rising four-seamer, a diving splitter, or a low-and-away slider. In fact, the overlap between the list of strikeout artists and legendary pitchers is very high—Walter Johnson, Bob Feller, Sandy Koufax, Nolan Ryan, Kerry Wood, Randy Johnson, Curt Schilling, Pedro Martinez, and Roger Clemens come to mind. Strikeouts are critical in certain situations, such as when there is a runner on third with less than two out. In general, the strikeout is the least efficient of outs because it requires three good pitches rather than just one.

To establish yourself as a power pitcher and not simply a power thrower, you'll need to focus more on location—taking the quick out rather than the strikeout. This means concentrating on hitting the inner and outer thirds and lower half of the strike zone, rather than simply pouring fastballs down the middle of the plate. You'll see fewer walks, lower pitch counts, more double plays, and not as many extra-base hits. Your strikeouts might go down, but so will your ERA.

"Strikeouts are highly overrated except for when they're needed. You have to identify strikeout situations and pitch accordingly, such as when you have a runner on second with nobody out or a runner on third with less than two outs. The only other time I ever think strikeout is when I already have two strikes on the hitter."

—Curt Schilling

There will be days when you don't have your best stuff. You won't have that extra zip on your fastball, or the sharp break on your slider or splitter. Those outings are ones that separate pitchers from throwers. You must rely on brains rather than brawn. Check your ego at the door and bait the hitter into getting himself out. Don't feel pressured to go for the strikeout. Remember, the hitter may not realize you don't have your best stuff. Use that to your advantage. When he's expecting the high heater (fastball), fool him with something off-speed.

"I became a good pitcher when I stopped trying to make them miss the ball and started trying to make them hit it."

—Hall of Famer Sandy Koufax, who was 36–40 in his first six seasons and 129–47 in his final six.

STRIKING OUT ON THE MOUND

Strikeouts alone are no guarantee of success. A list of the top strikeout pitchers during the 1998 season shows Hideo Nomo sixth overall, despite a 6–12 record. Nomo is not unique in the annals of baseball, which is littered with overpowering pitchers who've struggled through some underwhelming seasons.

The following 10 pitchers are on the short list of pitchers who've fanned a batter per inning in a season. Yet their combined record for those seasons is 120–140 with no ERA lower than 3.46. What happened?

In the cases of Randy Johnson, Sandy Koufax, Hideo Nomo, Nolan Ryan, Darryl Kile, Mark Langston, Tom Griffin, and Sam McDowell, control problems for these young pitchers left them with a sub-.500 record to show for all those strikeouts. In the cases of Andy Benes and Sid Fernandez, an inability to make the big pitch when it was needed left them with two of the three worst won-lost marks of the group.

Pitcher	W–L	K/9	BB/9	ERA
Randy Johnson, 1992	12–14	10.3	6.2	3.77
Randy Johnson, 1991	13–10	10.3	6.8	3.98
Sandy Koufax, 1960	8–13	10.1	5.1	3.91
Hideo Nomo, 1997	14–12	10.1	4.0	4.25
Nolan Ryan, 1978	10–13	10.0	5.7	3.71
Andy Benes, 1994	6–14	9.9	2.7	3.86
Tom Griffin, 1969	11–10	9.6	4.5	3.54
Mark Langston, 1986	12–14	9.2	4.6	4.86
Sid Fernandez, 1990	9–14	9.1	3.4	3.46
Darryl Kile, 1996	12–11	9.0	4.0	4.19
Sam McDowell, 1967	13–15	9.0	4.7	3.85

COMMANDING THE STRIKE ZONE

"Never the same pitch twice, never the same place twice, never the same speed twice."

—Eddie Lopat, who won 166 games in his career, including 80 for the 1949–53 Yankees teams that won five consecutive world championships

Is your velocity only average relative to other pitchers at your level? Are your best pitches a change-up, a fastball with movement (cutter or sinker), or a breaking ball? If you can hit corners, keep the ball down, and change speeds, you could have much more success than the radar-gun readings might suggest. In fact, the first thing you should probably do is forget about radar-gun readings completely. Velocity is secondary to developing good command of the strike zone.

The worst thing a pitcher with "crafty stuff" can do is to try to get strikeouts. Even one of the best nonstrikeout pitchers in recent memory, Bill Lee, struggled with the urge to overthrow. Lee says, "Nobody had to tell me that my strength was hitting the corners and keeping the ball low. But there were days when the adrenaline would be racing and the ball would say, 'Come on, Bill, throw me through that wall,' causing me to rear back and do my Sandy Koufax impersonation. It would work for about two batters. I'd blow both guys away, walk the next batter, and give up a satellite to a .220 hitter."

The prototypical crafty veteran lefty, Eddie Lopat of the Yankees, used to drive the game's best hitters to distraction with a steady diet of off-speed and breaking pitches. The Barry Bonds of Lopat's day—Ted Williams—would yell at him from the batter's box to challenge him with a fastball, but Lopat had already decided that Williams could take the walk or swing at Lopat's pitch.

You don't need to be a veteran or a lefty to be crafty. Crafty pitchers can be young (Brian Moehler and Carlos Perez), in their prime (Andy Ashby), or battle scarred (Jamie Moyer). They can be a consistent winner (Tom Glavine) or someone who'd been written off (Kenny Rogers). But here's what all of those pitchers have in common: low pitch counts, few walks, a lot of groundouts, and hits and runs kept to a minimum without piling up the strikeouts. They rely on change-ups and on well-located fastballs that have more movement than velocity. As a result, they are also a lot more likely to induce a double play, with Moehler and Rogers each getting about one per start.

When you're a "crafty" pitcher, you don't overpower hitters, you frustrate them. You make batters get themselves out, getting weak grounders or soft flies on off-balance or defensive swings. They may call you a "junkballer," because you only seem to throw fastballs when the hitter isn't looking for it. But one man's junk is another man's out pitch.

Crafty Pitchers	W–L	ERA	BA	K/9	BB/9	P/IP	Out Pitch
Tom Glavine	20–6	2.47	.238	6.2	2.9	15.7	Change-up
Andy Ashby	17–9	3.34	.259	6.0	2.3	13.9	Cut fastball
Kenny Rogers	16–8	3.17	.242	5.2	2.5	14.7	Cut fastball
Jamie Moyer	15–9	3.53	.256	6.1	1.6	15.2	Change-up
Brian Moehler	14–13	3.90	.260	5.0	2.3	15.0	Cut fastball
Carlos Perez	11–14	3.59	.264	4.8	2.4	14.3	Change-up
ML Average		4.44	.267	6.6	3.4	16.1	

1998 season.

"I don't ever try to throw a ball over the middle of the plate. There is no reason to. The middle six inches is just as wide as the six inches on the inside corner and just as wide as the six inches on the outside part of the plate."

—Curt Schilling

Power pitchers thrive on velocity and crafty pitchers on movement and changing speeds. What if your greatest strength as a pitcher is your ability to put a fastball exactly where you want it? Whether you throw it hard or soft, there will be room for you on any staff. Gain the same control of your change-up as you have of your fastball, mix up your pitches well, and you'll be able to compete at a higher level than a hard thrower without command. Do all of that while throwing hard and you could make the big leagues.

Having command of all your pitches does not simply mean you're able to throw strikes. Issuing zero walks in a pitcher's box score can be a deceiving statistic. It doesn't necessarily indicate pinpoint control. Pitchers can be wild *in* the strike zone, which at times can be more damaging than

Bret Saberhagen has above-average stuff, but his ability to work hitters in and out and up and down has made him one of the best pitchers of his time.

throwing a pitch *out* of the strike zone. Blue Jays pitcher Pat Hentgen learned this early in his career, realizing certain areas of the strike zone can be dangerous: "There was a situation where a veteran pitcher threw two innings without walking anybody. He came in the dugout with a real sour expression on his face. So I went over to him and asked him what was wrong. He said, 'I was wild. I was all over the place.' I asked how many guys he walked and he said, 'No one, but I was wild in the strike zone.'

"I remember thinking, 'Wow.' The way he looked at the strike zone was completely different from the way I looked at it. At that time, all I was trying to do was throw strikes, where he was throwing to one side of the plate or the other, up and down in the strike zone. It was at that point in my career that I realized that simply throwing the ball in the strike zone was not enough."

CATFISH HUNTER: CONTROL PITCHING

"I'm going to make them hit it. They gotta hit it out, and I don't care if they do. I'll keep throwing it in there, and I'll keep getting most of them out."

—Hall of Famer Catfish Hunter

Catfish Hunter is remembered by many now for being the first "free agent," going out on the open market and triggering a bidding war that George Steinbrenner's Yankees eventually won. But Hunter's true baseball legacy is as a pitcher with great command of the strike zone.

As a 19-year-old, he went 8–8 for a 100-loss team. He threw a perfect game in 1968, one of only 16 ever thrown in the modern era. He led the A's to three consecutive world championships, going 7–2 with a save in the postseason for Oakland. His finest season was 1974, when he won 25 games, completed 23, and led the league in ERA by forcing batters to hit his pitch—striking out only four batters per nine innings while walking only 46 in 318 innings.

In the 1978 World Series, Hunter was on the mound for the Yankees in Game 6 in Los Angeles with a chance to wrap up the series. Early in the first inning, Yankees catcher Thurman Munson called time and visited the mound. Munson told Hunter, "You don't have squat tonight, so you better throw the ball where I put my glove."

As always, Hunter did just that, holding the Dodgers to two runs before turning the ball over to Goose Gossage in the eighth inning. It would turn out to be his ninth postseason win and his fifth world championship.

Commenting on his induction into the Hall of Fame in 1987, Hunter offered a straightforward description of how to succeed: "I was a control pitcher who hit spots. I had players behind me to back me up."

His former manager, Dick Williams, was even more succinct: "What he does best is win games."

As a control pitcher, you may actually end up yielding a lower batting average than a harder-throwing, wilder pitcher. Throw strikes and you actually become more difficult to hit, as batters can't sit on 2–0 and 3–1 pitches or count on seeing first-pitch fastballs down the middle. The average hitter will make an out two out of three times when hitting the ball. Throw strikes and good things are likely to happen.

If you're serious about being a control pitcher, hone your mechanics (Chapter 2), master a change-up (Chapter 4), and pay special attention to the following section on pitch selection. You could end up as one of those pitchers who make their living "on the black"—only throwing strikes on the corners.

> **Throw It Again**
> You need to choose a pitching style that is appropriate to your personality and repertoire. The three most common styles are the power pitchers who rely on velocity, the crafty pitchers who rely on movement, and the control pitchers who rely on location. Don't try to be a strikeout pitcher with groundball stuff, and don't try to get cute when you have an excellent fastball.

PITCH SELECTION

"Pitch selection is the most important and creative part of catching. When it's right, it's like the batter's a puppet. I decide what strings to pull, and the pitcher pulls them."

—Carlton Fisk, former major league catcher

It's no accident that pitch selection hasn't been covered until now, the final chapter, after all other aspects of pitching have been discussed at length. Excellent pitch selection doesn't mean much if you haven't developed sound mechanics, command of your pitches, the right mental approach, and the concentration to maintain it all in the heat of battle.

The first thing to do is to keep it simple. Move your fastball around in the strike zone until the hitters have shown that they can handle it. Robin Roberts kept things this basic for most of his career, and he ended up in the Hall of Fame. For Roberts, it was more about location than type of pitch. Early on in his career, he stuck almost exclusively to a good fastball, which he could put wherever he wanted. Later on, he added a curveball. His pitching style was little more than working hitters high and tight or low and away—and

Never underestimate the importance of good communication between a pitcher and his catcher.

when he did throw a curveball, he kept it down. Hitters knew what was coming, but couldn't do much with it because of his exceptional control. As he liked to say, "Keep your life and your pitching real simple, and you'll get along."

Keeping it too simple can lead to easily detected patterns to which hitters can adjust. Making it too difficult can lead to bad choices at the worst possible time. Fortunately, you have a catcher and a manager to fall back upon.

> *"I used to like to set guys up for screwballs and then throw a slider inside to get a soft ground ball.... I walked a lot of guys and got the bases loaded and stuff all by trying to design outs. I wanted to get a hitter out in a certain way, and if I couldn't, sometimes it was worth putting him on and pitching to the next guy. There was a method to my madness."*
>
> —Tug McGraw, former Mets and Phillies closer, who pitched for 19 seasons and recorded 180 saves

Some pitchers call their own game—Greg Maddux and Don Sutton, for example—but many pitchers entrust pitch selection almost entirely to their catcher. Younger pitchers, especially, will shake off a veteran catcher at their own risk. Veteran pitchers who find themselves struggling with their mechanics often lighten their load by letting their catcher take over the pitch calling.

After a no-hitter, chances are you'll hear a pitcher giving much of the credit to his catcher, who he "only shook off once or twice." Jim Abbott pulled batterymate Matt Nokes out of the Yankees dugout to share a curtain call after Abbott's 1993 no-hitter. A catcher you can trust is an invaluable asset.

Nevertheless, a pitcher knows his stuff better than anyone, including his catcher, and should not abdicate the responsibility of pitch selection completely. Throwing a pitch you don't believe in is one of the best ways to give up runs. As manager Davey Johnson puts it, "[A pitcher] has to believe in what he's throwing. If he doesn't want to throw a certain pitch, he won't throw it well."

THE CARE AND FEEDING OF CATCHERS

Hall of Famer Ed Walsh's advice for pitchers: "Hook up with some good catcher."

Hall of Famer Bob Feller: "If you believe your catcher is intelligent and you know that he has considerable experience, it is a good thing to leave the game almost entirely in his hands."

Future Hall of Fame catcher Carlton Fisk: "I've caught for pitchers who thought that if they won it's because they did such a great job, and if they lost it's because you called the wrong pitch. The good pitchers know that it isn't just their talent that's carrying them out there."

Bill Lee: "[Carlton Fisk] had learned the importance of working a pitcher and nursing him along when he didn't have his best stuff. Fisk also demanded your total concentration during a game. If you shook him off and then threw a bad pitch that got hit out, he had a very obvious way of expressing his displeasure. After receiving a new ball from the umpire, he would bring it out to you, bouncing it on the grass all the way to the mound. There would be an expression on his face that said, 'If you throw another pitch like that, I'm going to stuff this ball down your throat.'"

Johnny Oates: "In the end, it's the pitcher who has to throw the pitch. As a catcher, my goal was to call the pitches so that the pitcher didn't have to think about what to throw. The relationship is much like that of a husband and wife. The relationship depends on two-way communication. You have disagreements and battle a little sometimes, but there has to be good communication all the time."

"The best pitch you can throw is a comfort-able pitch, the pitch that you believe in, even if it's the wrong pitch."

—Greg Maddux

Pitch sequencing—or "designing outs," as Tug McGraw puts it—is not just about knowing your repertoire, it's about knowing the count, the hitters, and the game situation. In the following pages, you'll get to see it from all of these different perspectives.

GAME SITUATIONS

When it came to game situations, Hall of Famer Warren Spahn linked pitch selection to control. To him, control meant not just throwing strikes or not issuing walks but understanding what you needed—a double-play ball, a popped-up bunt, or a grounder to the left—and responding by pitching a sinker, a high fastball, or something up and in to a lefty that's hard for him to pull.

David Cone is a master of improvisation. He mixes speeds, changes arm angles, and induces hitters to offer at pitches out of the strike zone.

"If he had a guy on first base, less than two out, he'd take the fastball, turn it over a little bit to a righthanded batter. Boom! He'd hit a one-hop shot to me. Bing-bang! A double play."

—Mike Shannon, former Cardinals third baseman, on Bob Gibson

You also need to recognize where your team's defensive strengths are. Former catcher Jerry Grote said that in his early days with the Mets, his infield had only one good fielder so he'd "call a game to get every batter possible to hit the ball to [shortstop Bud] Harrelson."

In addition to recognizing when a double play is needed or where he'd like the ball to be hit, a pitcher should also be aware of other situations—such as when a batter might be bunting, trying to hit behind the runner to move him along, thinking about jerking a ball over a short fence, or when the game is on the line.

Bunt. How a batter squares will reveal his weakness. If he holds the bat low, throw a high fastball. If he stands straight up without flexing his knees, throw a low fastball. Watch where he takes his stance in the batter's box. If he stands too far from the plate, he may not have full plate coverage. Throw a strike on the outside corner. Avoid throwing breaking balls unless you are very confident that you can get them over the plate. The last thing you want to do is walk a batter trying to sacrifice.

Hitting Behind the Runner. With no one out and a runner on second base, most hitters will be looking to hit the ball to the right side of the infield. To keep them from doing this, try to jam right-handers and pitch left-handers away.

Short Porch. When Bill Lee pitched for the Red Sox, one of their biggest rivals was the New York Yankees. Facing them in home games meant pitching with a short porch in left. Going to Yankee Stadium meant a short porch in right and a cavernous left field. Lee pitched the Yankees' hitters differently in each stadium.

Lee says, "When facing their lefty hitters in New York, I would throw a lot of soft stuff in their kitchens. They would try to pull it over the right-field fence, and the result would be a lot of two-hoppers to my second baseman. When they came to Fenway, they'd shoot for the wall [the famous "Green Monster" in left field]. I'd nail them with hard sinkers inside. They never were able to adapt, and after a few wins against them, I felt like I owned them."

Even if you don't ever get a chance to pitch in Fenway Park or Yankee Stadium, chances are you'll pitch on a field with dimensions that tempt hitters to hit everything a certain way. The same principles apply.

Pitching in a Pinch. Christy Mathewson advised young pitchers to "always hold something in reserve, a surprise to spring when things get tight." It would take a special pitcher to have a deep enough repertoire that he could hold a pitch in reserve just for use in a crucial situation—such as Mathewson and his "fadeaway"—and to then be able to hit his spot with it. So what other surprises can a pitcher spring?

You can throw a pitch that a particular batter hasn't yet seen that game, but that's no guarantee of success. There may be a good reason why he hasn't seen it—he crushes it! Good hitters will be studying how a pitcher works others in the lineup. They'll observe what the pitcher uses as his "out" pitch or his critical-count pitch (3–2 especially). They'll also watch the 2–0 and 3–1 pitches to see if a pitcher is "giving in," that is, throwing the hitter's pitch (usually a fastball).

Sometimes you can just try to get a hitter thinking by shaking off your catcher—and then throw what the catcher had called for in the first place. When you see a catcher give a sign while shaking his head, he's telling the pitcher to give the fake shake.

Hall of Famer Rollie Fingers pulled a fast one on fellow Hall of Famer Johnny Bench in Game 3 of the 1972 World Series. Bobby Tolan had just stolen second base to put runners on second and third with a 3–2 count on Bench. After a visit to the

Hitters at Fenway Park often set their sights on the big Green Monster in left field. A smart pitcher should use that temptation to his advantage.

mound from manager Dick Williams, catcher Gene Tenace returned to his place behind the plate, where he held out his arm to indicate an intentional walk. Fingers began his delivery, Tenace took a step out of the catcher's box to receive the pitch, and Bench relaxed. Tenace ducked back in as Fingers threw a strike that Bench could only stare at for strike three. In the ultimate irony, Fingers had thrown a slider on the black that was probably unhittable anyway!

Another form of trickery involves changing your arm angle. David Cone has been known to create pitches on the spot, usually by simply dropping down and coming sidearm. This different look can be just enough to freeze a hitter, and he's been known to get many called third strikes on sidearm sliders.

"That's what makes him so successful—you never know what to expect. He'll drop down sidearm and sneak a sidearm fastball on you, or a sidearm slider. You see him drop down and you're like, 'Oh no, what's coming now?' He has more different looks than anybody.

And the stuff from those different looks is as good as anyone's."

—Dean Palmer, Detroit Tigers third baseman, on David Cone

That's great for Mathewson, Fingers, and Cone. What should *you* do? For one thing, you need to give your stuff that day an honest evaluation, consider who is at the plate, then determine whether you even need to spring a surprise at all. Maybe you should simply challenge the hitter. In general, most pitchers don't challenge hitters enough, and they get too cute. And there are a few pitchers who get caught up in the macho thing and want to challenge every hitter every time. Avoid both pitfalls.

After you decide the approach that makes sense for you, it again comes down to velocity, movement, and location.

VELOCITY

If they haven't caught up to your fastball yet, challenge them. Keep throwing it. But trying to throw the ball past the batter and through the catcher is almost always a mistake. Former Cy Young Award winner and current Chicago Cubs broadcaster Steve Stone points out that when in a tough spot, *a pitcher is almost always better off taking a little off the pitch than putting a little more on.*

Unfortunately, many young pitchers at all levels fail to follow this advice. For example, rookie pitcher Carlton Loewer of the Phillies pitched one of his best games in 1998 when he beat the Milwaukee Brewers at the Vet in July. He was consistently at 91–92 miles per hour with his fastball, but his fastest pitch of the day (94 miles per hour) was hit out of the park by a .230-hitting catcher.

Rather than try to hump up your fastball, consider throwing a change-up instead. It takes a lot of practice throwing on the side to get comfortable enough with the pitch to lay it in there during a game, and it takes a lot of guts to go to it in a critical situation. It'll all be worth it when you can use that pitch to completely neutralize a tough hitter when the game is on the line.

MOVEMENT

Overthrowing happens on breaking balls just as much as fastballs, if not more so. You can squeeze the ball too hard and have it fly out of your hand. When pitching for the Indians in the early 1980s, Len Barker put one on the screen behind home plate at Fenway Park doing that.

Another common problem is rushing your arm through; these pitches end up as 55-foot curveballs that eat up your catcher or as sliders scooting back to the screen. Obviously, overthrowing a breaking ball with a runner on third can be a *big* mistake. With a breaking ball in a tough situation, it's better to concentrate on keeping the ball down than making it break two feet.

You can also add movement to a pitch that is ordinarily straight. Maybe you typically throw four-seam fastballs. Practice throwing a two-seam fastball. If you can get even a little sinking, running, or tailing action on it (see Chapter 3), you'll be able to fool a lot of hitters who are expecting your straight fastball.

LOCATION

Try for too much velocity, and you lose movement. Try for too much movement, and you lose location. When "pitching in a pinch," location is more important than either velocity or movement. The bottom line is that the more pitches you can control, the more the hitter has to think about—and the greater your chances for success.

You can focus on hitting a spot that has worked for you all day, or you can try to cross up the batter by throwing to a different part of the plate. For example, many right-handed off-speed pitchers throw their breaking stuff low and in to lefties to set up their fastball away. Perhaps you were very successful with that the first time through the lineup, but found the hitters starting to lay off your breaking stuff off the plate. They started getting good swings at breaking balls that got too much of the strike zone and began taking your average fastball the other way. Maybe it's the third time through the lineup and the last batter

Set a hitter up with something thrown hard and inside, and he often becomes susceptible to an off-speed pitch thrown low and away.

has just golfed your curveball down the right-field line for a triple. Say you've got two strikes on the next hitter, but the tying run's on third with no one out and you need a strikeout. Maybe you cross him up by hitting the outside corner with a "back-door" breaking ball. Or maybe you've got enough guts to challenge him with your mediocre fastball on the inside black, knowing that it's the last thing he'd expect in that situation. Either way, it won't be the pitch that gets him—it will be the location.

> *"Even in the major leagues, you can throw the wrong pitch at the wrong time, but put it in a good location and you can get the batter out."*
>
> —Bob Apodaca

ATTACKING HITTERS WITH A PLAN: THE VALUE OF INFORMATION

> *"[Koufax and Maddux] both have a love for the art of pitching. That's the only similarity they have, and the only similarity they really need to have. They both have an appreciation for their craft, and both worked very hard at getting better at it—finding out more information and using that information."*
>
> —Hall of Famer Don Sutton on the greatest pitchers of two different generations, Sandy Koufax and Greg Maddux

Pitchers have been observing and exploiting hitters' tendencies for years. No one knows who was the first to enter this information in a "black book," though it may have been a veteran pitcher named Howard Ehmke. He won 166 games in a 14-year big league career, but his biggest win was his last in the majors. Ehmke was about to be released by the Philadelphia Athletics, who were on their way to the 1929 pennant. He appealed to manager/owner Connie Mack, who sent him off for a month to scout the front-running Chicago Cubs.

When the two teams met in the World Series, Mack made Ehmke his surprise choice to start Game 1. Knowing the Cubs' weaknesses inside and out, he responded with a baffling 13-strikeout (a World Series record at the time), 3–1 victory. In more modern terms, imagine if the Atlanta Braves sent a veteran like Bob Tewksbury off for a month to scout the New York Yankees, then used their fifth starter to pitch Game 1 of the World Series after being idle since September—only to have him throw a gem.

> *"[Pitching is] a memory test, like playing a game of cards where you must remember every card that has been played."*
>
> —Howard Ehmke

When you're pitching more than one game against the same competition, you need to start keeping what's called a "black book" (though today's pitchers often use computers). In your "book," you need to record each at bat for each batter you faced, noting what you threw, what he took, what he offered at, what he hit, and what he missed. Some pitchers take meticulous notes, others simply indicate what worked (such as "chases the breaking ball away"). Some pitchers can enter this information solely from memory— a tribute to their concentration level during the game—while others need to rely on the pitch charts kept by the next game's starter. The important thing is that you take a disciplined approach to retaining and using information on the hitters you face.

There are countless stories of hugely talented players who never reached their potential as pitchers because they never learned how to adapt to the adjustments the hitters were making to them. They never studied the hitters enough to know how. Curt Schilling acknowledges that he made it to the majors on talent alone, but he has since worked hard to develop into one of the greatest strikeout pitchers in baseball history. In fact, only Sandy Koufax of the 10-strikeouts-per-game club has dominated hitters with better control than Schilling.

Curt Schilling's success has coincided with his becoming a student of the game. He keeps detailed files in his computer on opposing batters. He prepares for games by visualizing the lineup he will be facing and how he will pitch to them. As he puts it, "If I get a hitter to swing at a certain pitch in a certain situation it's not because I'm lucky. It's because I'm prepared." Schilling's preparation does not end with the hitters; he also studies umpires: "If it's the seventh inning in a crucial situation and I want to freeze a hitter inside, I better know that the umpire is a guy who will call that pitch."

GAME-TIME OBSERVATIONS

"I know there are a lot of pitchers out there who say that they refuse to have their pitching approach influenced by the strength of the hitter. But sometimes, you've got to use common sense. If you're facing a low-ball hitter, it makes sense to throw the ball up in the strike zone. That doesn't mean you're changing your game for him, it just means you're being a smart pitcher."

—David Wells

Well before batter-tendency charts, videotapes, and laptops, pitchers were students of hitters. What hasn't changed between then and now is the importance of observation. With a fastball that couldn't break glass, Eddie Lopat had to be extremely attentive to anything the batter might reveal: "The reflexes of a batter tell you what he's looking for. I watch his reactions, watch the hands on the bat. If I threw a fastball, did he show me that he was a little late?"

Even if you haven't faced a hitter before, you can tell a lot just by where he stands. Don Sutton would observe when hitters stood close to the plate and ask himself, "Are they trying to lure me inside or can they not handle anything inside? Experience taught me the answer." A hitter who stands well off the plate may make it tempting for a pitcher to try to get him out away. Hal McRae used to stand far back from the plate, then drive outside pitches the other way for doubles in the gap. The same with Jim Leyritz. What may look like an opportunity is actually a trap. He wants you to go away; he's standing back there so he won't get jammed on inside pitches.

Watch hitters' practice swings, too, and look for holes in their swing. If the front shoulder dips, the hitter will probably have a hard time with fastballs up and in. If it rises, he'll hit a lot of balls in the air and will struggle with breaking balls down in the strike zone. Does he have a long, looping swing? Feed him inside fastballs. Does he have a hitch in his swing? Throw him fastballs up in the zone.

"During the 1988 World Series [Dodgers vs. A's], we faced Canseco and McGwire and the mighty Oakland lineup. I watched the way McGwire and Canseco manipulated their feet. When they stood pigeon-toed, I knew they were looking for something middle-away to drive the ball to right-center field. So we pitched them inside. When they opened up or pulled back the front foot a little, they were looking for something middle-in to pull. So we pitched them away. Our staff dominated that series because they gave themselves away by their stances in the batter's box."

—Rick Dempsey, former Dodgers catcher, commenting on the 1988 World Series, in which the Dodgers shocked Oakland by defeating them four games to one. The Bash Brothers (Canseco and McGwire) went a combined 2-for-36 in the series with just two home runs.

with other pitchers, which isn't a good way to learn how hitters think.

> *"Hitters take pitches certain ways, they foul off pitches certain ways, and they get hits certain ways. You try to anticipate what they're looking for as best you can. But you're never sure. Anticipate the best you can and pitch accordingly."*
>
> —Greg Maddux on reading hitters' minds

With better hitters, you may have to face them several times before you notice any patterns you can exploit. Does he try to take everything the other way? Throw him fastballs inside. Does he try to pull everything? Work him away. Does he sit on the fastball? Miss with a fastball, then throw a change-up in the strike zone.

What do you do when the hitter you've been observing seems to have no weaknesses? He fights off the tough pitches or takes them the other way, and he crushes fastballs middle-in and hanging

Ryan Klesko (in an open stance) frequently struggles with pitches in the outside half of the strike zone.

Sometimes you'll need to actually see a hitter take some swings for real before you can learn anything. His front foot will tell you a lot. If it moves away from the plate, he'll be vulnerable to breaking balls away. If it moves toward the plate, throw him a fastball inside. If he takes a long stride or if his weight shift is poor and he hits off his front foot, he'll have a harder time with pitches down and inside and off-speed.

Try to learn something in the very first at bat. The first time through the lineup, one of Greg Maddux's many tricks is to give a hitter a ball he can take the other way—just to see if he will. Maddux, perhaps more than any pitcher in the game today, really works at understanding hitters. It's no coincidence that he spends most games sitting alongside the Braves' *hitting* coach. Some say he knows hitters better than they know themselves. Too many pitchers spend all of their time

Hitters who hold their hands low and away from their body commonly have trouble handling pitches up in the strike zone.

breaking balls. At times like these, remind yourself that two-thirds of all balls that are put in play end up as outs. Limit the damage. Pitch him away and avoid throwing the same pitch twice in a row. Do the best you can to vary your pitch patterns and locations. Most importantly, throw strikes early in the count. Too often young pitchers give good hitters too much respect and nibble. Suddenly, you've fallen behind 2–0 or 3–1 and that good hitter now becomes a great hitter.

Hitters know they're being observed, and they're watching the pitcher just as closely. Some of the smart ones have been known to set traps. A common one is to take a number of pitches early in the game, especially the first pitch, then jump on a first-pitch fastball late in the game. The best defense against this is to assume nothing. The only patterns you reveal should be traps of your own.

DEVELOPING A YOUTH LEAGUE PITCHING PLAN

Hitters study pitchers endlessly, looking for pitch patterns, release points, and discrepancies in their motion that tip pitches. All of this investigative research is practiced with the hopes of gaining an advantage at the plate. So if you're a pitcher, why not focus your attention on what the hitter might be telling you. Hitters tip their strengths and weaknesses with regularity. If you're observant, you can expose them and reduce them to an easy out.

Major league pitchers enjoy the benefit of seeing hitters time after time. They're able to establish a pitching plan by analyzing the results of previous encounters. A collegiate or high school pitcher may face hitters who play within their conference only a few times. Babe Ruth and Little League pitchers may recall a hitter's tendencies when facing them from year to year or possibly in neighborhood games. But it's rare for amateur pitchers to see opposing hitters over a three-game series like in the big leagues.

So how do you establish a scouting report on a hitter in youth leagues? Well, in Little League and Babe Ruth, don't ignore what you hear by word of mouth or about the reputation of a hitter. Any information is useful information. If you know which team you're scheduled to pitch against, have Mom or Dad take you over to the field and watch one of their games. Take notes on pitches each hitter handles well and also pitches he struggles with. Pay attention to whether he swings early in the count or if he takes a few pitches. Record the type of pitches as well as the pitch location each hitter likes and dislikes. Will he chase a pitch out of the strike zone? Does he take outside strikes until he has two strikes in the count? Does he have trouble handling good fastballs? Is he easily fooled by off-speed pitches? Be your own scout. It will help you become successful, and you'll even have fun doing it.

At times, you'll have no information on an offense heading into a game. Say, for example, you're competing against unfamiliar teams in an out-of-town tournament. In this case, you can use the most basic information you have available— the opponent's batting order. In youth leagues, the best hitters are usually loaded at the top of the lineup and the weaker hitters are placed toward the bottom.

The leadoff and number-two hitters are generally players who make consistent contact, have the discipline to swing at pitches only in the strike zone, and possess speed on the bases. It's a good idea to concentrate on throwing strikes to these hitters. The number-three hitter is the team's best hitter, and the cleanup and five hitter hit for power. These three hitters will have good bat speed, excellent hand-eye coordination, superior strength, or all of the above. Because they have talent, they'll be aggressive and eager to swing the bat. Stay on the outside edges of the strike zone and change speeds. Keep them off balance and swinging at borderline pitches, and you'll keep them under control.

The seven, eight, and nine hitters are in those slots for a reason. They may have poor hand-eye coordination, or they may not have enough bat speed to be able to catch up to your fastball. Be aggressive and challenge these hitters. If they beat you with a base hit, tip your cap to them and make an adjustment the next time you face them.

What about the six hitter? Well, the ability of the batter in the six hole usually depends on the strength of the team. Against a strong offensive team, the quality of hitters probably runs a little deeper. Approach the six hitter like you would the five hitter; with caution. When facing a weak offensive team, the talent pool will be a bit shallow. In this case, go at the six hitter as if he is their seven hitter.

Remember, young hitters like to hit early in the count. They have not yet learned how to work counts and hit with two strikes. Induce them to swing at a tough pitch instead of laying in a fat one right away. Their greatest fear is getting to two strikes and eventually striking out. Use their fear to your advantage.

As you advance through Babe Ruth, high school, American Legion and college-level base-ball, the hitters will get better and better. The ability of hitters rises with each level. If your ability doesn't rise commensurately, you could be in for some long days on the mound.

COUNTS

"I like to get ahead of a hitter by starting him off away, especially if it's the first time I've faced him in that particular game. My theory is that you pitch in when you're ahead in the count, and pitch outside when you're behind."
—Nolan Ryan

WORKING THE UMPIRES

"You'll run into umpires that are 'pitcher's umpires', but you'll also run into those who aren't. It's in your best interest to acknowledge what the ump's strike zone is early in the game and throw to it. If you think his judgment is questionable, the bottom line is, it doesn't matter what you think. Deal with it, or you may be in for a long, long day on the hill."—David Wells

Arguing balls and strikes or becoming frustrated with an umpire creates nothing but negative results. In the history of baseball, no umpire has ever heard a complaint from a pitcher and then said, "You know, you're right; that did catch the corner. Let me change my call to a strike." It has never happened and it never will. Your job is to pitch, and the umpire's job is to call balls and strikes. Concentrate on doing your job and don't worry about his.

It's the catcher's job—not yours—to ask an umpire how close a ball came to nicking the inside corner. He can do it much more discreetly than you can. If nothing else, it can serve to place in the umpire's head that the pitcher plans to go after that corner again. If you're breaking off especially nasty curveballs in warm-ups, it's up to the catcher to let the umpire know that you've got a good bender working today. You don't want your pitch ending up fooling *him*, too.

You can make a good guess about an umpire's tendency before you even throw a pitch. Watch where he sets up, because that determines how well he'll see different parts of the strike zone. Is he looking over the catcher? Chances are he'll give you the high strike and squeeze you a bit on the low ones. Is he setting up lower, to one side of the catcher or the other? He'll see the low strike better than the high strike. And if he's to the batter's side of the catcher, he's got an excellent view of the inside corner and a fuzzier view of the outside corner. Most likely, he'll be less consistent on the outside corner, but he could end up giving you a few inches off the plate if you hit the catcher's glove.

"If the umpire upsets your pitcher, go calm him. Say, 'I'll handle that bum.' Then go to the umpire and say, 'Ignore that bozo. He's a space cadet.' You've got to be the buffer."—Steve Yeager, former Dodgers catcher

Calling balls and strikes is the responsibility of the umpire. Any effort expended worrying about his calls is wasted energy.

"First, throw strikes. Get ahead of the batter and then make him hit your pitch. Second, if you do get behind in the count, change speeds. Don't give in and groove a fastball. Third, when you must throw the fastball, keep it low."

—Scout Bill Werle

When pitching to the count, the choices that pitchers must face can be boiled down to what to throw on the first pitch, what to throw when you're ahead, and what to throw when you're behind.

FIRST PITCH

The most important pitch is strike one.

There is a misleading statistic you might hear thrown around that can make some pitchers afraid to throw a first-pitch strike: gaudy batting averages for first-pitch swingers. Big leaguers do hit around .330 on the first pitch, as opposed to .265 overall. You'll see this increase in high school, college, the minors, everywhere. But that's the batting average of hitters who *connect* with the first pitch, and it should be compared to the overall batting average of hitters who make contact with *any* pitch. The two are virtually identical. The same holds true for slugging average. First-pitch swingers do not lose anything—it may be the best pitch they see—but they also do not *gain* any real advantage by hacking. At lower levels, in fact, first-pitch swinging is often indicative of being impatient and not very selective—traits a pitcher should notice and exploit.

Batters may not be gaining much if anything by swinging at the first pitch, but pitchers are gaining a lot by throwing a first-pitch strike. In the big leagues, hitters' batting average will drop by 10 to 15 points when a first-pitch strike is thrown—even if that first pitch is hit—and it will go up by 15 to 20 points when a pitcher falls behind 1–0. A called first strike will drop a batter's average by 30 to 40 points. The same thing happens with slugging average. A pitcher who throws a first-pitch strike is less likely to yield a home run during the course of the at bat than a pitcher who throws a first-pitch ball. The effects tend to be even more extreme at lower levels.

In short, the importance of the first pitch cannot be overstated. Other than first-ball fastball hitters, many hitters aren't all that aggressive. At lower levels, hitters tend to be less patient—but you'll still find coaches from high school to college to the minors who are frustrated by hitters not swinging at hittable, first-pitch strikes. So if you can hit your spots with your fastball, and keep it from catching too much of the plate, it can be a very effective pitch even against a fastball hitter.

Don't be nervous throwing a first-pitch fastball for a strike the first time through the lineup. Put yourself in the hitter's shoes. In most cases, a hitter wants to see a fastball before swinging at one. He'll want to gauge its speed, see what type of movement it has, recognize whether it has late life or if it's sneaky fast, and also observe what type of plane it travels on to the plate. A hitter acquires most of this information even if the pitch is off the plate. So do yourself a favor and throw it for strike. Get ahead in the count early, and put the hitter at your mercy.

When facing an aggressive hitter, use his aggressiveness against him with a fastball a little bit off the plate. He might chase it. Or bring a fastball up and in off the plate. Chances are they're sitting on a fastball and won't be able to lay off. The result could be a long foul, but that's still strike one. Be careful about this pitch as the game progresses, especially when facing sluggers—the more tired you are, the easier it will be for you to leave that pitch out over the plate. A change-up at the knees late in the game, after he's seen and timed your fastball, can also be effective.

As a middle reliever during his major league career, Larry Andersen had good-enough command of his slider to throw it for a first-pitch strike. Some of them were called strikes while others were well-hit strikes. Anderson says, "When I faced a left-handed hitter, I would often start them off with a slider on the inside corner. When a hitter sees a hard pitch on the inside part of the plate, he's got to start his swing early. When the pitch breaks in and has a little less velocity than a fastball, the head of the bat gets out in front of the plate and there's nothing they can do but pull it foul. That's a free strike."

Taking it one step further, there are advantages to throwing a breaking ball for strike one and following it up with a fastball. Andersen described a common pattern he sees frequently from the broadcast booth: "Even if it's the third time through the lineup, if you can get the first-pitch breaking ball for a strike, come back with a fastball. Very rarely will you see that fastball get put into play. You'll see it fouled off time and time and time again."

AHEAD IN THE COUNT

"I worked long and hard to master the control of my breaking ball and change-up. As my confidence in those pitches improved, I was able to set hitters up, get ahead in the count, and apply strategy instead of sheer force."

—Nolan Ryan

There is good reason why the fastball is referred to as "old number one."

There are managers at all levels who get so aggravated by 0–2 base hits that they will fine pitchers for throwing a ball over the plate in the situation, even if it's strike three. Some pitchers get so traumatized by these managers that they won't even come near the strike zone with the pitch. Hitters soon learn this and it truly becomes a "waste pitch." The best pitchers will tell you that there is *never* any reason to waste a pitch.

"What are you accomplishing if you throw the ball a foot over the batter's head? What are you setting him up for when you do that? He's not going to swing at it. All you have done is waste a pitch. When I get to 0–2 on a hitter, I like to get him out with the next pitch. I throw a lot of pitches as it is, I don't need to throw any extra ones."

—Hall of Famer Bob Gibson

A pitcher should use the 0–2 pitch to set up the hitter for something else, or make him hit the pitch you want him to hit. You can also try to get in the batter's head by "showcasing" a pitch early in the game—even if it's a third or fourth pitch that you didn't have much command of in the bullpen warming up, you've given the hitter that much more to think about later in the game.

By getting ahead in the count, you put the hitter on the defensive. If you fall behind, he won't swing at anything but fat pitches.

None of these is a "waste" pitch. They're "purpose" pitches. An 0–2 or 1–2 count is *not* an invitation to try to blow a batter away—unless the game situation calls for it, such as a runner on third and less than two outs. When facing a hitter without the bat speed to catch up to your fastball, it makes sense to bring more heat anywhere over the plate. The higher the level of competition, the more rare this luxury will be. You'll need to start looking at the 0–2 or 1–2 count not as two-thirds of a strikeout, but an opportunity to capitalize on the fact that the hitter must protect the plate and expand his strike zone.

When thinking about what to throw the better hitters in the opposing lineup, keep in mind how you got to two strikes in the first place.

- Did the batter just get out in front of an inside fastball and pull it foul? Good time for a change-up in the strike zone.
- Is he swinging through the fastball? Bring it again, aiming for the outer third—since missing away is a lot less dangerous.
- Have you gotten strikes with fastballs or breaking balls away? Freeze him inside with a fastball.
- Has he gone after a fastball at the belt followed by a fastball at the letters? Climb

the ladder. Throw another fastball chin-high and watch him chase that one, too.
- Has he gone after a breaking ball down and then a fastball up? Go up and down the ladder. Throw another breaking ball down or a fastball up, depending on the location of the second strike.
- Has he gone after breaking pitches down and out of the strike zone? Throw another breaking ball in the same spot until he proves he can lay off of it.

Los Angeles Dodgers starter Darren Dreifort believes throwing a purpose pitch can complement your "out pitch" by creating a psychological advantage: "A purpose pitch is setting a guy up for a strikeout pitch or something you want to get him out with. In certain cases, you may want to move a guy back off the plate by throwing something hard and inside so you can come back with an off-speed pitch away.

"It is important to pay attention to how a hitter reacts to your purpose pitch. If you throw him something hard and in and notice he's still leaning out over the plate, you may want to come back with another fastball even farther inside. You've got to give the hitters credit sometimes for thinking along with you. If they recognize a pitch hard and inside as a purpose pitch, they may realize they're being set up and counter it by looking for the next pitch to be something away."

Is there a pitch besides your "out pitch" that you think you can get the hitter out on? If you can get him out without it, you'll still have the element of surprise on your side later in the game in what might prove to be a more critical spot. Maybe you just stay with the fastball, moving it around in the zone, until he shows he can hit it. Or maybe you go to your third best pitch here, making sure it's located where you're less likely to get hurt—keep the change-up away and the breaking ball down.

On 0–2, sometimes you'll need to think about using two pitches to get the batter out (though with runners on, you need to be careful not to let an 0–2 or 1–2 count get to 3–2; by failing to put the hitter away, you're letting the base runners move with the pitch and your margin for error has disappeared). The two-pitch combination is usually just a matter of mixing up velocity (fastball, change), movement (slider, fastball), and location (inside, outside or high, low). You need to be careful not to fall into predictable patterns, though. Show a hitter too many inside/outside combinations and as soon as he sees the 0–2 fastball on his hands he'll be practically diving across the plate for the 1–2 slider away.

By setting up hitters in this manner, you will not have to rely on the same pitch in the same spot to get batters out. Here's how a three-pitch (fastball, change-up, breaking ball) pitcher could use all three as his out pitch five different ways in five different at bats:

- fastball outer half (0–1), breaking ball outer half (0–2), fastball away (1–2), fastball inner half
- breaking ball (0–1), fastball outer half (0–2), fastball in (1–2), change-up
- fastball lower half (0–1), fastball lower half (0–2), breaking ball low (1–2), fastball upper half
- fastball inner half (0–1), fastball inner half (0–2), fastball up and in (1–2), breaking ball outer half
- fastball upper half (0–1), change-up down (0–2), fastball up (1–2), breaking ball lower half
- fastball low in the strike zone (0–1), fastball high in the strike zone (0–2), fastball up and out of the strike zone

BEHIND IN THE COUNT

"The real good pitchers are the guys who on 2–0 and 3–1 don't have to throw the fastball. They can get their change over, their slider, whatever."

—Whitey Herzog, former manager

Many hitters—and most power hitters—approach an at bat with a very simple strategy. Get the pitcher in a position where he has to throw a fast-ball. Some dead-pull hitters will even give up the outer third early in the at bat, and sit on a fastball middle-in. As a pitcher, all you can do is try to get your breaking ball over and paint the outside black with your fastball. If you could do that every time, you'd be Greg Maddux. But even Maddux has to deal with hitter's counts on occasion—2–0 and 3–1. In finding the best way for you to get out of them, think about velocity, movement, and location.

Velocity. Most hitters who are sitting on your fastball can't do much with your change-up. You'll certainly have more success taking something off your fastball than trying to throw it through the backstop. This is called a batting-practice (BP) fastball. It's simply a fastball thrown at about 85 to 90 percent effort. To throw it, take a deep breath to relax your body, and throw a fastball at less than maximum effort. The challenge is to work on it enough that you can control it, not telegraph it, and develop the guts to throw it—then to not throw it so much that hitters start sitting on *it*.

"How dumb can the hitters in this league get? . . . When they're batting with the count two balls and no strikes, or three and one, they're always looking for the fastball. And they never get it."

—Eppa Rixey, a change-up specialist who won 266 games in a career that spanned from 1912 to 1933

Movement. Many pitchers go to a breaking ball on offensive counts simply because they don't have much confidence in their fastball. The hitter isn't just sitting on a fastball, he's sitting on a fairly mediocre one. On 2–0 and 3–1, Tim Wakefield still has to throw his knuckleball and hope for the best—as Phil Niekro did before him. Jim Bouton attempted a comeback as a knuckleballer in the mid-'70s without the fastball he had when he went 21–7 for the 1963 Yankees. He spoke for most soft-tossing, breaking-ball specialists, and not just knuckleballers, when he explained his philosophy of pitching: "I'd rather walk the guy with my best pitch than let him beat me with one swing at my worst."

Location. Greg Maddux's pitching coach, Leo Mazzone, encourages his pitchers to "go inside on offensive counts." To a fastball hitter who's been watching junk float by down and away, an inside fastball can look very appetizing even if it's too far in to do anything with except rip foul. And a pitcher like Maddux, who has both a tailing fast-ball (breaks toward righties) and a cut fastball (breaks toward lefties), can make those unhittable inside fastballs look even more appealing by start-ing them out over the plate. Even if you don't have Maddux's pinpoint control or outstanding move-ment, you can turn offensive counts to your advantage by challenging hitters inside.

Hitters frequently get themselves out when served an inside fastball, even when they're look-ing for one. When a hitter sits on an inside pitch and gets it, he'll often "muscle up" on his swing, which diminishes his bat speed. The barrel of the bat will be just a bit late getting to the ball, and the result will be a lazy fly ball to the opposite field. On his way back to the dugout, the hitter will be shak-ing his head mumbling, "I just missed that one."

Brady Anderson does a fine job of getting the bat level through the hitting zone, but the barrel is an instant late, causing him to hit a routine fly ball to left field. Challenging the hitter is often a pitcher's best option.

Don't get too cute with the inside corner, though. Remember, stay away from predictable pitch patterns. There is an expression that hitters use about pitchers who come inside too often and eventually pay the price: "You can come into my kitchen, but don't be sitting down to eat."

"They would be ready and anxious on the 2–0 count. But they'd try to pull that outside pitch and would hit a fly ball to center field. I was lucky to have good outfielders with the Yankees, so even if they hit it deep it was just an out. I don't know how many times one of them would say to me, 'You lucky so-and-so, I just missed getting that one.' They didn't have any idea what had happened."

—Hall of Famer Allie Reynolds on the
outside fastball

Sometimes you need to be more careful when behind on the hitter. If first base is open and the on-deck hitter isn't quite so dangerous, pitch around him. If you walk him, so be it. You can avoid insulting the on-deck hitter by using the "unintentional walk." Try to throw unhittable pitches and maybe you hit the corners, or maybe he pops one up. If not, he takes his base and you go after an on-deck hitter who doesn't have smoke coming out of his ears.

If the bases are empty, a speedy hitter who lacks power should be challenged with fastballs. Walking a good base stealer practically puts him in scoring position. With slap hitters, the best location behind in the count can be right down the middle with a fastball.

LEARN FROM EXPERIENCE

When major league pitchers get better with age, it's often because they are putting their experi-ence to use. Everyone *has* experience, but not everyone *uses* that experience. Every time you step on the mound, you gain experience. Be aware of *why* things are happening, and you can begin to *use* that experience. This will help you make adjustments during the game, work out of trouble, and attack hitters with a plan.

For illustration, compare some 1998 results for three veteran pitchers—Greg Maddux, Chuck Finley, and Orel Hershiser—to those of a talented rookie (Eric Milton) being forced to learn at the major league level.

GREG MADDUX: IN-GAME ADJUSTMENTS

Greg Maddux will drive batters nuts by working them differently each time he faces them in a ballgame. As a result, he actually gets tougher to hit as the game goes along, and if you don't get to him in the first inning you might not get to him at all. Eric Milton, on the other hand, enjoyed his best success in the first two innings—better even than Maddux, in some respects—then got knocked around on his second time through the lineup.

At most levels of competition, you should pitch a hitter the same way until he proves he can do something with it. At the highest levels, as Maddux shows, you may need to get a batter out one way while setting him up for another way in his next at bat.

CHUCK FINLEY: WORKING OUT OF TROUBLE

In 1998, veteran lefty Chuck Finley put almost as many runners on base as rookie Eric Milton. Nevertheless, his ERA was more than two runs per game lower than the rookie's. Why? He was better at working out of trouble than Milton. He had a downward-breaking pitch he could use to coax more ground balls out of opposing batters. He had a reliable strikeout pitch, making him much tougher on hitters once he got two strikes on them. And his experience helped him to relax and remain focused—rather than panicking—which, in turn, allowed him to make better pitches at critical moments.

The techniques demonstrated by Finley could and should be used by pitchers at all levels.

	Eric Milton	Greg Maddux	ML Average
BA, First 30 Pitches,	.242	.261	.260
SA, First 30 Pitches,	.381	.362	.404
BA, Second 30 Pitches,	.289	.192	.271
SA, Second 30 Pitches,	.514	.265	.428

	Eric Milton	Chuck Finley	AL Average
ERA	5.64	3.39	4.65
Ground balls per Inning	.9	1.3	1.4
BA, Two Strikes	.219	.164	.193
% of Two-Strike Counts Resulting in Strikeouts	28%	44%	36%
BA, Runners on 2nd or 3rd	.338	.217	.270
% of Batters Struck Out with Runners on 2nd or 3rd	10%	28%	17%

As you use them and have success with them, you will add another technique: self-confidence.

OREL HERSHISER: THE PLAN BEGINS WITH STRIKE ONE

You don't need John Smoltz's slider or Greg Maddux's pinpoint control to be able to work a hitter. Even at the age of 40, Orel Hershiser could get ahead of hitters and use the count to his advantage. Though Eric Milton threw more first-pitch strikes than Hershiser in 1998, Orel got significantly more first-pitch outs and yielded much less first-pitch damage. As the chart below shows, Eric Milton was one of the few pitchers to be more effective by throwing a first-pitch ball—and that kind of random result can only happen when you aren't attacking hitters with a definite plan.

What can you take away from this? That your plan begins with strike one. A first-pitch strike— swinging or called—sets up your next pitch and will dramatically improve your chances of getting the batter out. A ball put in play will be an out two-thirds of the time. As you get better at throwing strikes to a particular part of the plate, your success rate will only get higher. A first-pitch ball gets you nothing.

> ········ **Throw It Again**
> Pitch selection is an art and a science. You need to consider the count, the strengths and weaknesses of the hitter, the game situation, and your stuff on that particular day. If you play in a league where you will pitch against the same team more than once, you should begin to gather and use information on the opposing lineups to help you make the proper pitch selections.

	Eric Milton	Orel Hershiser	ML Average
1st-Pitch Outs per 9 Innings	2.8	3.4	3.2
SA, 1st Pitch	.587	.398	.525
BA, 1st Pitch	.325	.287	.333
BA After 0–1	.284	.229	.231
BA After 1–0	.268	.280	.283

MODERN PITCHING:
FIVE-MAN ROTATIONS, EXPANSION, AND THE SPLITTER

Perhaps it was the calling of the low strike that enabled a crop of pitchers to emerge in the 1970s and early 1980s who could win without striking out batters, something baseball hadn't seen since the 1940s. Pitchers like Clyde Wright (father of hard-throwing Jaret), Scott McGregor, Ross Grimsley, Lary Sorensen, Paul Splittorff, Larry Gura, Mike Caldwell, Jim Barr, and Randy Jones were getting by on low strikes, off-speed pitches, and the inevitable parade of groundouts. The best example was Bill Lee, the third-winningest left-hander in Fenway Park's history—a park that southpaws such as Wilbur Wood, John Tudor, and Bobby Ojeda had to escape before experiencing any real success. The only pitcher of Lee's era to win 100 games with a lower rate of strikeouts was Jim Barr, his teammate on USC's 1968 NCAA championship squad.

THE RIGHT STUFF VS. THE WRONG STUFF

Bill Lee couldn't match Nolan Ryan's longevity, and his junk certainly couldn't compare with Ryan's heat, but for three years in the mid-'70s, "Spaceman" held his own with the "Ryan Express." It shows that you don't need overpowering stuff to get batters out.

1973–75	Nolan Ryan	Bill Lee
W–L	57–44	51–35
Win Pct.	.564	.593
Innings	857	827
Hits	611	869
Walks	496	212
HW/9	11.63	11.76
ERA	3.01	3.38

In addition to the low strike, the other significant development of the era in pitching occurred in 1977 when a Cubs relief pitcher with an average fastball was one of the most unhittable pitchers in big league history. In a league that hit .262, Bruce Sutter held batters to a .182 batting average. In 107 innings he struck out 110 batters and recorded an ERA of 1.35, almost single-handedly keeping the Cubs in the pennant race until he broke down after the all-star break. His secret weapon was a new pitch called the split-fingered fastball. It was similar to the forkball thrown by Lindy McDaniel and Elroy Face—relief aces of another era—only thrown much harder. The original forkball served as a change-up, while the splitter offered the movement of a "dry spitter." It looked just like a fastball, but dove down at the last split second—usually beneath the big swing of a fooled batter. Sutter came back in 1979 to hold hitters to a .186 batting average in 101 innings. At the time, he was the only pitcher in history to hold hitters to that low an average for that many innings *twice* (Nolan Ryan did it for the second time in 1991, 19 years after doing it for the first time). *That* was how devastating Sutter's splitter could be.

> *"Most of the time they'd be called balls if the batters would only leave 'em alone."*
>
> —Bruce Sutter, Cy Young Award winning reliever, on his split-fingered fastballs

The best news for pitchers, however, was that the splitter was fairly easy to throw—provided your hands were large enough to hold a ball between your fingers. It was a strikeout pitch for pitchers without strikeout stuff. Unlike other briefly unhittable breaking balls, like Ron Guidry's 1978 slider or Fernando Valenzuela's 1981 screwball, the splitter didn't lose its bite as quickly and hitters didn't adjust to it as easily. The pitch spread quickly, especially in the National League, and big league ERAs and batting averages fell while strikeouts climbed. The pitch of the 1980s, the splitter even helped turn Mike Scott, a journeyman with a 29–44 career record, into an overnight sensation who won the 1986 Cy Young Award with 10 strikeouts per game and a 2.23 ERA.

> *"[It has] the velocity of a Sandy Koufax fastball and the movement of a Koufax curve. It's like a fastball with a bomb attached to it."*
>
> —Umpire Doug Harvey on Mike Scott's split-fingered fastball

SPLITTING THE DIFFERENCE

American League	Runs	Home Runs	Walks	Strikeouts	Batting Average	Slugging Average
1977	734	144	521	805	.266	.405
1988	706	136	515	883	.259	.391

National League	Runs	Home Runs	Walks	Strikeouts	Batting Average	Slugging Average
1977	713	136	541	874	.262	.397
1988	629	107	484	922	.248	.363

Average team, 162 games.

The downside to heavy use of the splitter is the strain it places on a pitcher's arm, making it a "deal with the devil" that marginal major leaguers are willing to jump at while others hesitate. The anecdotal evidence supports the fears, with a probable list of split-finger casualties including Jack McDowell, Dan Petry, Mike Scott, just about Roger Craig's entire San Francisco Giants pitching staff, and Bruce Sutter himself. Today, many splitter devotees such as Roger Clemens, David Cone, and Shane Reynolds use it sparingly as an out pitch—much like Christy Mathewson learned to do with his fadeaway.

Fewer pitchers throwing fewer splitters is just one explanation for why hitting has taken off again in the 1990s. Expansion has reduced the quality of pitching to very low levels, with talented rookies such as Eric Milton being forced to learn at the big league level. The move to the five-man rotation during the 1970s—prompted in part by the early retirement of work-horse pitcher Sandy Koufax—diluted pitching by another 20 percent. New, intimate parks such as Baltimore's Camden Yards have replaced larger, older stadiums. And eighty-one games a year are played in Denver, where thin air takes the break out of curveballs and allows fly balls to carry 10 percent farther.

Regardless of the stadium, hitters swing for the fences in the hopes of showing up on someone's highlight reel, while pitchers raised on unbreakable aluminum bats in high school and college hesitate to throw inside. Weight training does more for bat speed than arm speed, while many of the game's best young arms are often pampered rather than strengthened at all. Most overpowering pitchers are turned into relief specialists who throw only 70 innings per year. Tight strike zones and the high cost of making a mistake cause many starters to run deep counts, reaching 100 pitches in six innings or less and forcing the game to be turned over to a middle reliever. Though the days of the 300-inning pitcher are long gone, today's starters are throwing just as many pitches, if not more, than Grover Alexander did when he polished teams off in under one hour.

"What do you want me to do? Let those SOBs stand up there and think on my time?"

—Grover Alexander on working fast

TAKING THE OFFENSIVE

American League	Runs	Home Runs	Walks	Strikeouts	Batting Average	Slugging Average
1988	706	136	515	883	.259	.391
1998	811	178	552	1,031	.271	.431

National League	Runs	Home Runs	Walks	Strikeouts	Batting Average	Slugging Average
1988	629	107	484	922	.248	.363
1998	745	160	544	1,090	.262	.410

Average team, 162 games.

In the 1990s, pitchers are taking a page out of Grover Alexander's book and going back to the basics of changing speeds to get batters out—turning batters' quick bats against them. Greg Maddux and Tom Glavine are acknowledged masters of this, but even power pitchers such as John Smoltz and Kerry Wood include a change-up in their repertoire. Pedro Martinez's ability to take the step to Cy Young Award status in 1997 was attributed by many to his mastery of the change-up.

Albert Goodwill Spalding would be proud.

"The smart pitchers today can capitalize on the hitter's fondness for home runs."

  —Hall of Famer Bob Feller

GREAT PITCHING NICKNAMES

The Hoosier Thunderbolt (Amos Rusie)

Old Hoss (Charles Radbourn)

Cyclone (Denton True "Cy" Young)

Icebox (Elton Chamberlain)

Iron Man (Joe McGinnity)

Big 6 (Christy Mathewson)

Three-Finger (Mordecai Brown)

The Big Train (Walter Johnson)

Ol' Stubblebeard (Burleigh Grimes)

Dazzy (Clarence Vance)

Dizzy (Jay Hanna Dean)

Daffy (Paul Dee Dean)

Satchel (Leroy Paige)

Schoolboy (Lynwood Thomas Rowe)

The Meal Ticket, King Carl (Carl Hubbell)

The Arkansas Hummingbird (Lon Warneke)

Rapid Robert (Bob Feller)

The Barber (Sal Maglie)

The Chairman of the Board (Edward Charles "Whitey" Ford)

Big D (Don Drysdale)

Sudden Sam (Sam McDowell)

The Monster (Dick Radatz)

The Vulture (Phil Regan)

The Ryan Express (Nolan Ryan)

Mudcat (Jim Grant)

Catfish (Jim Hunter)

Blue Moon (John Odom)

Spaceman (Bill Lee)

The Bird (Mark Fidrych)

The Emu (Jim Kern)

The Mad Hungarian (Al Hrabosky)

The Terminator (Tom Henke)

Gator (Ron Guidry)

Doctor K (Dwight Gooden)

El Presidente (Dennis Martinez)

Wild Thing (Mitch Williams)

The Rocket (Roger Clemens)

The Professor (Greg Maddux)

The Big Unit (Randy Johnson)

El Duque (Orlando Hernandez)

Index

ABOUT THE AUTHORS

Mark Gola is managing editor of Mountain Lion, Inc., a sports book packager located in Princeton, New Jersey. He is coauthor of *The Louisville Slugger® Ultimate Book of Hitting* and author of the forthcoming book *The Louisville Slugger® Complete Book of Hitting Faults and Fixes*. He is also an assistant baseball coach at Rider University, where he was an all-conference and northeast regional All-American in 1994.

Doug Myers lives in Delaware with his wife and newborn twins, who—despite his best efforts—are not named Nolan and Ryan, and a cat who has not been renamed Koufax. He has written three other books on various aspects of baseball, including *Louisville Slugger® Presents Batting Around*, *Essential Cubs*, and *The Scouting Report: 1997*. He would have benefited greatly from this book back in his Little League days when he missed three consecutive pitchout signs and threw three perfect strikes, leading to the only instance in the history of organized baseball of a catcher charging the mound.